D1544538

WISDOM NECTAR

Dudjom Rinpoché's Heart Advice

THE TSADRA FOUNDATION SERIES
published by Snow Lion Publications

TSADRA FOUNDATION is a U.S.-based nonprofit organization that was founded in 2000 in order to support the activities of advanced Western students of Tibetan Buddhism, specifically those with significant contemplative experience. Taking its inspiration from the nineteenth century nonsectarian Tibetan scholar and meditation master Jamgön Kongtrül Lodrö Tayé, Tsadra Foundation is named after his hermitage in eastern Tibet, Tsadra Rinchen Drak. The Foundation's various program areas reflect his values of excellence in both scholarship and contemplative practice, and the recognition of their mutual complementarity.

This publication is part of Tsadra Foundation's Translation Program, which aims to make authentic and authoritative texts from the Tibetan traditions available in English. The Foundation is honored to present the work of its fellows and grantees, individuals of confirmed contemplative and intellectual integrity; however, their views do not necessarily reflect those of the Foundation

Tsadra Foundation is delighted to ally with Snow Lion Publications in making these important texts available in the English language.

❧ Wisdom Nectar

DUDJOM RINPOCHÉ'S HEART ADVICE

The Spontaneous Song of Kuntu Zangpo's Wisdom Mind:
Secret Wisdom Mind's Vast Treasure of Luminous Realization,
The Unobstructed Sound of the Nature of Phenomena,
A Collection of Self-Manifest Vajra Speech by Padmasambhava's
Representative of the Supreme, Secret Early Translations, the Great Treasure
Revealer, King of Dharma, Lord Dudjom Drodül Lingpa Yeshé Dorjé

gsang chen snga 'gyur pad ma'i rgyal tshab chos kyi rgyal po gter
chen khyab bdag bdud 'joms 'gro 'dul gling pa 'jigs bral ye shes rdo rje
mchog gis thugs gsang 'od gsal dgongs pa'i klong mdzod las chos
nyid kyi rang sgra 'gags med rang byung rdo rje'i gsung 'ga' shas phyogs
gcig tu sdeb pa kun bzang dgongs pa'i thol glu zhes bya ba bzhugs so

His Holiness Dudjom Jigdral Yeshé Dorjé

Translated by Ron Garry

SNOW LION PUBLICATIONS
ITHACA, NEW YORK/BOULDER, COLORADO

Snow Lion Publications
P.O. Box 6483
Ithaca, NY 14851 USA
(607) 273-8519
www.snowlionpub.com

Printed in Canada on acid-free recycled paper.

ISBN-10 1-55939-224-X
ISBN-13 978-1-55939-224-2

Library of Congress Cataloging-in-Publication Data

Bdud-'joms (Jigs-bral-ye-śes-rdo-rje, 1904
    Wisdom nectar : Dudjom Rinpoche's heart advice / Dudjom
Jigdral Yeshe Dorje ; translated by Ron Garry.
      p. cm. — (The Tsadra Foundation series)
    Includes bibliographical references.
    ISBN-10: 1-55939-224-X (alk. paper)
    ISBN-13: 978-1-55939-224-2 (alk. paper)
    1. Rdzogs-chen (Rñiṅ-ma-pa) 2. Spiritual life—Rñiṅ-ma-pa
(Sect) I. Title. II. Series.
BQ7662.4.B3529 2005
294.3'444—dc22
                                        2005008280

Text designed and typeset in Aldus by Gopa & Ted2, Inc

Taking to heart what your Lama has said
Is like seeing a treasure in the palm of your hand.

Saraha[1]

Without my Lama's blessings—like earth, water, and warmth
[necessary for seeds to grow]—having entered me,
Recognition of my true nature is impossible.
Now that I've come to the direct path, not taking the long way around,
May I persevere in my practice of the sublime Dharma!

Although hundreds or thousands of explanations are given,
There is only one thing to be understood—
Know the one thing that liberates everything—
Awareness itself, your true nature.

Dudjom Rinpoché[2]

Contents

Dedication

This book is dedicated to the long life of the Jewel of Activity; may all beings have the great good fortune to make a connection with him. May our precious Lamas live long; and may the lineage of His Holiness Dudjom Rinpoché spread far and wide, bringing lasting joy and happiness to all beings.

Foreword

BY LAMA THARCHIN RINPOCHÉ

Lord of one hundred families of enlightenment,
illustrious holy spiritual master, at your feet I bow!

ALL PAST, PRESENT, and future victors who live in the ten directions converge in the same glorious form: the great master from Oddiyana, Lotus-Born. With his vajra command, he enthroned, empowered, and confirmed the reincarnate great treasure revealer Lord Dudjom Jikdral Yeshé Dorjé Drodul Lingpa Tsal as his representative. Moreover, many ancient treasure texts' scriptures fully laud Dudjom Rinpoché as a great personage, the crowning jewel of the sublime secret Original Translations' entire doctrine, the king of Buddhist teaching throughout the three realms. He is like the newly dawning sun amidst the constellations of learned, accomplished awareness- holding masters of the snowy Himalayan region. Completely without rival in the past, present, or future, his name's renown reverberates unceasingly throughout the breadth of this great globe's realms. In incomparable kindness, this supreme master accepted the task of being the holy protector and supporter of beings and the Buddhist doctrine during this era of decline. Here, I will write a brief account of this master's history.

In the past, great individuals not focused on extremes were imbued with the strength of familiarization with intense, forceful compassion, and entered sentient beings' realms with endless intent. On the level of definitive meaning, since primordial, original time, they were liberated in the basis, and epitomized the youthful vase body, the body of ultimate enlightenment's great exaltation, the non-conceptual wisdom of all buddhas' minds within the expanse of ever-excellent awareness. They arise into form as the original lord glorious Héruka or other chief deities of oceans of infinite sacred circles, then dwell in the midst of an endless retinue, their wisdom's natural manifestation, without death of change throughout the four times. Without movement, they unceasingly diffuse naturally-arisen elaborations—unimaginable, excellent miraculous displays that perform inconceivable good for others.

In general, on this subject of their enlightenment's manifestations, some are related in a linear progression, from former to latter; some are manifestations that appear at the same time; and others include the appearance of blessed manifestations. These cannot be restricted to a single, definite pattern: in as many water vessels of disciples as there are, their moon's compassionate form will appear; they are unlimited. Thus, my mind, limited to my own experience, is incapable of fathoming this lord's physical incarnations, and naming them as this one or that one.

Nevertheless, here I will follow the common histories of his series of lifetimes, arranged in a linear fashion from former to latter. I will use as my basic source the supplication to his own series of incarnations, *Pearl Necklace*, written by this great treasure revealer, king of Buddhist teaching throughout the three realms. Further, this treasure revealer's son, whose realization is of one taste as his father's, Lord Jikmé Trinlé Norbu Gélek Nampar Gyalwé-dé, wrote a volume of detailed commentary to *Pearl Necklace*, entitled *The Ruby Garland, A Necklace That Delights Awareness-Holding Dakinis*. Moreover, the most senior of all this great treasure revealer's direct disciples, a great learned, accomplished master of the definitive meaning, Chadral Sangyé Dorjé Rinpoché, wrote a supplication to the life of the incarnate great treasure revealer Jikdral Yeshé Dorjé Drodul Lingpa Tsal called *The Seed of the Three Kinds of Faith*. Apart from these texts, this supreme great treasure revealer's own treasure texts contain information concerning his past lives in such places as the treasure texts' proclamations and histories, where I ask that you learn the details.

In this case, I will write a short outline of his lifetimes according to the meaning of a supplication made in this great treasure revealer's own vajra speech, in rhinoceros-numbered verse [i.e., solitary]. The first line states:

In the past, you were awareness holder Capable Vajra Adept.

This refers to a time during this present age, one in which one thousand and two buddhas have accepted disciples and lit the lamp of the sacred Teachings. Thus, this age is called the age of illumination or the fortunate age. The spiritual master whose empowerments, predictions, and profound blessed aspirations consecrated this fortunate age's thousand and two buddhas, and who became the chief of these thousand guides' family, was the great lord of contemplative adepts named Capable Vajra Bearer: the first in this great treasure revealer's series of lifetimes.

During the life of our teacher Shakyamuni, his heart son whose realization equaled the Victor's own and who was foremost among the Buddha's disciples in transcendent knowledge, known as exalted Shariputra, was the second in his series of lifetimes.

Amoxho dwelled on a great stage of awakening yet intentionally took rebirth and ruled powerfully the entirety of Tibet was the Buddhist king known as Drogön Pakpa, eleventh in his series of lifetimes.

The great treasure revealer who mastered forceful miraculous powers, known as Drum-gyi Khar-nak, was the twelfth in his series of lifetimes.

The master who used the wrathful activity of manifest conduct to eradicate evil, untamed demons, and who mastered the strength to liberate them upon the ground of lasting happiness and definite excellence, was known as Hépa Chö-jung, the thirteenth in his series of lifetimes.

An emanation of Drok-ben became the spiritual master of the learned, accomplished masters throughout Tibet who were known as great lamas of the Original Translations, and he had dominion over innumerable treasure sites, including those of sacred places, teachings, and substances. He was known as the great treasure revealer Dudul Dorjé, fourteenth in his series of lifetimes.

Dudul Dorjé's subsequent emanation, who preserved the Victor's Katok Monastery with the three cycles of teaching and meditation practice, was known as Gyalsé Sönam Déu-tsen, fifteenth in his series of lifetimes. Gyalsé Sönam Déu-tsen's reincarnation held the treasury of teachings of great mystery, from which the dakini's breath had not evaporated, and raised the victory banner of the Victor's Katok Monastery's doctrine. He was known as the great treasure revealer Dudul Rolpa-tsal, sixteenth in his series of lifetimes.

Dudul Rolpa-tsal's reincarnation did not have to rely in his lifetime on the fleeting hardship of diligent training: from teachers that were non-human beings' natural manifestations he received the ultimate lineage. Thus, he naturally liberated the seal of the great treasury of the nature of reality's expanse of space within the basic space of Ever-Excellent's wisdom mind. This was the great treasure revealer Garwang Dudjom Lingpa, seventeenth in his series of lifetimes.

Thus, the words "in the past" imply this series of lifetimes until the present, although the name of Capable Vajra Bearer is the one explicitly mentioned. This concludes a short commentary to the first line of this supplication.

The second line states,

In the future, you will be Joyful Buddha Infinite Devotion.

This great person's rebirth is the reincarnate master named Sangyé Péma Shépa Drodul Rikzin Trinlé Drupé-dé or Péma Ösel Pal-zangpo, whose father is the holy, great treasure revealer's own son, named Dola Choktrul, Jikmé Chökyi Nyima. His mother, who shows all the marks and signs of being a dakini, is named Péma Khandro. In the Iron Horse Year (1990), the lotus of his enlightened form's marks and signs of physical perfection blossomed anew amid numerous amazing portents. From a young age, his positive propensities awakened, igniting the dynamic power of his innate transcendent knowledge, the domain of exalted beings' exceptional lives. Thus, he learned such things as reading and writing at a mere glance. From many lineage-bearing, learned, and accomplished masters (including his uncle, the treasure revealer's son, sublime lord Jikmé Trinlé Norbu; the senior master among all his past life's direct disciples, lord of refuge Chadral Sangyé Dorjé; and the treasure revealer's disciple Gonjo Tulku, Orgyen Chémchok) he drank to his satisfaction the nectar of the Canon's and Treasures' empowerments, transmissions, and pith instructions. The force of his recollection of past lives has given him prodigious knowledge of boundless approaches to the Buddhist teachings of scripture and realization. Now, at the age of fifteen, the qualities of his learning, nobility, and excellence are unrivalled in every way, and his blessed activity that flourishes in every direction has made him a living holy lord, supporter of sentient beings and of the Original Translations' very secret doctrine.

Not only that, his manifestations will appear in the future as art, as incarnate beings, and as supreme manifestations who will work for sentient beings' good, appearing spontaneously, without movement or effort, in whatever form can tame each being. This results from two causes—his compassion's blessings and beings' flourishing positive acts, appearing in the same way as water, the moon's reflection, and the moon's circle. Just as the moon can leave a reflection, the body of perfect rapture's moon can appear as a manifestation to its disciples. Likewise, just as a vessel of water can contain the moon's reflection, disciples have the merit to perceive enlightenment's manifestation. Just as the moon appears effortlessly on water when there are disciples, the autumn moon's emanated reflection appears without being veiled for an instant; thus, this lord's dance of emanated magical displays will continue uninterrupted and boundlessly until the ocean of the wheel of life runs dry.

Specifically, among the six regions of this world, the Land of Jambu, the northern kingdom of Shambhala is an especially exalted region. There, bodhisattvas on awakening's tenth stage of culmination appear as a series of kings. This lord will take rebirth as the lineage bearing monarch Wrathful Sharp Vajra with an Iron Wheel. He will defeat armies of wild barbarians who always impair living beings' happiness and have both hostile attitudes and violent behavior. That king, guide on the path to awakening's peace, will be an emanation of this great treasure revealer.

Further, in the past, when this fortunate age's buddhas each formulated vows and aspirations to work for sentient beings' benefit, the youngest of the thousand guides, Boundless Intellect, said, "The Buddha's qualities are like space and sentient beings as well are endless; therefore, I make the aspiration to equal the sum of all your acts as buddhas, including your longevity." The moment he said this, gods' voices arose from space proclaiming, "Excellent!" The force of this aspiration will result in Transcendent Buddha Infinite Devotion being the last buddha of the thousand; that buddha is definitely this great treasure revealer's future emanation.
This concludes a very brief presentation of the second line's meaning.

The third line states,

At present, you are Lotus-Born's representative, Drok-ben incarnate.

Our supreme, incomparable spiritual guide, the king of the Buddhist teaching throughout the three realms, the sublime Dudjom Jikdral Yeshé Dorjé, was an emanation of Drok-ben Translator's body, an emanation of the queen of the basic space of phenomena Yeshé Tsogyal's speech, and an emanation of the powerful sovereign Padmakara's mind. He has been thus lauded by Guru Rinpoché, Dudjom Lingpa, and others in the texts of many ancient treasures. As foretold, the lotus of his marks and signs of physical perfection newly blossomed in the hidden land of Péma-kö during the

Wood Dragon Year (1904). His father belonged to a family descended from the Buddhist king Trisong Déutsen; his mother belonged to a family descended from Ratna Lingpa.

From an early age, the excellent patterns of his natural affinity awakened: Guru Rinpoché and his consort manifestly revealed their faces to him and empowered him as the chief of their profound treasures. When they enthroned him as Lotus-Born's representative, they gave him the name Orgyen Garwang Drodul Lingpa-tsal. He became satisfied drinking the nectar of ripening and liberating instructions, with supporting transmissions, granted him by many great, authentic learned, accomplished masters. His innate transcendent knowledge overflowed in relation to the view, meditation, and philosophical systems: he became a lord of scholars unrivalled in the past, present, or future. As a great bodhisattva, he used the six transcendent perfections and the four means of attracting disciples to lead beings to temporary uplifted states and to the ultimate definite excellence of awakening. Without having to take the path of hardships based on expedient meanings, he traversed the direct path of Ati's essence of luminosity and reached a high level of accomplishment where his manifest realization's qualities blazed together. The wisdom dakinis openly gave him such treasures as the inventory of his yellow parchment treasures, and the guardians and protectors of the Teachings watched over him as if he were their own son. His mastery of the three forms of blazing and three kinds of gathering led him to become worthy to be carried on the crown of the heads of all living beings, be they high, low, or middle.

During a degenerate time such as ours, his profound aspiration that the teaching and practice of the Ancient Translation School's doctrine not decline but spread in one hundred directions led him to build Buddhist institutions widely. He set aside the effort involved in overtly revealing the earth treasures designated as his, and turned his attention to very meaningful projects: to preserve the Kagyu and Nyingma doctrines, he raised to the four continent's skies the victory banner of teachings that unite all lineages, such as *Jamgon Kongtrul's Five Treasuries*. To serve as a place of offering for beings of the degenerate age, who need to accumulate merit, he built a replica of both the structure and contents of the palace of Lotus Light on Tail-Fan Island's Copper Colored Mountain, and a new retreat center connected to it. He thus completely relieved the doctrine and beings' decline.

He newly constructed an inconceivable number of the three sacred supports, such as nourishing the doctrine by reprinting ancient texts that had become very rare. He thereby became the single source of help and happiness throughout Tibet. The activity he fostered proved as true the scriptures that foretold him to be Lotus-Born's representative. Moreover, his feet touched the ground of every large area of this world, including Tibet, all provinces of greater Tibet, Bhutan, Nepal, India, China, America, and Europe. He fulfilled the prophecy that every being with whom he made a connection through sacred substances, seeing his face, hearing his voice, or talking with him would be led to Tail-Fan Island's pure land of Lotus Light.

Groups of learned and accomplished high lamas and high ranking monarchs, officials, and great leaders bowed their heads at his feet, yet pride or arrogance never influenced him. He remained in equanimity in relation to the eight worldly concerns and lived with the discipline of concealing himself in the guise of an ordinary person. He saw infinite arrays of visions, including those of inconceivable buddhas' pure lands, deities and spiritual masters, and receiving dakinis' prophecies, yet he bound these with a strict seal of secrecy and never allowed himself such acts as bragging, praising himself, or considering himself important.

When his disciples' karma and aspirations came to fruition, the seal of his realization's expanse was naturally released; this produced his cycles of mind treasures—the Three Roots' outer, inner, secret, and innermost secret practices, with those of the Teachings' protectors, their activity rituals, supportive instruction manuals, and other texts. These treasures, like the essence of the dakinis' heart blood, are concise, clear, come with the lineage's forceful blessing, and bring swift accomplishment. In these and other ways, these treasures satisfy whomever comes into contact with them, like the essence of nectar. He composed definitive texts, then granted their entire empowerment and transmission to their respective foretold responsible recipients and designated heirs of the lineage, filling this world's lands with these profound teachings' flourishing harvest. He became known as a great treasure revealer, chief of every accomplished treasure finder.

Further, the collections of many ancient treasures texts, such as the trio of practices of the spiritual master, Great Perfection, and Great Compassion, and another trio of the eight transmissions, the compendium of the spiritual master's intention, and Vajra Dagger had lost coherence: he revised them and made explicit what had been concealed, clarifying a whole range of rituals and pith instructions. These delighted the learned and prevented uneducated persons from performing rituals with omissions or additions by making them easy to perform correctly. For his own tradition's New Treasures and Ancient Treasures' cycles of ordered rituals, he composed such texts as outlines, replicas, commentaries to intensive mantra practice, vajra feast activity, manuals, and supplementary texts; concise or extensive profound texts of instruction related to the process of the four empowerments; histories, such as accounts of the Tibetan kings, the history of Buddhism, and the outline of the Nyingma doctrine; as well as records of his studies and supplementary teachings. In all, his collected works span twenty-five volumes. Moreover, he gathered dispersed ancient texts from the Original Translations' Canon, proofread them, produced definitive versions, and put them into order—a total of forty-eight volumes.

In brief, this example of his preservation of the Canon and Treasure texts' continuity exemplifies his elucidation and spreading of the teachings that lead to spiritual maturity and liberation, along with their supportive texts. Both India and Tibet have never seen such deeds, which is why he is known today as a second Lotus-Born Master. His kindness restored from its foundations the precious doctrine of the sublime secret essence of luminosity. At the completion of his enlightened activity, in the Fire Tiger Year (1986), the display of his wisdom form's miraculous appearance dissolved into the basic space of phenomena; the basis of his manifestation merged with the expanse of Ever-Excellent Lotus-Born Master's enlightened mind, to become of an identical flavor. This concludes a commentary on the third line's meaning.

The last line states,

Jik-dral Yeshé Dorjé, to you I pray.

"Jik-dral Yeshé Dorjé" is one of this great treasure revealer's names. A supplication he composed to his list of names states,

> The dakinis told my noble father Jampal Norbu, who belonged
>   to a royal family,
> "A son greater than his father will appear!"
> As predicted, this was my name before birth:
> To you known as Yeshé Dorjé, I pray.

As stated, his father, Jampal Norbu Tenzin, a Katok Monastery reincarnate master descended from King Trisong Déutsen, received his son's name "Yeshé Dorjé" in the dakinis' prophecy. "Jik-dral" was added by Karmapa: this is an oral account I have heard. In all, this is this noble master's most widely known name.

When you pray to this chief of enlightenment's family, the supreme refuge who has this name, with the certainty that he embodies all victors, and with the wish, "Grant your blessings to my stream of being and to that of all sentient beings!," the connection between your devotion and this spiritual master's compassion will blend his mind with yours. This will manifestly awaken the result that dwells in the basis of your being, the ultimate spiritual master—Yeshé Dorjé (literally, "vajra wisdom")—and you will attain enlightenment within the inner space of the youthful vase body, the deep and clear body of ultimate enlightenment.   This concludes a short commentary to the fourth line of this supplication and ends this foreword on an auspicious note.

I, an infirm vagabond from the region of Repkong (Tibet), Tsédrup Tharchin, the least among the servants of this lord great treasure revealer, the father and son of the Dudjom lineage, composed this. I used their writings as my source, and added on occasion whatever seemed suitable from my own mind, as a supplication. May my words cause readers to become the disciples of this ever-excellent lord spiritual master.

Translator's Preface

IT IS IMPORTANT TO ME at the outset to begin with a disclosure. I wish the reader to know that although I have translated these precious teachings, I am not portraying myself as a spiritual teacher, Lama, or accomplished senior student. I am just a simple practitioner and translator who, at the request of my Lama, has tried to the best of my ability to make these precious prayers and teachings available to the English reader. These teachings are, and have been, a crucial support of my spiritual practice, without which I would be hopelessly lost.

In this spirit, I have refrained from giving my own commentary to any of Dudjom Rinpoché's teachings. His words speak perfectly for themselves. I have added endnotes explaining various terms, Tibetan expressions, or other references that will be familiar to a Tibetan Buddhist but may possibly be unknown to some Western readers.

The purpose of my introductions that precede each chapter is to share with the reader a sense of the preciousness and profundity of His Holiness's teachings and to help the reader approach each page with an open heart and mind, thirsting for these nectar-like instructions that can bring liberation upon hearing or reading them.

Despite my limitations, I encourage you to have confidence in the translation of His Holiness's words, as I have extensively and carefully reviewed this work with many of our precious Lamas, such as Lopön Jigmé Rinpoché, Khenpo Orgyen Thinley Rinpoché, Lama Tharchin Rinpoché, Tulku Thubten Rinpoché, Lama Chönam, and Sangyé Khandro. I have also been fortunate to have Lama Ngawang Zangpo review my entire work. Because of this the reader can have confidence in the present translation. Any mistakes that remain are entirely my own.

Acknowledgments

I wish to express my deep gratitude to Lama Tharchin Rinpoché whose kindness I can never ever repay for all the pure teachings I have received, and for being a thoroughly pure connection to Dudjom Rinpoché and his New Treasures lineage (*Dudjom Tersar*). I especially wish to thank him for being the pure connection for the reader through writing the introduction to His Holiness's works contained in this book.

Sincere thanks to Lopön Jigmé for always being available to answer questions concerning the translation as well as for his explanation of the profound meaning of His Holiness's teachings. Without him this translation could not have been brought to proper completion. My appreciation cannot be expressed.

I also had the great privilege to consult with both Lama Chönam and Sangyé Khandro on several of the works included in this book, including many important key terms. I am honored by the opportunity. Thank you.

My continual thanks to Tulku Thubten Rinpoché, from whom I learned to translate many years ago, and for his ongoing kindness and assistance in my translation projects.

I wish to thank the Tsadra Foundation and especially Eric and Andrea Colombel for their support given through the Tsadra Foundation that made possible the translation of these most important teachings. I also would like to acknowledge the historical role they are playing in facilitating the transmission and preservation of these most important Buddhist texts and teachings that contain wisdom flawlessly preserved in the Tibetan tradition in unbroken lineages for over 1,300 years. In funding and bringing many resources together, the Tsadra Foundation is making a serious impact that will ensure the preservation of these pure teachings for present and future generations. This is an extremely noble and inspiring endeavor. Thank you. I also wish to thank Lama Drupgyu, Tsadra Foundation's Director of Programs, for the excellent example he sets for all Western practitioners and for all his direct and indirect support of my work. Thanks also to my vajra sister Christiane Buchet, Tsadra Foundation's Executive Assistant, whose administrative support makes the process so seamless that it appears the translation process occurs without any administrative support whatsoever (which isn't so). I also wish to thank my colleagues, the Tsadra Foundation fellows, for all I continually learn from them about translation, writing, and the Dharma.

Though I am not the first to give my accolades, I would be remiss not to thank Jeff Cox and Sidney Piburn who are doing an incredible job making available to an ever-growing number people a vast array of the most precious Buddhist teachings (including not allowing these teachings to go out of print). Their noble mission is worthy of the insight of a bodhisattva. I wish to also thank my editor, Connie Miller, for her patience and the excellent work she has done in covering up my poor writing style with her incredible editing job; and also I wish to thank Steven Rhodes for help reviewing the bibliography, and the entire Snow Lion staff working diligently behind the scenes.

Thank you, Michael Herr, for helping me find my writing voice, and for your insightful edit of my writing. Special thanks to Sonam for her support throughout this entire project, especially the excellent job done with the English-Tibetan word list. And last but not least, I want to express my appreciation to Cassandra English for her incisive help with the general introduction.

Ron Garry

Conventions

NOTES

MOST OF HIS HOLINESS'S WRITINGS found in this collection were written in direct response to requests from his students and were written for the most part in a direct, poetic style. He was writing for an audience already familiar with the Buddhist teaching and its diverse terminology, not to mention the many references to Tibetan culture, including people, places, landmarks, and the various Tibetan idiomatic expressions. This assumption of familiarity cannot necessarily be made regarding all Western practitioners, particularly those new to Buddhist teachings, especially the Vajrayana teachings. Therefore, I have added extensive endnotes, not to clarify His Holiness's writings, but to address this unique situation.

As Richard Barron aptly wrote:

> Every translation brings its own set of problems and compromises. Works such as Kongtrul's accounts of his life and lives were written for people of his time and his cultural background, so there is the implicit assumption that an educated readership among his peers would understand the implications of the statements and observations he made. The same assumption cannot be made about an educated English-speaking readership.[3]

LITERAL TRANSLATION VS. MEANING-TO-MEANING TRANSLATION

The translation of Buddhist texts into Tibetan began over thirteen hundred years ago, when Guru Rinpoché was in Tibet. Many enlightened beings were involved in this process, including the sublime master Guru Rinpoché and the great translator Bérotsana. The distinctive feature of these translations was their emphasis on translating meaning-to-meaning (*don sgyur*) from the Sanskrit texts, and not translating word-for-word (*tshig sgyur*). Fortunately, both the masters and their translator-disciples were fully enlightened buddhas. This meant that they fully, completely, and thoroughly understood the teachings of Buddha, as they were of one mind, and the translation of the meaning occurred naturally. There's the rub. Although the Lamas I have consulted and worked with in review of this translation are, from my perspective, of one mind with His Holiness Dudjom Rinpoché, I am not. Therefore, although I have tried my best to render this translation according to its meaning, using literary English as opposed to a hybrid Tibetan-English jargon, there are still a few key terms that I do not yet have confidence in translating into English. Key terms not translated into English are, for example: *dharmakaya, sambhogakaya, nirmanakaya, tantra, mantra, vajra,* and *nada.* My feeling is that when commonly accepted translations of these key words occur, they will reflect a meaning-to-meaning translation. Many of our finest and most brilliant translators have coined excellent translations for these key terms, which will soon probably become standard. Still, I am timid. The first occurrence of a translated key term will be accompanied with its corresponding Tibetan or Sanskrit in parenthesis. These key terms will also be listed at the end of the book in a word list that contains the English translation and the original Tibetan.

Key Terms: A Note about Use of Tibetan or Sanskrit

Sometimes the translation of a key term into English can leave the reader as mystified concerning its real meaning as he would be by the original Sanskrit or Tibetan, with the loss of the levels of meaning found in the original. In those instances, I chose not to translate the word into English. In almost all instances when an English translation is not used, I have chosen the Sanskrit term since in most cases the Sanskrit word is easier to pronounce and is more familiar to the English reader than its Tibetan equivalent. Terms left in Sanskrit are italicized at their first appearance except in cases in which they've made their way into the English language, such as Buddha, bodhisattva, karma, and samsara.

I do believe the English language will someday become a sacred language, blessed by both Tibetan and Western fully enlightened Buddhas, in which all key terms will be translated into English (with only a few remaining in Tibetan and Sanskrit). Although at the moment the process is going well, it is still a work in progress.

TEXT TITLES

I have chosen to translate most titles of texts and collections into English while giving the corresponding Tibetan or Sanskrit title in parenthesis on first occurrence.

PROPER NAMES

In general, proper names have been left in their most recognized rendering in Tibetan or Sanskrit. In cases where they are translated, I include the appropriate Tibetan or Sanskrit in parenthesis on first occurrence. Proper names and deity names, such as Jigdral Yeshé Dorjé, Amitabha, and Chenrezi are usually not translated but are instead rendered in their original Tibetan or Sanskrit, or whichever name is in common usage with English readers. Place names are sometimes left in the original language (Oddiyana, for example) unless there is an obvious English rendering, such as Tibet for the Tibetan name *Bö*.

Regarding deities and pure lands, because these names carry profound meaning and may aid in the English reader's understanding, I have translated into xEnglish some of their names. For instance, Tsokyé Dorjé is translated into English with the aid of Sanskrit as Lake Born Vajra, (Guru Rinpoché's name given by the dakinis upon his birth in the center of Danakosha Lake). The first occurrence of a translation in English of a deity name, proper name, or place name is accompanied by the Sanskrit or Tibetan given in phonetics.

Translating names (Lake Born Vajra) and places (Glorious Copper-Colored Mountain) into English is a work in progress. I have chosen not to wait until the correct translation of every name or place is found but to enter this shaky ground on a case by case basis.

TRANSLITERATION AND PHONETICIZATION

Transliteration refers to the closest corresponding letters of a different alphabet or language, while phoneticization is the approximation of the pronunciation of a language. Throughout this book I have adopted the Wiley system of transliteration. As for phoneticization, there are as many systems as there are translators and dialects of the Tibetan language, none entirely satisfactory, including my own. In the use of phonetics, I hoped to approximate the sound of the Tibetan as spoken by my teachers—southeastern Tibetan with a dash of Amdo and Kham. I have used a system that is as simple as possible, so as not to distract the reader from the material itself.

TABLE OF CONTENTS

The initial table of contents provides a detailed overview of the entire book and lists each and every work contained herein. Many of these writings were not given a title by Dudjom Rinpoché. To help the reader easily identify these writings, each work without a titled is denoted in the table of contents by the first line or the first significant line of the text.[4] In cases where Dudjom Rinpoché titled his work, it is capitalized in the table of contents, such as "Blessings Swiftly Received: A Prayer Calling the Master from Afar." On the other hand, titles listed for identification purposes only will have just the first letter capitalized, such as "My kind, precious root Lama."

The explanation presented in Appendix 1: An Explanation of the Nine Vehicles is directly and indixrectly (in the form of my translation of this text and my own paraphrasing) based upon Dudjom Rinpoché's text called *The Festival of Delight in Which the Expression of Eloquent Teachings Manifest: A Concise Detailed Classification of the Nyingmapa Teachings, the Ancient Translation School of Secret Mantra*, located in volume 2 of his *Collected Works*. (An English translation of this entire work can be found in *The Nyingma School of Tibetan Buddhism*, translated by Gyurme Dorje).

Each of the four chapters of translations has the same format: a quotation from a text from within that section; the translator's brief introduction to that section; and the translation itself.

EDITION OF TEXT

The edition of the text used for this translation is: *Collected Works of H. H. Dudjom Rinpoché* (*bdud 'joms 'jigs bral ye shes rdo rje yi gsung 'bum dam chos rin chen nor bu'i mdzod*) in twenty-five volumes, published by Dupjung Lama, Madhav Nikunj, Kalimpong, W.B., 1978. It was compiled by His Holiness Dudjom Rinpoché.

General Introduction

THIS BOOK, *Wisdom Nectar*, is arranged in four chapters: Heart Advice (*zhal gdams*); Songs of Realization (*mgur*) and Songs of Tantric Gatherings (*tshogs*); Supplication Prayers (*gsol 'debs*); and Aspiration Prayers (*smon lam*). Each chapter begins with a translator's introduction, followed by the translation of Dudjom Rinpoché's teachings.

My intention in writing this introduction to Dudjom Rinpoché's teachings is to provide a context for the reader to realize what a gift we literally hold "in the palm of our hands," in the form of this book that contains a collection of His Holiness's pith instructions. I find for myself that reading with an open heart—reading with faith and devotion—is the key that allows the mastexant. For instance, right now I hear the songbirds of springtime outside my window, while morning sunlight shines through shimmering green bamboo leaves blown by a warm, fragrant breeze. It is Saturday morning, and I decide to stay home and enjoy this gorgeous time. These circumstances create a feeling that is hard to describe; perhaps words that come close are peacefulness, serenity, and happiness. I have a strong sense of enjoyment, and I try to recreate it, consciously and unconsciously. This attempt underlies my choices of the house I live in, the type of garden I cultivate, and the car that I drive.

Due to our individual karma, this process does not manifest in the same way for everyone. We have diverse feelings that we try to engender or avoid, and we sometimes react differently to similar external phenomena. Whatever our personal likes and dislikes are, they are all based upon feelings that arise within. These feelings are, in turn, based upon circumstances such as those just mentioned. Therefore, we then attempt to create and sustain circumstances that will result in internal feelings we enjoy, such as love, inspiration, and happiness. We attempt to change or avoid circumstances that may result in feelings we dislike, such as suffering, disappointment, and fear. But isn't it actually the feeling itself that we enjoy and want to recreate and maintain? Don't we actually spend our entire lives grasping after pleasurable inner experiences, attempting to create and sustain these feelings through creating and sustaining outer circumstances, just as we push away unpleasant inner experiences, trying to change and avert these feelings through changing and averting outer circumstances?

So we then engage in our life project to set up external circumstances that give us the internal feelings we want; and our joys and sorrows throughout our life are very much related to how well we succeed in doing this. Unfortunately, sooner or later, all these projects based upon grasping and avoidance end in failure, due to unforeseen circumstances beyond our control, such as illness, unwanted separation from loved ones, or imminent death, whatever the case may be. Our attempts at maintaining or avoiding external circumstances will almost certainly bite the dust, especially when death occurs.

According to the Buddhist Vajrayana teachings, when we die, we enter a series of experiences called the intermediate state (*bardo*). This series of experiences will culminate in our rebirth in one of six realms of cyclic existence, unless our previous practice and the blessings of our Lama results in liberation during this intermediate state. Clearly, at death, when our mind separates from our body, we no longer have the ability to create the circumstances that support feelings we enjoy or to prevent the feelings that cause us suffering. In the intermediate state between this life and the next, our experiences and the feelings related to these experiences arise based on conditions that are the results of the cause and effect of our past karma. This is the bad news.

Fortunately, there is also very good news. Through practicing the Buddha's teachings with faith and devotion, it is possible to become free of all circumstances, both positive ones that lead to feelings we enjoy and negative ones that lead to feelings we dislike. Buddha skillfully taught many methods that take us beyond circumstances, progressively leading us to the realization of our true nature, which is Buddha Kuntu Zangpo (Always Noble), primordially pure, great exaltation. Dudjom Rinpoché's writings compiled in this book are the essence of all Buddhist teachings and are the quintessence of the wisdom mind of Kuntu Zangpo, present from the beginningless beginning. His direct and simple pith instructions on view, meditation, and conduct are a sure guide upon the path of Dzogchen (Great Perfection), leading to this realization in a single lifetime. As His Holiness writes in his preface to *Essential Advice for Solitary Meditation Practice*:

> My words will place direct instructions for the practice of inner-most secret Great Perfection in the palm of the hands of fortunate individuals.

Sometimes, to read endless volumes and to listen to numerous lengthy teachings only creates more confusion, while at other times reading or hearing just one line of profound teachings is enough to change your entire life. These teachings and prayers of His Holiness Dudjom Rinpoché are of this latter type: They are so direct that every word has the power to change our lives in a very positive and profound way. Each line, read slowly and taken to heart, has the ability to turn us away from the meaninglessness and spiritual poverty of our time and move us toward the vast wealth of our true nature, which lies within us, present from the very beginning.

≈§ I

Heart Advice

Self-manifest Buddhahood, this awareness,
Is original dharmakaya, never separate from you.
You've never been separate from it, so just recognize it right now.
It is very important to remain settled in the ground
    of this recognition.[5]

Introduction:
Heart Advice (*zhal gdams*)

This section offers the reader a translation of one of Dudjom Rinpoché's most important works, the heart advice (*zhal gdams*) called *Essential Advice for Solitary Meditation Practice* (*ri chos bslab bya nyams len dmar khrid go bder brjod pa grub pa'i bcud len*), found in the *Collected Works of His Holiness Dudjom Rinpoché*, volume *pa*, pp. 443–68. Also included in this chapter is the entire heart advice (*zhal gdams*) section entitled *Nectar for Fortunate Disciples' Hearts: A Compilation of Essential Words of Advice*, as found within the *Collected Works*, volume *ah*, pp. 291–342. *The Mirage of Nectar* is the only work not included. I decided not to include my translation in this book because it has already been beautifully translated by the Padmakara Translation Group and can be found in *Counsels from My Heart*, pp. 77–82, under the title "Magical Nectar."

All heart advice is given as direct instructions, which are the pith instructions of Grexat Perfection. In most cases, Dudjom Rinpoché wrote these instructions in metric verse, the two notable exceptions being *Essential Advice for Solitary Meditation Practice* and *Heart Gem for Fortunate Disciples: Pointing Out Instructions of the Great Perfection*, which he taught in prose. This series of heartfelt advice span all areas of practice and are taught from the Great Perfection point of view, directly pointing to one's own experience and one's own mind. Many of the works included here are concise instructions that point out the nature of mind. In some cases, such instructions are given in just a single verse, such as:

> Rest at ease within the uncontrived nature of mind.
> By looking, nothing is seen;
> Seeing nothing is actually to see naked awareness.
> That itself is Buddha Kuntu Zangpo.

Heart Gem for Fortunate Disciples lives up to its title's promise. This text is a practical manual for the practice of the Great Perfection. The instructions are direct and concise, written in an accessible, comprehensible style. Dudjom Rinpoché gives us pith instructions regarding view, meditation, and conduct, and heart advice on how to work with whatever arises during meditation and conduct.

ESSENTIAL ADVICE FOR SOLITARY MEDITATION PRACTICE

The first text presented in this collection, *Essential Advice for Solitary Meditation Practice*, was written by Dudjom Rinpoché at the behest of a retreatant, Rikzang Dorjé, in residence at Dudjom Rinpoché's three-year retreat center, Ogmin Péma Ösel, in Tibet. This profound teaching contains within it the entire path of Great Perfection (*Dzogchen*), including how to prepare oneself for retreat and how to discern a proper location, as well as key instructions on view, meditation, and conduct with direct advice on how to bring your experiences onto the path. During my three-year retreat, my teacher, Lama Tharchin Rinpoché—who was one of those fortunate retreatants for whom Dudjom Rinpoché wrote this text—would refer us to this text over and over again. It seemed that the answer to every question on meditation that we posed could be found in *Essential Advice for Solitary Meditation Practice*. We all discovered this to be true, and this text continues to be my treasured companion.

As a preface to this text, Dudjom Rinpoché explains why he wrote it:

> In this text I present essential advice for solitary meditation practice in an easily accessible way. My words will place direct instructions for the practice of innermost secret Great Perfection in the palm of the hands of fortunate individuals. Their previous lifetimes' positive aspirations and pure karmic propensities have led them to feel heartfelt trust in the teaching of the profound secret Great Perfection and in the Lama who reveals it; and they wish to take their practice to completion. For them, this text will provide an open gate to the path of Great Perfection.

I would like to use these words by Dudjom Rinpoché as a framework for introducing the entire Heart Advice section, and in a sense, as an introduction to all the writings in this book. As I previously mentioned, the purpose of this introduction is to engender in the reader a sense of the preciousness and profundity of these teachings—heart advice, songs of realization, songs of tantric gatherings, supplication prayers, and aspiration prayers. This will be done with a discussion in three parts based upon the above quotation:

* Rinpoché's purpose for writing this text: To give "essential advice for solitary meditation practice"
* Type of instruction: Essential advice that is "direct instruction for the practice of the innermost secret Great Perfection placed in the palm of the hands," that is, the Pith Instruction Class of the innermost secret Great Perfection
* To whom it is revealed: Fortunate individuals, those "who feel heartfelt trust in the teaching of the profound secret Great Perfection and in the Lama who reveals it and who wish to take their practice to completion"

RINPOCHÉ'S PURPOSE FOR WRITING THIS TEXT

Dudjom Rinpoché states that his purpose for writing this text is to give a practitioner "essential advice for solitary meditation practice." "Essential advice" means direct advice, based upon experience, on how to practice meditation. This is not a theoretical or intellectually based teaching given by a scholar, but the direct transmission of pith instructions to be applied in practice given by an accomplished master.

"Solitary meditation practice" is usually understood literally: meditation in an isolated physical environment such as mountains, forests, or any place secluded from the activity and distractions of daily life. In this case, "solitary meditation practice" is also meant to be taken figuratively, as Dudjom Rinpoché later mentions in the text:

> In a solitary place, the thought of death penetrating [the practitioner's] heart...

This statement refers to inner retreat, which is based upon an attitude that allows a practitioner to be in the true solitary place—mindful of one's own impending death—regardless of one's outer physical location.

Therefore, although the context in which Dudjom Rinpoché gave these teachings was a specific three-year retreat center in Tibet, these teachings are not limited to that situation but apply to long and short-term retreats anywhere and are relevant to those of us whose "retreat" occurs in the context of our work and family life. This text is a manual that guides us in every aspect of practice, whether in an isolated retreat setting or in the context of our daily life's responsibilities. This dual purpose makes this text unique and invaluable.

Type of Instruction: Pith Instruction Class of the Innermost Secret Great Perfection

Essential Advice for Solitary Meditation Practice is a "direct instruction for the practice of the Great Perfection." All tantric teachings are especially precious—they shine the light of wisdom in our world darkened by ignorance and delusion and lead to enlightenment in one lifetime. Great Perfection is the summit of all Buddhist teachings and is the most direct and easy path to achieve this goal. In *The Festival of Delight*[6] Dudjom Rinpoché explains that the Great Perfection is superior to the lower vehicles:

> This king among vehicles holds stainless space—the originally pure nature of mind whose nature is clear light, the naturally present, changeless, self-manifest wisdom that is naturally and spontaneously present in oneself—to be the original ground of the Great Perfection.

In contrast, the eight lower levels of Buddhist teachings are based upon intellectual contrivance and fabrication. Dudjom Rinpoché explains this from the perspective of the Great Perfection:

> The eight lower levels have intellectually fabricated and contrived that which is changeless solely due to fleeting thoughts that never experience what truly is. They apply antidotes to and reject that which is not to be rejected. They refer to as flawed that in which there is nothing to be purified, with a mind that desires purification. They have created division with respect to that which cannot be obtained by their hopes and fears that it can be

obtained elsewhere. And they have obscured wisdom, which is naturally present, by their efforts in respect to that which is free from effort and free from needing to be accomplished. Therefore, they have had no chance to make contact with genuine, ultimate reality as it is (*rnal ma'i de kho na nyid*).

Dudjom Rinpoché further explains:

> In this way, the natural Great Perfection is present as the nature of mind that transcends ordinary mind, the uncompounded clear light of wisdom that is awareness, in which all noble qualities of the essential nature are spontaneously present.

Great Perfection is categorized into three classes—Mind Class, Vast Expanse Class, and Pith Instruction Class (*upadesha*). "Direct instructions" falls within the category of the Pith Instruction Class, the most profound of the three. Dudjom Rinpoché supports this point of view by citing the *Supreme Array of Ati* (*a ti bkod pa chen po*):[7]

> O Vajrapani!
> If the Pith Instruction Class is not established,
> There will be those who cling to deliberate examination [Mind Class],
> And in particular, those who will believe in nothing at all [Vast Expanse Class].
> Therefore, this definitive secret essence [Pith Instruction Class]—
> Like a butter lamp amid darkness,
> Like an elephant among oxen,
> Like a lion among wild animals,
> Or like a horseman among those on foot—
> Is superior to them all.

The Pith Instruction Class of Great Perfection constitutes the essential key teachings that a Lama reveals to his disciple in a direct way, heart to heart. In previous times, in India and Tibet, great practitioners had to go through many hardships—accounts of their travails are depicted in their life stories, some now available in English—to receive these very teachings.[8] Here, Dudjom Rinpoché literally places these profound teachings in the palms of our hands, without us having to undergo hardship. We are all so incredibly fortunate. Reflection on this fact naturally fosters appreciation for these teachings.

The Vehicles of Buddhism

For a proper foundation to be laid for a practitioner to further cultivate appreciation for these teachings—Great Perfection's vast and profound pith instructions imbued with the ability to bring us to enlightenment in this very lifetime—I feel it is very helpful to give an account of the nine Buddhist vehicles according to the Nyingma school as taught by His Holiness Dudjom Rinpoché. For an extensive explanation of the nine vehicles please see Appendix 1.

The Buddhist teachings are very precious at every level, as the essence of the Hinayana teachings is never to harm any sentient being. The essence of the Mahayana teachings is to have compassion toward all sentient beings. The essence of the Vajrayana teachings is to have pure view, which is to see all phenomena as wisdom phenomena—all forms as the wisdom deity's body; all sounds as the wisdom deity's mantra; and all thought as the display of the wisdom deity's mind. In our world so full of various sufferings and problems, these are extremely precious teachings. Each vehicle is a lamp that illuminates the darkness of this world. For a person to receive and practice any of these teachings is a profound blessing in and of itself. In our case we are extremely fortunate: among the plethora of teachings and styles of transmission, Dudjom Rinpoché in *Essential Advice for Solitary Meditation Practice*—and for that matter, in all of his teachings, prayers, and songs of realization contained in this book—chose to teach the essence of all teachings, Great Perfection, in the most direct style possible, as pith instruction.

I refer the interested reader to Appendix 2, which is an overview of the place these pith instructions have within the classification of Buddhist teachings.

TEACHINGS GIVEN FOR FORTUNATE INDIVIDUALS

Although Dudjom Rinpoché wrote *Essential Advice for Solitary Meditation Practice* based on a request related to a specific three-year retreat, these teachings are not limited to those retreatants but have relevance for all fortunate individuals.

"Fortunate individuals" does not refer to those with high social status or to those who are wealthy, well-educated, famous, or well-connected; nor is Dudjom Rinpoché referring only to those who are Lamas nor to those who have spent years in retreat. Instead, he specifically states that fortunate individuals have three characteristics:

1. heartfelt trust in the teaching of the profound, secret Great Perfection
2. heartfelt trust in the Lama who reveals it
3. the wish to take their practice to completion

These are the qualifications that make someone a fortunate individual to receive these profound Great Perfection teachings. Let's explore why these three qualities are so outstanding.

Heartfelt Trust in the Great Perfection

Heartfelt trust in Great Perfection's teachings is vital; without it, full enlightenment on this profound path is impossible. Patrul Rinpoché writes in his *Song of Encouragement to Read the Seven Treasuries, The Excellent Words of Omniscient Longchen Rabjampa*:

> Simply reading one line of such an excellent text
> Can leave your worldly experience in ruins.
> Having met with the good fortune to read it entirely,
> What will you think if you throw it away?[9]

Patrul Rinpoché wrote these words to describe *The Precious Treasury of the Space of Phenomena* (chos dbyings rin po che'i mdzod). Reading Patrul Rinpoché's praise to all *Seven Treasuries*[10] transports us close to the experience of the meaning held in these texts. We feel inspired. For me, the above quotation aptly applies to all the precious teachings collected within this book. "Simply reading one line of such an excellent text can leave your worldly experience in ruins"—this is very true. It is necessary to trust the teachings and to take the time to read them slowly and carefully, allowing time for both reflection and meditation.

In a way, it is obvious that we must trust in those things we wish to utilize, even in relationship to ordinary things, let alone the Great Perfection. Who would take a flight without the belief that the plane could get off the ground, fly, and land safely? Who would study to become a heart surgeon— endless years of schooling—if there was doubt in the efficacy of heart surgery, or if there was doubt that the doctor training you knew how to perform surgery himself? If you are a surgeon who constantly doubts and worries whether the procedure will actually work or not, you will not be successful, nor will you last long as a doctor. As dangerous as this might be to yourself and the patient, there is an even greater potential danger if you enter Great Perfection's path without trust, because not only can this life turn into a disaster, there may even be negative consequences in your future lives.

Having doubt in the view, meditation, and conduct of the Great Perfection is an obstacle that will keep you from achieving any result. When practicing within the context of the lower eight vehicles, dualistic mind is used as the path—either to reject, apply antidotes, or transform the passions. But when practicing in the context of Great Perfection, awareness itself is used as the path. In awareness there are no activities of ordinary dualistic mind. If doubt occurs, that is dualistic mind and is not the practice of Great Perfection.

In *Heart Advice of My Always Noble Spiritual Master*, Patrul Rinpoché quotes Guru Rinpoché:[11]

> Confident faith allows blessings to enter you.
> When you are free of doubt, whatever you wish will be accomplished.

Heartfelt Trust in the Lama Who Reveals It

Why is it important to trust in the Lama who reveals these precious Great Perfection teachings? It is said that on the path of Secret Mantrayana, all spiritual attainments come from relying upon your Lama. Dudjom Rinpoché writes in his commentary to the preliminary practices called *The Chariot for the Path of Union*:[12]

> All spiritual attainments of the profound Secret Mantra arise
> from nowhere else but through reliance on the Lama.

Patrul Rinpoché explains the importance of having faith in one's Lama:

> This is also necessary in this vajra essence vehicle, the heart
> essence of the Natural Great Perfection. It is not taught that the
> profound truth should be established through the process of
> analysis and logic as is done in the lower vehicles. Nor is it taught
> that common accomplishments should be relied upon in order to
> obtain supreme consummation, as in the lower tantras. It is also
> not taught that you should emphasize reliance upon the illustra-
> tive wisdom of the third empowerment to introduce ultimate
> wisdom, as it is in the higher tantras. In the Great Perfection tra-
> dition, you rely upon prayer made with fervent devotion to the
> supremely realized Lama alone, whose lineage is like a golden
> chain untainted by the defilement of broken tantric commit-
> ments, and consider him to be an actual Buddha. If you simply
> pray to him in this way, your mind will merge inseparably with
> his wisdom mind. By the power of the transference of his bless-
> ings to you, it is said that realization will arise within you.[13]

Saraha has said:

> Taking to heart what your Lama says
> Is like seeing a treasure in the palm of your hand.[14]

As we can see, trust in one's Lama is crucial for the Vajrayana practitioner.
Dudjom Rinpoché describes the three types of faith as follows:

> Faith is classified as three: clear faith, enthusiastic faith, and con-
> fident faith.[15]

Patrul Rinpoché himself emphasizes the importance of faith:

> The compassion and blessings of the Triple Gems are inconceiv-
> able, but whether these enter our mindstreams depends entirely
> on our faith and devotion. If you have immense faith and devo-
> tion, the compassion and blessings that enter you from your
> teacher and the Triple Gems will also be immense. In the same

way, if your faith and devotion are just moderate, the compassion and blessings that enter you will also be moderate. If you have only a little faith and devotion, only a little compassion and [a few] blessings will enter you. If you have no faith and devotion at all, absolutely no compassion or blessings will enter you. If you do not have faith, even meeting the actual Buddha and being accepted as his disciple will be of no benefit...[16]

Although it is essential to have complete trust in the Lama from whom you receive Great Perfection teachings, this trust develops gradually. It is essential for a beginner to examine thoroughly his or her teacher. As Patrul Rinpoché has said:

First, skillfully examine a Lama;
In the middle, skillfully rely upon a Lama;
Last, skillfully emulate his realization and action:
A noble person who does this is on the authentic path.

Having examined a Lama and having been accepted by him, it is important to maintain faith and respect. As Tobden Chöying Dorjé writes in *The Invaluable Treasury of Discourses and Tantras*:

First examine a Lama or teaching; then once you have accepted them, maintain faith and respect without fatigue, discouragement, or fluctuations. Rely upon the Lama and the Dharma with tenfold faith:
1. unchanging, like the king of mountains
2. vivid and without shadows, like the sun
3. endlessly deep, like the ocean
4. without an ulterior motive, like a mother
5. without limit or center, like space
6. without relaxation, like a bowstring
7. without discouragement and fatigue, like a ship
8. unperturbed by events, such as others' influence or scolding [by the master], like a bridge
9. continual, like a stream
10. respectful but supple and embellished with politeness, like a silken cord[17]

At the Hinayana and Mahayana level of practice, students see their teacher as a spiritual friend and can choose to weigh advice received. Once you practice within the context of the higher tantras, you promise to do what your Lama says. As Dudjom Rinpoché points out in *Essential Advice for Solitary Meditation Practice*:

> Therefore, everyone is at first independent until a Lama has accepted them. However, once you rely upon a Lama and are connected through empowerments and instructions, you are not free to disregard your tantric commitments (*samaya*). Didn't you bow before your Lama, lord of the *mandala*, at the end of the four empowerments and say:
>
> > As of now, I am your servant,
> > And I offer myself to you.
> > Having taken me as your disciple,
> > Please use every part of me.
>
> With this promise, no matter how great or powerful you are, aren't you subject to your Lama? You also said:
>
> > Whatever my lord commands,
> > That I will do.
>
> Once you took this promise, do you have the power not to do what he says? If you do not keep your promise, it is not appropriate to call you anything other than a vow-breaker, no matter how unpleasant a name this is.

For a practitioner—whether from the East or West—to progress on this path, trust in the Lama is essential because sometimes his or her advice will help bring you beyond your current limitations, thereby being a great aid on your path. Let's take a simple example: When a person decides to practice in the Vajrayana Buddhist tradition, that person first searches for a Lama with whom he or she feels a connection. The student requests this Lama to accept them and give them a practice and related teachings. Perhaps the master suggests that the student begin with the preliminary practices.

Initially, the student may become very excited at being accepted and given a practice. The master then explains that the preliminary practices include four parts: taking refuge and engendering *bodhicitta*, mandala offerings, Vajrasattva practice, and guru yoga, and that the student must accumulate 100,000 recitations of each.

People react differently to this suggestion. Some become excited by the opportunity and, due to their pure faith in their teacher, request teachings on how to do these practices without even the thought, "That's a lot to accumulate." Others, upon hearing about the accumulations, hesitate at first, but due to faith and trust in their Lama, they go beyond their initial hesitation and request instructions for practice with the thought, "That's a lot to accumulate, but if my Lama makes this suggestion, there must be a good reason for it." These people enjoy the benefits of these foundational practices early in their path, and the foundation for their practice becomes rock solid, an appropriate basis upon which to build their practice further. Still others may feel overwhelmed upon learning about the practice and may think, "That's a bit too much for me at the moment; maybe in the future I can try." Perhaps many years down the road they may begin their preliminary practices. And then some people never take their master's advice due to hesitation and lack of faith; after many years, having never begun, they will have accumulated only regrets. In this simple example, we can see how having even a little faith in one's Lama can lead to following his advice, thereby yielding huge benefits.

Traditionally, after completing the preliminary practices, one then practices Mahayoga. This includes practices contained within the categories of the three roots: Lama, wisdom deity, and dakini. Some people undertake these practices in the context of a three-year retreat; others, in other forms of long-term retreat. For example, at the retreat center Péma Ösel Ling where I live, many people begin one of these practices in the context of a public summer retreat and then complete it at home throughout the course of the next year or two.

We can see, based upon the words of these sublime wisdom teachers, how important it is to develop genuine and sincere trust in our Lama so we will be ready to receive the profound Great Perfection teachings when the opportunity arises. For an excellent explanation on how to rely upon a Lama I highly recommend the chapters on how to follow a spiritual friend and on guru yoga in *The Words of My Perfect Teacher* by Patrul

Rinpoché; and also *The Teacher-Student Relationship*, written by Jamgön Kongtrul.

The Wish to Take Their Practice to Completion

The third characteristic of a fortunate person is the wish to take their practice to completion. As we have seen, Dudjom Rinpoché states that a fortunate person feels

> ...heartfelt trust in the teaching of the profound, secret Great Perfection, and in the Lama who reveals it; and they wish to take their practice to completion. For them, this text will provide an open gate [to the path of Great Perfection].

What does Dudjom Rinpoché mean when he speaks of "taking their practice to completion"? This means to practice until attaining full and complete enlightenment. It is very important that a person in the Great Perfection tradition have as their motivation for receiving and practicing these profound teachings the aim to attain full enlightenment for sentient beings' benefit, not for selfish or limited motivations.

Our motivation is like an eye that takes aim when shooting an arrow at a target. What we really aim at, we will strike. Therefore, it is of the utmost importance to choose a proper target before letting our arrow fly. It is also important that once we have made that choice, we make sure we aim accurately at the target. In the same way, if we wish to receive and then practice the Great Perfection teachings, we must first choose the proper, finest target—full enlightenment for others' benefit. Next, we must make sure that, due to our selfishness or limitations, we are not surreptitiously aiming at a target other than the chosen one.

Limited motivations include the wish to attain the otherwise worthy goal of the state of an arhat or solitary sage, goals that fall short of fully enlightened Buddhahood. For many of us, the most common obstacle preventing us from bringing our practice to completion (that is, full enlightenment) is not that we focus upon the limited goals of the arhat or solitary sage but that our motivation is tainted with selfish drives. It seems to me that this is the most dangerous potential hazard we confront. If our motivation is pure and set on the goal of attaining enlightenment for others' benefit, sooner or later this will come true, and there is no way we can become sidetracked. As my Lama always says:

> If your motivation is pure, there is no way to make a mistake.

On the other hand, if our motivation is selfish or limited, we will never free ourselves from the pain and sufferings of the ever-spinning wheel of life.

Although we may voice the proper words, "May I receive these teachings in order to attain enlightenment for others' benefit," if our real underlying motivation is otherwise, we will not be able to achieve our stated goal, since aiming at lesser targets based on selfishness is an obstacle to spiritual progress. Therefore, it is crucial not to practice Great Perfection with an underlying motivation mixed with worldly concerns, or with a motivation unintentionally mixed with desire for our own personal gain, for example, to become a spiritual teacher with many students, a famous workshop leader with a large income, or a respected spiritual teacher in "new age" circles that will provide us with a career, money, fame, and prestige. It is important always to check our motivation to protect our practice from becoming merely a way to prop up the ego within a Buddhist community or from becoming an unintended method for creating the self-delusion of being a great practitioner. Checking our motivation also protects us from using our practice as a way to run away from painful life experiences and responsibilities. Whatever the case may be, if this is our underlying motivation, these limited goals may be accomplished but never the goal of full enlightenment for others' benefit.

Therefore, we must become aware of our underlying agendas in order to guarantee that our motivation is not tainted by selfishness or self-promotion. If we find it is tainted, we can take that recognition as an opportunity to purify it. My teachers emphasize this point over and over again, and it is one that is very important for the sincere practitioner to remember. I write this with no one but myself in mind, as self-criticism and as a reminder.

CONCLUSION

The teachings Dudjom Rinpoché presents in the Heart Advice section and throughout this book are extremely precious and very rare. They are the essence of the vast body of Buddhist wisdom; historically, they were very difficult to obtain. Traditionally, in the Himalayan region, to receive Great Perfection teachings, a person must first have practiced for many years within the context of the Hinayana, Mahayana, and Vajrayana teachings. There was no such thing as "Great Perfection workshops" or "Monday evening teachings" available. Instead, a meditator would receive these teachings after an arduous journey beginning with the gradual development of trust in his or her Lama. Based upon that developed trust, further instructions would be given on how to meditate. The student then would set out upon the progressive stages of the path, including: extensive preliminary practices; creation stage Mahayoga—outer, inner, secret, and innermost secret extensive practices related to the Lama, wisdom deity, and dakini; transmission stage Anuyoga—working with channels, winds, and bodhicitta; and then the preliminary practices specific to the Great Perfection.

After many years of practice, accumulating merit, and a close, pure connection with your Lama, if you were one of utmost good fortune, you may have received the precious Great Perfection teachings. It was always this difficult and rare to receive these precious teachings.

Traditionally, when one treads the path in this way, a deep trust in the teachings and the Lama who reveals these teachings would come naturally. This process would refine the practitioner's motivation until its target would be only the attainment of complete and full enlightenment. Buddhist practice propelled by selfish motives is ultimately self-defeating and pointless. As Dudjom Rinpoché says, whoever has these three qualities— faith in the Great Perfection teachings, faith in the Lama who reveals these teachings to you, and the goal only to become fully enlightened—is the fortunate person to whom he reveals the pith instructions of the Great Perfection, in a form of direct instructions placed in the palm of your hand.

Whether we are "fortunate individuals," truly qualified to receive the precious and profound Great Perfection teachings, is entirely up to us.

Nowadays, there are many teachings available in bookstores and libraries and numerous talks and workshops offered by qualified (and unqualified) people; consequently, it is very easy for the sincere student searching for a pure teacher or a pure, unbroken lineage to be overwhelmed and confused. I myself searched for such a lineage for many years, while being exposed to a vast array of spiritual teachers and teachings. In my youth, I studied

Western spiritual traditions, including Plato and the Pre-Socratic philosophers, leading to practice in Western mystical traditions. Later, I received an M.A. in integral psychotherapy and studied the theories and practices of Jungian, Gestalt, and existential paradigms, to name a few. Later, I received a Ph.D. in Indo-Tibetan Buddhism and afterward continued to search carefully for a pure, unbroken lineage that holds the wisdom and methods for attaining enlightenment in one lifetime.

I know without a doubt that Dudjom Rinpoché is the holder of such a lineage and that his pure lineage continues to this day, held by some of his heart disciples, whom I have the greatest good fortune to have as my teachers. This lineage is entirely complete within itself. It is not necessary to add anything from Western pyschology, New Age philosophies, nor any other tradition.

Therefore, the Heart Advice teachings found in this book—and for that matter all the writings contained herein—are the spiritual inheritance of humanity: the living realization, and the methods to attain it, passed down from master to disciple for over 2,000 years in an unbroken lineage. I searched for many years to find this lineage, undergoing both effort and hardship. Here, Dudjom Rinpoché places these teachings, this lineage, along with its blessings right in the palms of our hands. We are indeed very fortunate.

So please, find a comfortable chair, or your practice seat, and slowly, carefully, read these profound words of Dudjom Rinpoché, which have the ability to change our lives in a profound way, teachings that are an invaluable support for spiritual life and a light illuminating the darkness of our world. These teachings can relieve us of all our pains and sorrows and bring us to the final goal of ultimate freedom.

Essential Advice
for Solitary Meditation Practice

*Direct instructions on practice explained in a manner
easy to understand called* Extracting the Very Essence
of Accomplishment

*I go for refuge and bow with devotion at the feet of my incomparably
kind, glorious, sublime Lama.*
*Grant your blessings to my followers and me that the flawless realiza-
tion of the profound path arises swiftly in our mindstreams and that we
may then reach the unassailable state in this very life.*

IN THIS TEXT I present essential advice for solitary meditation practice in
an easily accessible way. My words will place direct instructions for the
practice of the innermost secret Great Perfection in the palms of the hands
of fortunate individuals. Their previous lifetimes' positive aspirations and
pure karmic propensities have led them to feel heartfelt trust in the teaching of the profound, secret Great Perfection, and in the Lama who reveals
it, and they wish to take their practice to completion. For them, this text will
provide an open gate [to the path of Great Perfection].

This can be understood through three general topics:

1. Preparation
   How to purify your mindstream, and how to direct your mind toward
   the teachings after having severed all ties of attachment.
2. Main practice
   How to directly cultivate the experience of Great Perfection, and how to
   resolve any misconceptions regarding the view, meditation, and conduct.

3. Post-meditation
   How to keep your vows and tantric commitments (*samaya*), and how to include all activities of this life within the Dharma.

First, the Preparation

Now I will say a little about the first topic. That which is called mind—this so very vivid awareness—appears from the very beginning at the same time as Buddha Kuntu Zangpo.[18] Nevertheless, Buddha Kuntu Zangpo knew this awareness as his own. Alas! Sentient beings endlessly wander in samsara because they do not recognize this, taking rebirth in countless forms of the six types of beings. Everything they have done has been meaningless.

Now, one time out of hundreds you have obtained a human form. If you do not do what you can now to avoid rebirth in the lower realms, your place of rebirth might be unknown, but wherever it might be among the six classes of beings, suffering will be its only sure feature.

It is not enough to have just obtained this human form. You must at once practice the authentic Buddhist path since the time of your death is unpredictable. Furthermore, at death you should have no regrets and should not be ashamed of yourself, like Jetsun Milarepa.

> In my, Milarepa's, religious tradition,
> We live so as not to be ashamed of ourselves.

When entering the Buddhist path, it is not sufficient to be a person who only adopts the outer appearance of a person on the path. Cut all entanglements to desirable things and to this life's affairs. When you enter the gate to Buddhist practice without having cut these ties, you will lack determination but not attachment to homeland, wealth, possessions, lovers, spouses, friends, relatives, and so forth. Your attitude of attachment becomes an underlying cause; the objects of your attachment, catalysts. When these meet, negative forces[19] will create obstacles. You will once again become an ordinary worldly person and will turn away from creating positive karma.

Therefore, reduce your food, clothing, and talk to the bare necessities and one-pointedly unite your mind with the Dharma without attachment toward the eight worldly concerns.[20]

In a solitary place, the thought of death penetrating his heart,
The practitioner, deeply averse to grasping,
Sets the retreat boundaries by giving up thoughts of this life
With a mind that does not encounter anyone, the eight worldly
  concerns.[21]

You should do just as Gyalwa Yang Gönpa advised; otherwise, mixing the eight worldly concerns with your spiritual practice is extremely dangerous, like eating food mixed with poison. The eight worldly concerns in concise form can be reduced to two things, hope and fear, which are, in fact, desire and anger. Inner desire and anger take apparent outer form as male demons (*gyalpo*)[22] and female demons (*senmo*). As long as your mind is not free from desire and attachment, you will not be free from these demons, and obstacles will never end.

Therefore, question your innermost thoughts repeatedly, "Do I harbor the eight worldly concerns or conceited attachment to this life?" Strive to give up these faults. Once you sustain the eight worldly concerns in your outlook, you invent the false semblance of spiritual practice: the things acquired in such deceit amount to wrong livelihood.[23]

In accord with the saying "You accomplished half of the Buddhist teachings when you left your native land," you turned your back on your homeland to wander in unfamiliar lands. Now that you have parted company from your friends and relatives in a positive way, do not listen to those who try to discourage you from pursuing your spiritual practice. Now that you've given away your possessions, rely upon whatever meritorious donations[24] come your way. Once you've recognized all your pleasures as obstacles created by bad habits, cultivate an attitude without desires.

If you are not contented with few possessions, as long as one "need" after another arises, the deceptive demon of your pleasures will enter without much trouble. Do not take as true anything others say, good or bad: Do not regard it with hope or fear; do not affirm or deny it. Allow others to say whatever they like, as if they are talking about a corpse. Except for a qualified Lama, no one can give correct advice, not even your father or mother. Be the judge of your actions and do not let others lead you around by the nose.

Outwardly, be persevering, and know how to live in harmony with everyone without being annoying.[25] In fact, should anyone high or low try to interfere with your practice, you should be as unaffected as an iron boulder flayed with a piece of silk. Do not be weak, someone whose head bends whichever way the wind blows, like blades of grass on a mountain pass. From the beginning until the conclusion of your cultivation of any practice, whether lightning strikes from above, lakes rise from below, rocks rend asunder on all sides, or your life is in danger, think, "To stop would break my promise!" You should do as you vowed until the end of that practice.

From the very beginning of your retreat, gradually establish a structure for sessions and sleep, down to the slightest details such as meals and breaks. Do not allow yourself to lapse into bad habits. In particular, whether your practice is simple or complex, ensure that it is not sporadic. Make your practice regular and even, and do not leave even a moment's space for anything ordinary. During retreat, seal your cave's entrance, or if that doesn't apply, do not meet with, talk to, or be on the lookout for others.

Completely discard all distractions of your restless mind, expel the stale breath, and assume the correct physical posture for meditation. Your dualistic mind must firmly stay on awareness with mindfulness, without moving for even an instant, like a solid oak stake planted in the ground. A strict outer, inner, and secret retreat will quickly produce all signs of accomplishment and noble qualities.

When in retreat you may have the thought "This is very important. I will meet with someone, and even speak to him; then afterward, I'll be strict." If you violate your retreat boundaries in this way, you will lose the richness of your practice, and it will become more and more lax. Therefore, if you made a firm initial decision to remain in retreat, your determination will become progressively firmer, and obstacles will not undermine your practice.

Selecting the Location for Retreat

Although there are numerous methods for examining the special characteristics of the location for retreat, generally, a suitable location is one blessed by previous accomplished masters (*siddha*) such as Guru Rinpoché, a place where those who have broken tantric commitments do not live, or any very isolated place suited to your character, such as one in which all basic necessities are easily available. If you have the inner strength to control quickly the malevolent local spirits who live in graveyards or other terrifying places using the appropriate outer and inner interdependent links, this will greatly enrich your meditation. But if you cannot control them, many obstacles will occur. When your realization becomes as vast as space, all adverse conditions arise as allies, so at that time it is most excellent for you to engage in the secret practices in graveyards or other such places. Continuously give up all outer and inner distractions, for the real solitary place is to abide in non-action.[26]

The Actual Purification of One's Mindstream

The common practices are the four thoughts that turn the mind away from samsara.[27] The uncommon practices are taking refuge, generating bodhicitta, purifying obscurations, and gathering the accumulations of merit and wisdom. Exert yourself according to each of their commentaries until experiences arise.[28] Especially, embrace guru yoga as the vital essence of practice, and practice diligently. If you do not, your meditation will grow slowly, and even if it grows a little, obstacles will arise and genuine realization will not manifest in your mindstream. Therefore, forcefully pray with uncontrived devotion. After some time the realization of wisdom mind will be transmitted to your mindstream, and an extraordinary realization that cannot be expressed by words will definitely arise from within yourself.

As it has been said by Lama Shang Rinpoché:

> To nurture stillness,
> To nurture spiritual experiences,
> To nurture *samadhi* and other spiritual states—
> These are common.
>
> But by the strength of your devotion,
> For realization to arise from within
> Due to the Lama's blessings—
> This is rare.

Therefore, for the ultimate truth of the Great Perfection to appear in your mind is dependent upon the preliminary practices. This is what Drigungpa meant when he said:

Other spiritual teachings regard the main practice as being profound.

We regard the preliminary practice as being profound.

It is just as he said.

Second, the Main Practice

The main practice is to cut through misconceptions regarding view, medi-
tation, and conduct, and how to put our practice to the test.

The View

To begin, the view is recognition of ultimate reality as it is.

As for this view, your mind's nature is the ultimate nature of reality. Once
you have concluded this with certainty in awareness free from all characteristics of intellectual mind's fabrications and contrivance, awareness
nakedly manifests as self-manifest wisdom. Words cannot express it.
Metaphors cannot illustrate it. It does not get worse in samsara nor better
in enlightenment. It has not been born, nor will it come to an end. It has not
been liberated nor deluded. It does not exist or not exist. Awareness is
unlimited and impartial.

In short, from the very beginning, awareness has never been established
as being material and having characteristics that can be conceptualized,
because its essence is primordially pure, sublime, all-pervasive emptiness.
The ocean of realms of phenomena of existence and enlightenment naturally manifest as the display of unobstructed emptiness, like the sun and its
rays.[29] Therefore, awareness is neither partial nor a completely empty void
because its nature is the supreme spontaneous presence of wisdom and
noble qualities.

Thus, awareness, the indivisibility of appearance and emptiness, epitome
of the three kayas, is the primordial nature of reality. Precise recognition of
awareness, ultimate reality as it is (*yin lugs*), is what is called the Great
Perfection's view beyond the intellect.

Our sublime master [Guru Rinpoché] said:

The dharmakaya, beyond the intellect, is ultimate reality.

We actually hold in our hands the wisdom mind of Buddha Kuntu Zangpo. How wonderful! This is the very essence of the six million, four hundred thousand Great Perfection tantras, themselves the consummation of all eighty-four thousand divisions of the Victorious One's collection of teachings. There is nothing beyond this. You should resolve all phenomena in this awareness. Definitively conclude that all phenomena [are contained] within this awareness.[30]

Meditation

Now, once you have resolved all your inner doubts and misconceptions regarding this view, to sustain its continuity is called meditation.

All other meditations with reference points are conceptual meditations fabricated by the mind. This is not how we meditate. Do not lose hold of this view previously described, and in that state release all consciousnesses of the five senses within the natural state (*rang babs*) and rest at ease.

Do not meditate to arrive at a conclusion: "That's it!" If you meditate in that way, it becomes intellectual activity. Here, there is no object of meditation whatsoever nor even an instant of distraction. Distraction from resting in awareness is true delusion. Don't be distracted!

Whatever thoughts arise, let them arise. Do not follow after them and do not suppress them. If you ask "In that case, what should I do?" whatever objective phenomena arise, whatever appears, do not grasp phenomena's appearing aspect as you rest in a fresh state, like a small child looking inside a temple.31 When all phenomena are left as they are, their appearance is not modified, their color does not change, and their brilliance does not diminish. If you do not spoil phenomena with clinging and grasping thoughts, appearances and awareness will nakedly manifest as empty and luminous wisdom.

However, many teachings considered to be very deep or extremely vast have left individuals of lesser intelligence mystified. If I put my finger on the concise essential meaning, it is this: In the gap between the last thought's cessation and the next's arising, isn't there a fresh, present knowing (*da lta'i shes pa*) that has not been modified even in the slightest— luminous, naked awareness? That itself is awareness's abiding state![32]

But one does not permanently abide within the nature of reality (*de kho na*). Doesn't a thought suddenly arise? That is the natural display of awareness. However, if you do not recognize thoughts as soon as they arise, they will naturally spread. This is called "the chain of delusion," the root of samsara. Simple recognition of thoughts as they arise breaks their flow. Release thoughts within that recognition. When you remain in that state, arising thoughts will all be liberated equally within awareness, the expanse of dharmakaya. This is the main practice in which the view and meditation of Cutting through Solidity (*khregs chod*) are cultivated as one.

Garab Dorjé has said:

> From within the nature of originally pure stainless space,
> Awareness suddenly manifests. That moment of mindfulness[33]
> Is like finding a jewel at the bottom of the ocean.
> This is dharmakaya, not fabricated nor created by anyone.

Persevere in this way. You must meditate without distraction day and night—do not leave emptiness in the domain of mere understanding. Bring everything back to awareness itself.

Conduct

Now, I will describe how conduct can enhance meditation and how to put our practice to the test.

The main point, as I previously explained, is never to part for an instant from the perception of your Lama as a true Buddha; make heartfelt, intensely focused prayers to your Lama. This is known as "devotion that is the sole sufficient cure"; it is superior to any other method to remove obstacles and enhance your practice. You will forcefully and decisively travel all paths to enlightenment.

Faults in Meditation

If you experience dullness and drowsiness, arouse awareness. If you experience excitement and agitation, relax your mind. Always, the meditator's vivid mindful awareness should not impose a disciplined mindfulness. Mindfulness is simple recollection of the recognition of your own nature.

Continuously sustain vivid mindful awareness at all times as you go about your daily activities, whether eating, sleeping, moving, or sitting, whether during meditation or post-meditation. Never harbor hope or fear toward whatever thoughts arise, such as those of happiness or suffering or those of the passions.[34] Do not accept or reject them; and do not destroy them using antidotes, and so forth. Instead, whatever feelings of happiness and suffering are there, settle in their naked, vivid, lucidly present essence. This single vital point, and none other, applies to everything. Do not confuse yourself with a lot of thinking.

A separate meditation upon emptiness as an antidote to what must be relinquished—thoughts and passions—is unnecessary. Awareness of what must be relinquished liberates it naturally with that recognition, like a snake's knot uncoiling.

Most people know how to say the words "the ultimate concealed meaning of the clear light vajra essence," like a parrot's chatter, but don't know how to practice it. We are all so incredibly fortunate! Carefully consider this once again—there's something to be understood. During our beginningless series of lives until now, our mortal enemy, dualistic clinging,[35] binds us to samsara. Now, thanks to our Lama's kindness, his introduction to naturally abiding dharmakaya releases both poles of grasping,[36] like a feather consumed in fire, with nothing following and without a trace. Isn't that really satisfying?

If you do not practice once you've obtained the profound instructions of the swift path such as these, it is as if a wish-fulfilling jewel were placed in a corpse's mouth. What a waste! Practice without being discouraged![37]

Furthermore, beginners will lose their mindfulness in distraction due to unwholesome thoughts that get out of control; these thoughts coalesce in the form of underlying mental activity. At some point, a piercing mindfulness returns, and the thought of regret arises, "Oh, I'm distracted!" Nevertheless, do not do anything whatsoever at that moment, such as stopping the flow of previous thoughts or regretting having been distracted. When this vivid mindfulness returns, it is sufficient merely to sustain naturally resting in precisely that mindfulness.

A famous saying advises, "Do not reject thoughts; see them as dharmakaya." However, until you perfect the subtle power of higher insight, you might dwell upon the thought, "This is probably dharmakaya!" and remain in a blank state of peaceful abiding. You thus risk getting trapped in a spaced-out, indifferent, unreflective state. Therefore, in the beginning look directly at whatever thoughts arise; do not examine, analyze, or reflect upon them at all. Rest upon the recognizer of thoughts, without making it a big deal, disinterested in what arises, like an old man or woman watching children at play.

Once you've placed your mind as I described, the deepening of the experience of stillness in a non-conceptual natural state will be suddenly, abruptly destroyed. At that instant, wisdom beyond mind will nakedly and clearly manifest.

While you tread the path, [this experience of wisdom] will not come untainted with one or another of three meditative experiences—bliss, clarity, or conceptionlessness.[38] Nevertheless, placing your mind without the slightest bit of hope, fear, attachment, or conceit due to holding such experiences as supreme prevents errors. It is very important constantly to give up distraction and to meditate with one-pointed vigilant mindfulness. When you lapse into sporadic practice and mere intellectual understanding, arrogance will arise out of just a little peaceful abiding. If you do not carefully observe your spiritual experiences, you will merely be skilled in pretense and knowledgeable of the right words, which is not beneficial.

As the Great Perfection tantras state:

> Intellectual understanding is like a patch,
> It will fall off.

And,

> Spiritual experiences are like mist,
> They will evaporate.

As this says, even some slight positive and negative objective event has deceived great meditators,[39] and many lose their bearings in the midst of circumstances. Even when meditation is planted within your stream of being, the profound instructions will remain on the pages of your book if you do not meditate consistently. Your mind will become insensitive: You will become insensitive to the teachings, you will become insensitive to practice, and genuine meditation will never arise. Even old great meditators are in danger of dying completely lost,[40] in the state of a newcomer to practice. Therefore, be very careful.

When you continually familiarize yourself with this over a long period of time, devotion or some other suitable catalyst will at some point cause these spiritual experiences to overflow into realization, and you will vividly see naked awareness, as if a veil were instantly lifted from your head. You will become utterly free and spacious. This is called "the supreme seeing that does not see anything." Thereafter, thoughts arise as meditation; mental stillness and movement are simultaneously liberated. Moreover, at first, recognition of thoughts liberates them, like meeting someone familiar.[41] In the middle period, thoughts are liberated by themselves, like a snake's knot uncoiling. Finally, thoughts are liberated without benefit or harm, like a thief entering an empty house. These three ways of liberation will occur gradually. A deep, decisive trust manifests within you that all phenomena are the magical display of your awareness alone—waves of realization of emptiness and compassion will surge. Choosing between either cyclic existence or enlightenment ends. You realize that Buddhas are not "good" and sentient beings are not "bad." Whatever you have done, you will be carefree beyond words without knowing how to move from the sole nature of phenomena (*dharmata*), and therefore, you will uninterruptedly abide in this infinite space day and night.

As it is said in the Great Perfection tantras:

> Like the sky, realization is changeless.

This kind of Great Perfection practitioner[42] appears to have an ordinary human form, but his or her mind is dharmakaya. He or she abides in wisdom mind free from effort and activity and, without doing anything, traverses all paths and stages. Finally, ordinary mind and phenomena exhausted, like the space of a broken vase, the body vanishes into atoms, and the mind vanishes into the nature of phenomena. This is called attaining[43] the immortal vase body (*gzhu nu bum sku*), which is the inner clarity of the original ground, stainless space (*dbyings*). This will come about. Since this is the ultimate consummation of view, meditation, and conduct, it is called the fully manifest unattainable result. The stages of spiritual experiences and realization arise either in a progressive order, without a progressive order, or all at once. This occurs according to the particular faculties of people, but there is no difference when the result is achieved.

Post-Meditation

How the teachings encompass keeping vows and tantric commitments, and applying them in your daily life.

Although you applied yourself in the practice of view, meditation, and conduct as described above, if you were unskillful in post-meditation's conduct, and your vows and tantric commitments were damaged, impediments and obstacles will hinder your progress on the paths and spiritual stages in the short term, and ultimately you will certainly fall to the lowest hell called Incessant Pain. Therefore, it is extremely important never to be separate from vigilant mindfulness, not making any mistakes regarding what kind of conduct to accept and what to reject.

The great master Guru Rinpoché has said:

> My view is higher than the sky;
> My attention toward karma and its consequences is finer than
>   flour.[44]

Thus, once you give up a coarse blank state of mind, act with circumspection to the cause and effect of your actions. Guard your vows and tantric commitments so that not even the slightest one is damaged; ensure that faults and downfalls do not taint you. Secret Mantra's tantric commitments have many categories, but in a concise form they can be subsumed into one—the tantric commitments of the wisdom body, speech, and mind of your root Lama. A mere instant of having considered the Lama to be a human being[45] is said to postpone spiritual attainment (*siddhi*) by years and months. Why is this so? Because the relationship with your Lama is very serious.

Vajrapani has said:

> Spiritual attainment is received from the Lama.

Therefore, everyone is first independent until a Lama has accepted him or her. However, once you rely upon a master and are connected through empowerments and instructions, you are not free to disregard your tantric commitments. Didn't you bow before your Lama, lord of the mandala, at the end of the four empowerments and say:

As of now, I am your servant,
And I offer myself to you.
Having taken me as your disciple,
Please use every part of me.[46]

With this promise, no matter how great or powerful you are, aren't you subject to your Lama? You also said:

Whatever my lord commands,
That I will do.

Once you took this promise, do you have the power to not do what he says? If you do not keep your promise, it is not appropriate to call you anything other than a vow-breaker, no matter how unpleasant a name this is.

Furthermore, it has not been taught that you should keep your tantric commitments especially with a Lama of higher status, who has a large retinue, who is wealthy, powerful, and prosperous but that it is unnecessary to keep your tantric commitments with a Lama of lower status, who takes a humble position, who engages in the fearless conduct (*brtul zhugs*) of a beggar. Whatever the case may be, you must understand the potential risks and profit of a commitment with any Lama, since it won't suffice to remain standing around like a dim-witted old horse. This being so, carefully consider whether the purpose of keeping your tantric commitments is for your Lama's sake or for yours. Reflect on this with a composed mind, just as when one prepares medicine.[47] If you think you do so for your Lama's sake, you can completely give them up as of right now. If doing so is not for his sake, it doesn't make sense to deceive yourself.[48]

In relation to tantric commitments with your spiritual companions, in general, view positively whosoever has entered the gateway of Buddha's teachings, and train in pure vision (*dag snang*). Give up sectarian bias, slander, and so forth. Specifically, the full extent of everyone who gathered before the same Lama in the same mandala is your vajra brothers and sisters. Give up mistreatment, competition, jealousy, deceit, and so forth; be sincerely loving and caring toward them.

All sentient beings are none other than our kind parents, but alas! the intense, inescapable suffering of samsara torments them. Think, "If I do not protect them from this, who will?" and train your mind by cultivating unbearable compassion. Only accomplish what is beneficial for them in body, speech, and mind, and dedicate all your virtuous acts to others' benefit. You should continuously think of nothing apart from the teachings, your Lama, and sentient beings. Do not allow your motivation and actions to contradict one another. Do not compete with anyone who has the title or outward appearance of a yogi or a monk. Since this is most important, do not foolishly do this. Shut your mouth and subdue your mind.

Deep down, if you only think about what will help you in future lives, what is called "the Dharma" is something that you yourself must do. If you hope or need for others to practice virtue in your name after you die, it will be difficult for that to help you.[49]

Therefore, turn your attention within and apply yourself. With a heartfelt attitude of renunciation, be extremely diligent, mindful, and determined to practice for as long as you live. The main practice is to strike the vital point in the cultivation of the profound view and meditation. Postmeditation is conduct that is consistent with conduct to be accepted or rejected, to correctly [keep] the tantric commitments of the Vajrayana, the precepts of the bodhisattvas' training, and the vows of individual liberation.[50] Such conduct's imprint is that noble qualities cannot help but arise within you. This is why the Great Perfection is the path upon which people who committed negative acts can become suddenly enlightened.

The Great Perfection is so profound that it also has obstacles, just as sources of great profit entail great risk. The reason for these obstacles is that the instructions' impact stirs up your previously accumulated negative karma; signs of this are the outward appearance of demons' magical apparitions of obstacles. It is possible that various unwanted outer and inner adverse conditions will appear, such as gods and demons showing their forms in your place of practice, calling you by name, and disguising themselves as your Lama and giving predictions. Various frightening magical apparitions may appear in your experiences or dreams. Also, unpredictable things may happen to you in person, such as being subject to attackers, robbers, thieves, or diseases. In your mind, you may experience intense suffering for no apparent reason and become despondent; intense passions may arise; devotion, love, and bodhicitta may diminish; and thoughts may arise as enemies—you feel you are about to go crazy. You may take good advice the wrong way. You may sincerely wish not to stay in solitary retreat but strongly wish to break your promise [to remain].[51] Wrong views toward your Lama may arise and you may entertain doubts about the teachings. Further, you may be unjustly accused although you are innocent. You may acquire a bad reputation. Friends may turn into enemies. It is possible that various unwanted outer and inner adverse conditions such as these will appear. Oh, these are upheavals (*lhong*); recognize them as such! You've reached a crossroads between spiritual gain and loss. If you apply the vital points of meditation to these obstacles, they become spiritual attainments. If they overpower you, they become hindrances.

When confronting upheavals, be courageous and turn your mind to your Lama with pure tantric commitments and unrelenting devotion. Give him your heart. Pray fervently to your Lama: "Whatever I do, think of me." If you take these adverse circumstances as something desirable and intensely apply yourself to practice, at some time these circumstances' solidity will naturally collapse and your practice will be enhanced. You will perceive appearances as being insubstantial like mist. More than ever before, you will trust your Lama and his instructions. Henceforth, even if upheavals appear again, you will find confidence thinking, "This is no big deal." Yes, this is the point of resolution (*tshar tshad*)! Your acceptance of these adverse conditions on your path has corresponded to the resolution of these upheavals. A la la! This is exactly what we old fathers want! So do not be like a fox creeping up on a human corpse, craving to eat it but with knees trembling in fear. Develop a strong mind.

People whose supportive accumulation of merit is small, who are careless toward their tantric commitments and vows, whose wrong views are great, whose doubts are many, whose promises are lofty, but whose practice is poor—their hearts stink like farts, and they invite the Lama's instructions to remain on their bookshelf. They hold on to and chase after those adverse conditions[52] until they die, and thus Mara takes the opportunity to lead them down the path to the lower realms. What a pity! Pray to your Lama that this does not happen to you!

Moreover, although it is fairly easy to bring adverse circumstances into the path, doing the same for positive circumstances is very difficult. Even those who vainly assume themselves to be highly realized beings risk enslavement by the son of Mara[53] and are distracted by devoting themselves to ways of becoming important in this life. Be very careful. Know that this marks the border line where you can go up or down, where the measure of great meditators is taken. Until you perfect the power of inner realization's noble qualities, it is inappropriate to tell whomever you meet the stories of your spiritual experiences. Keep your mouth shut.

Furthermore, don't count hardships of months or years in retreat; take your entire life as the only measure for the duration of your practice. Devote yourself to practice. Do not use the pretext of emptiness to mislead yourself—do not disdain virtuous practice on the relative level of cause and effect. Do not stay long in villages for the purpose of making money for food, such as performing home ceremonies or performing the pacification of demons. Reduce meaningless activities, unnecessary talk, and useless thinking about things. Do not act in ways that contradict the Dharma, such as fraud or deceit, to fool others. Do not gain wrong livelihood through flattery, indirect requests, or other means, because you have strong desire for pleasurable things. Do not associate with bad friends or with those whose view and conduct are disharmonious with your own. Expose your own faults, and do not speak about others' hidden faults. Any kind of smoking is said to be a lure of oath-breaking demons, so wholeheartedly give it up. Although alcohol is used as a tantric commitment substance, do not drink carelessly merely to get drunk. You should bring into the path all those who have a good or bad connection with you without making any distinction whatsoever, be they faithful persons who serve you or faithless persons who revile or abuse you. Care for them with pure prayers of aspiration.

At all times, do not lose courage in your inner awareness; uplift yourself, while assuming a humble position in your outer demeanor. Wear old, worn out clothes. Place everyone, good, bad, and in-between, above yourself. Rely upon the bare essentials, and resolutely remain in your solitary retreat. Fix your ambition on the life of a beggar. Follow the example of the life and complete liberation of previous accomplished masters (*siddha*). Do not blame your past karma; instead, be someone who purely and flawlessly practices the Dharma. Do not blame temporary negative circumstances; instead, be someone who remains steadfast in the face of whatever circumstances may arise.

In brief, taking your own mind as witness, make your life and practice one, and at the time of death, with no thought of anything left undone, do not be ashamed of yourself. This itself is the pith instruction of all practices.

Eventually, when the time of death arrives, completely give up whatever wealth you possess, and do not cling to even one needle. Moreover, at death, practitioners of highest faculty will be joyful; practitioners of middling faculty will be without apprehension; and practitioners of the lowest faculty will have no regrets. When realization's clear light becomes continuous day and night, there is no intermediate state (*bardo*): death is just breaking the enclosure of the body. If this is not the case, but if you have confidence that you will be liberated in the intermediate state, whatever you have done in preparation for death will suffice. Without such confidence, when death arrives, you can apply your previous training to master transference of consciousness[54] to send your consciousness to whichever pure land you wish and there traverse the remaining paths and stages to become enlightened.

Therefore, in our precious lineage this is not just some old tale from the past. Even these days, those who reach the ultimate consummation of realization on the paths of Cutting through Solidity, or *trekchö* (*khregs chod*), and Direct Vision, or *tögal* (*thod rgal*), have their material body vanish into a mass of rainbow light. Follow their example. Don't toss away a gem to search for a trinket. Since we have the extreme good fortunate to have met with such profound instructions, the heart blood of the dakinis, be inspired. Give rise to joyfulness, then meditate.

Disciples, treasure this book in your heart; it might prove very helpful to you.

The intended purpose for writing this book was to help the solitary retreat practice of all the retreatants in the three-year retreat center Ogmin Péma and was based on the request of the diligent practitioner Rikzang Dorjé who possesses the jewel of indivisible faith and devotion, the catalyst; thus, I, Jigdral Yeshé Dorjé, spoke this heart advice in the form of direct instructions. May it become the cause for the wisdom of realization to manifest powerfully in the mindstreams of fortunate disciples.

From Dudjom Rinpoché's public shrine room
in Dordogne, France

Dudjom Tersar Refuge Tree
© 1998 Kumar Lama (Yelmo)
kumarlama @ juno.com

right:
Sign outside HH's home
(Dordogne).

below:
HH's home with prayer flags
(Dordogne).

HH's home (Dordogne)

HH's practice seat and where he entered parinirvana
in his room (Dordogne).

Nectar for Fortunate Disciples' Hearts:

A Compilation of Essential Words of Advice

1. Lama, incomparable lord

Lama, incomparable lord of a hundred Buddha families,
I place your feet on a lotus at the center of my heart, forever inseparable
    from me.
Then, not to refuse the requests from you, my fortunate friends,
I will concisely teach you my essential advice in these few words:

Generally, the four thoughts that turn the mind from samsara
Inspire you to enter the gateway to all teachings;
You then exert yourself in the accumulations and purification of the
    common preliminary practices.[55]
This is the precious central pillar that precedes all practice.

Especially, evoke unbearably intense respect and devotion's energy:
Rely upon the profound path of guru yoga,
Take empowerment, merge your mind with the Lama's, settle in
    evenness.
This itself is the sovereign technique that removes hindrances and
    enhances your experience.

Purification of ordinary phenomena into the wheel of purity
Is the supreme path of skillful means, the creation stage.[56]
To have no material focus, even on attachment to pure appearances,
Is the incisive knowledge of emptiness, the crucial final decision, the
    completion stage.

All phenomena of samsara and enlightenment having neither base
    nor root,
Are rootless naked empty awareness, the original, natural state (*gnyug
    ma'i babs*),
And are unspoiled by contrived perceptions based on hope and fear.
Self-liberation sustained naturally is meditation's central point.

Self-manifest Buddhahood, this awareness,
Is original dharmakaya, never separate from you.
You've never been separate from it, so just recognize it right now.
It is very important to remain settled in the ground of this recognition.

The full measure of confidence in realization is to arrive at your
    essential nature,
Banishing hope, fear, anxiety, worry,
Joy, sorrow, desire, anger, or attachment
Toward anything whatsoever, such as virtuous acts, negative acts, gods,
    demons, happiness, and suffering.

Beginningless delusion's habitual patterns have fierce strength:
Mere understanding will not produce realization and liberation.
Once you've relinquished the nine physical, verbal, and mental activities,
Be diligent in attaining stability in one-pointed practice.

Whatever you have done is ordinary karma, whatever you have thought
    amounts to delusion.
Pursuit of delusion will never result in an undeluded state.
When clinging to any reference point whatsoever has collapsed,
The practitioner whose six senses are self-liberated is truly happy.

Once you have reached your goal, a carefree mind,
The state between death and rebirth is unknown, and "lower realms" is
    just a designation.
When you reach immortality at the level of phenomena's exhaustion,
You bid farewell to the three realms of existence.

Pray that Vajrakilaya dispels obstacles to your longevity;
That Great Mother Tröma grants you the highest accomplishment;
That Tsok-kyi Dakpo (Mahakala)[57] befriends you in accomplishing
    enlightened activity:
This will naturally aid others and yourself.

Thus, I, Jigdral Yeshé Dorjé, spoke these words to satisfy the wishes of Yeshé Rabsel, a tantric practitioner who keeps the vows of monastic discipline. May my words be medicine for you in every circumstance.

2. Incomparable Lama, wish-fulfilling jewel

Incomparable Lama, wish-fulfilling jewel,
To your feet I respectfully offer the crown of my head, before giving my
    disciple this counsel:
If you sincerely strive for liberation from your heart,
Apply an attitude of renunciation, needing nothing whatsoever.

With uncontrived faith and devotion, an excellent motivation,
Make supplications to your root Lama, inseparable from the wisdom
    deities;
Accept his empowerments and repeatedly merge your mind with his.
Remorsefully acknowledge your faults and downfalls and use antidotes
    to restore your vows.

There are countless things to be known in books;
Don't salivate at the many "deep, profound teachings."
Sustain, like a flowing river, creation and completion's tantric practices
Centered on Great Mother Tröma,[58] the embodiment of all the three
    roots.

Uncontrived, naked empty awareness is the supreme essential nature.
To sustain the natural state free from grasping is the view and
    meditation.
The vital points of conduct attuned to them are to be diligent and careful
    regarding your actions.
Cultivate the experience of whichever spiritual practice you trust.

Until you receive a specific indication from the wisdom deities or your
    Lama to engage actively in helping others,
Your activity for others' benefit may lapse into acts that help only
    yourself.
Therefore, always distance yourself from busy-ness,
And live in a solitary place, striving to engage in spiritual practice as long
    as you live.

At that time when you thoroughly cut clinging to this life,
The treasure trove of pure vision, devotion, and compassion overflows.
When spiritual experiences, realization, and noble qualities arise from
    deep within,
You will effortlessly and spontaneously produce a prodigious wave of aid
    for others and yourself.

When you keep this in your heart, it becomes heart advice.
I pray that these, my intimate confidences, merge with your mind.
I, crazy Dudjom Tulku,
Spoke this in response to the insistent request of the tantric practitioner
    Déchen Dorjé. May this be virtuous!

3. O friend! As you wander aimlessly

O friend!

As you wander aimlessly,
Or wherever you stay in unpredictable solitary places,
Pray to your Lama, receive empowerment, and merge your mind with
    your Lama's mind.

In continual inseparability with your wisdom deity, the mantra, and
    meditative state,
Conclude that samsara and enlightenment are resolved in the Great
    Perfection
And take uncontrived naked empty awareness as the path.

Give gifts of *tormas* and tantric feasts to the dakinis and protectors
    of the Dharma (*dharmapala*).
Make pure prayers of aspiration with compassion for beings.
Preserve your vows and tantric commitments as a pledge you make
    with your life.

Within a relaxed open state without physical, verbal, or mental activity,
You reach right now the citadel of Buddha Kuntu Zangpo's wisdom
    mind.
Happy in this life, happy in the next, happy continually.

Practice in this easy and effective way.
Make supplications: It will be impossible for us to be apart!

*I, Jigdral Yeshé Dorjé, spontaneously spoke this for Rikzang Dorjé as a
token upon his departure.*

4. Sublime nectar of profound meaning

O true friend, listen to these words!

The sublime nectar of the profound meaning of ripening and liberation
Has filled the full excellent vase of your vast and profound mind,
Increasing the celebration of the accomplishment of your own and
    others' good.

At all times, pray with longing to the great master from Oddiyana [Guru
    Rinpoché],
And repeatedly merge your mind with his.
Satisfy the three roots and the protectors of the Dharma (*dharmapala*)
    with torma and tantric feast offerings.
Turn your mind to others' benefit and don the armor of diligence.

Whatever good or bad events occur, gross or subtle concepts arise,
Leave far behind you hopeful or fearful consideration of them as solid.
Relax within the wide-open, original state of self-liberated, empty
    exaltation,
And integrate them into your experience as magical displays.

Especially, this wrathful practice of *Innermost Secret Gathering* (*gsang
    ba 'dus pa*),[59]
Like my very own heart, is your share of the teachings I gift to you,[60]
At this lowest point of malevolent times, it is the single trustworthy
    remedy
To subjugate legions of male demons and starving spirits and violators
    of tantric commitments.

Therefore, bring the approach and accomplishment stages to culmination
    for your own benefit;
To help others, perform various enlightened activities as appropriate.
Make this the essence of your continual tantric practice:
The treasure of the wish-fulfilling jewel will definitely open.

Do not be impatient nor let your courage be weak
In projects guided by the meaning of the scriptures that are of significant
    aid for the Buddhist doctrine and for beings,
Such as temples, the foundation of the doctrine.
With persevering effort, your projects will be spontaneously
    accomplished without hindrance.

Before long, we will meet repeatedly
In a celebration of joy and delight. This will occur without fail.
Right now, may Lake Born Vajra's unfailing blessings
Grant you auspicious fortune!

*Once as Tulku Orgyen Chemchok Düpa Tsal was leaving for his home-
land, I, Jigdral Yeshé Dorjé, wrote and offered these words of intimate
advice on his departure as a declaration of the truth. Siddhi rastu!*

5. Your present naked awareness

How amazing!

Your present, naked awareness—
Unspoiled by thoughts of past, present, or future,
Not fettered by mind grasping to so-called "meditation"
Nor falling into a pervasive blankness of so-called "non-meditation"—
The natural state nakedly sustained,
Is the practice of Great Perfection.

Regardless of what thoughts arise during that practice,
To reject negative ones or foster positive ones is unnecessary.
Mere recognition liberates them in their own ground.
Take this liberation upon arising as the path's key point.

Destroy whatever meditative experiences arise, and relax.
A tantric practitioner without fixation is deeply content.
You've reached your goal of contentment right now.
What is the use of numerous enumerations of Buddha's teachings
When you discover Buddha Kuntu Zangpo within yourself?
Keep the meaning of these words close to your heart.

I, Jigdral Yeshé Dorjé, spoke this to refresh Mahasukha's memory.

6. How wonderful! If you wish to embark

Kind Lama, at your feet I pay homage.

How wonderful! If you wish to embark upon the correct path, consider
   this advice:
The cause and effect of your cultivation of merit and wisdom and
   excellent prayers of aspiration throughout past lives
Have given you the freedoms and endowments of a precious human life
   and led you to a qualified Lama.

You have met profound instructions and enjoy the freedom to practice
   these teachings.
Now that you possess such good fortune and magnificent conducive
   circumstances,
Do not lose them in laziness or in meaningless activity.
Exert yourself in what is meaningful—reaching an everlasting state.

See your Lama as the Buddha incarnate and nurture respect and devotion
   toward him.
With pure vision toward your spiritual companions, care for them with
   love, affection, and respect.
Exert yourself in training your mind in compassion toward beings and in
   the mind of awakening.
At all times, encourage yourself with the recollection of impermanence,
   and further the certainty of your own release from cyclic existence.

Forthright keeping of your vows and tantric commitments
Is the single vital point so as not to be ashamed in your deity's or Lama's
   presence.
Your practice, the fusion of your life with the Dharma,
Is the single vital point so as to have no thoughts remaining at death.
Your constant reduction of concern with plans
Is the single vital point that prevents obstacles and laziness from
   overpowering you.

The root of the eighty-four thousand-fold teachings
Is found in one thing: subduing your own mind.
If you do not subdue your own mind, you might hear even a hundred
    thousand instructions,
Yet apart from a mere auspicious connection, it is difficult for such
    hearing to be useful at death.

Not only is lofty spiritual terminology no aid at the time of death,
It is even more difficult for it to help you in the next life.

Therefore, you do not need famous teachings;
Instead, to mingle your mind secretly with the teachings
Leads to gaining self-confidence in your practice.
At that point, regardless of who is unsatisfied with you, you are the
    highest practitioner.

I have no time to write a lot
And what I have written is the stuff of meaningless stacks of books.
    What is the use of them?
Thus, if you have kept just this in your heart,
You will surely accomplish the supreme essential meaning.

From my heart, I pray
That both the length of your life and the substance of your intentions
    reach culmination,
And that in the next life we meet
In Lotus Light Pure Land, at the feet of the guru.

*I, the madman Dudjom, spontaneously wrote and bestowed these words to
comply with the insistent request of the faithful nun Yeshé Kalden, who
had traveled a great distance from Shukseb Dakini's sacred place.*[61]

7. Listen, faithful nuns!

How amazing! Listen, faithful nuns!

You obtained free and fully endowed human bodies, so difficult to find,
Yet even these bodies are as fleeting as water bubbles.
You will infallibly experience the results of any positive and negative
    actions you amass.
Wherever you have been born in samsara is a land of suffering:
The wish for renunciation must arise in your heart.

Your eternal, infallible protectors are the Triple Gems,
Fused in a single person: your Lama.
That master who shows you freedom's path
Is far kinder to you than the actual Buddha.
Thus, even if he were to kill you now, your faith should remain
    unassailable,
And you should accomplish his wishes respectfully in thought, word, and
    deed.

Your tantric brothers and sisters united by commitments taken in the
    same empowerment received from the same Lama
Are your companions on the path until enlightenment.
You must not only give up anger, ill will, and wrong views toward them
But have pure vision, seeing them as male and female wisdom deities.

Conditioned phenomena's nature is impermanence;
Reduce your mental long-range plans.
Don't procrastinate until tomorrow, the next day, or the next life.
From now on, be diligent in your spiritual practice.

Moreover, enter the Victorious One's excellent path.
Having developed the intention to awaken for others' benefit,
Not with a motivation poisoned by consideration of your own
    selfish desires,
Be guided by high appreciation of compassion.

If your respect and devotion grows ever stronger as you rely on your
   Lama,
If your mind grows ever tamer as you study the sacred Dharma,
And if your anger, desire, and hatred progressively decrease,
These are signs that the Dharma have been very helpful to your mind.

As for the main practice, the experiential cultivation of Great Perfection,
Cut through to the depths your doubts and misconceptions
Concerning ultimate reality as it is, without recourse to hearsay.
It is crucial to gain certainty that is not just words.

All phenomena of samsara and enlightenment do not exist apart from
   deluded perception.
Dualistic phenomena—the grasping subject and grasped objects—
   are in essence empty.
When you recognize unaltered awareness as dharmakaya,
This itself is Great Perfection's view.

Knowing this, to settle naturally within the abiding nature
Without distraction, without meditation, without clinging, and without
   respite
And to sustain this in the natural state—fresh, unimpeded awareness—
Is uncontrived meditation.

Do not side with the view over conduct
Nor with conduct over the view.
While making your conduct harmonious with the Dharma,
Keeping the tantric commitments honestly is the best conduct.

Do not wrongly assume that enlightenment will be attained
Elsewhere than this present awareness.
To reach the ground of the immediacy of the essential nature of
   self-manifest awareness
Is the king of fruition.

Once you single-mindedly and flawlessly practice
All the crucial points of view, meditation, and conduct as described,
You will reach the unassailable state during this lifetime, have no doubt.
Vajra speech will surely not deceive you.

Teaching others without having subdued one's own mind,
Misleading others like a dog without having gained success oneself,
Giving others pointing-out instructions without having gained
    experience oneself—
Such immature conduct is the cause of shame.

Nevertheless, I spoke these words
So as not to refuse the insistent request, "We need your heart advice."
If these words have any virtue,
May it ripen in the minds of you who made this request: May your own
    and others' goals be fully accomplished!

*I, Jigdral Yeshé Dorjé, wrote this as both Sherab Zangmo and Tsultrim
Wangmo insistently requested. Virtue!*

8. Now that you have found a free and fully endowed human body

How amazing! Listen, my two friends!

Now that you have found
A free and fully endowed human body, so difficult to attain,
You should accomplish your everlasting goal.

You have met the one who is difficult to meet—
Your Lama, the Buddha incarnate.
You then received the profound instructions,
The swift path to liberation in this lifetime.

This fortune has been won with your previously accumulated merit's
    power,
Not with wealth of jewels.
Therefore, with intense diligence,
Have your practice accompany you to the end of your life.

The teachings' foundation is the mind of awakening.
The Victorious Ones' spiritual heirs spend their lives helping others.
Lacking this, the hearer's vehicle
Does not lead to enlightenment.

If anger's hailstones
Rain down upon virtue's bountiful harvest,
The fruit may be totally destroyed.
Keep the watchman of mindfulness alert!

Individual liberation vows without self-control;
Bodhisattva training without compassion;
Tantric practice without keeping samaya—
These cause rebirth in the hells.

Empowerment's foundation is samaya—
If you keep them, tantric practice is the nectar of immortality;
If you do not, it is like a deadly poison
You have already consumed.
With such potential advantages or disaster, such positive or negative
     effects,
Protect your tantric commitments as you would your life!

Having discarded one and seized another
Among the many deep, deep sacred teachings,
You will not accomplish even one ultimate result.
Therefore, be diligent in practicing one of them!

Apparent existence—all phenomena of existence and enlightenment—
Is the false design of your own mind's delusion:
Recognition of awareness as primordial dharmakaya
Is the view.

To settle in the evenness of the natural state
Within the fresh, continual state
Of unimpeded original awareness (*shes pa*)
Unbound by dualism's fetters: this is meditation.

To abide within a state of non-action
During the ninefold activities of body, speech, and mind[62]
And to conform your behavior to the Dharma
Are the essential keys of conduct.

Not searching elsewhere for what is to be attained
But to grasp within yourself
Buddha Kuntu Zangpo manifest, your own awareness—
This is the spontaneously present sovereign result.

Know the true nature of view, meditation, conduct, and result
Correctly as I described
And cultivate their experience single-pointedly.
You will definitely reach the unassailable state during this lifetime.

If my Lama's compassion
Prevents obscurations by negative acts and pollution due to accepting
    undeserved offerings
And gives the fortune to reach the pure lands
To one such as I—without spirituality, neither a lay person nor a monk—
I pray repeatedly that we, teacher and disciples,
Remain together as inseparable companions.

I, Yeshé Dorjé, spoke this so as not to refuse both Chöwang and Tsultrim's insistent request: "We need heart advice like this!"

9. Glorious Lama

Glorious Lama,
Incomparably kind lord of the Dharma,
At your lotus feet, I present the energy center of great exaltation
    [the crown of my head] as a supreme offering.
I will now relate some beneficial advice for your mind.

Unrestrained negative conduct is not the way of personal liberation.
Not working for others' benefit is not the bodhisattva path.
Not cultivating pure vision is not Secret Mantra.
Not destroying delusion is not a realized person.

If there is partiality, it is not the view.
If there are reference points, it is not meditation.
If there is a mere outward show, it is not conduct.
If there is hope and pretentiousness, it is not the result.

Those with faith have a refuge.
Those with compassion have an altruistic attitude.
Those with incisive knowledge have realization.
Those with respect and devotion have blessings.

Those with shame avoid carelessness.
Those who avoid carelessness have a guarded mind.
Those who have a guarded mind have vows and samaya.
Those who have vows and samaya have spiritual attainments.

Calm and self-control are signs of listening to the Dharma;
Few passions, signs of meditation;
Harmony with everyone is the sign of a practitioner;
Your mind at ease, the sign of accomplishment.

The root of phenomena is your own mind.
If you tame your mind, you are a practitioner.
If you are a practitioner, your mind is tamed.
When your mind is tamed, that is liberation.

I, Jigdral Yeshé Dorjé, wrote this.

10. The realization that all phenomena

The realization that all phenomena of samsara and enlightenment
   are emptiness inseparable from naked awareness is the view.

To release present awareness within the spacious natural state and
   then to sustain the self-liberation of thoughts without grasping
   is meditation.

All post-meditative activity done harmoniously with the Dharma is
   the conduct.

The complete manifestation of that abiding nature is the result.

I, Vajra Jñana, wrote this in response to the nun Jampa Chödron.

11. Irreversible faith

How amazing! Listen, fortunate woman!

Irreversible faith,
Keeping tantric commitments without deceit,
Undistracted diligence in practice—
These are the life blood of the sacred Dharma.

In having done virtues great and small,
It is crucial to complete the three stages of a practice: preliminary, main,
    and conclusion,[63]
And to cultivate compassion and the mind of awakening
For all sentient beings, once your mother.

The view is the realization that samsara and enlightenment's phenomena
    that appear in this way
Are one within emptiness
And the recognition of awareness itself as dharmakaya without
    formulation.

To settle naturally within the continual state
Of uncontrived, present awareness,
Unbound by reference points' chains, is meditation.

Impartial view and conduct
And all physical, verbal, and mental activity
Being in harmony with the Dharma
Are the crucial points of conduct.

Make this your essential practice.

I, Jñana, spoke this so as not to refuse Sukha's insistent request.

12. You have now obtained

How amazing!

Listen my excellent, holy companion!

You have now obtained a free and fully endowed human body, so
    difficult to find;
You have now met a qualified Lama, so difficult to meet;
And you've encountered tantric teachings, so hard to come in contact
    with:
At this time, it is important to take the first steps on the path to
    liberation in this life.

First, supplications imbued with irreversible faith and respect toward
    your Lama;
Second, pure vision and affection toward your tantric brothers and
    sisters;
Third, compassion and the mind of awakening toward all sentient beings;
Fourth, inspiring your mind to diligence in spiritual practice with
    reflection on impermanence:
These are a practitioner's lasting wealth. Treasure them in your heart.

To realize that all phenomena of samsara and enlightenment that appear
    in this way
Are great emptiness is the view.
To sustain a state of non-meditation and non-distraction
Without uncontrivance or intervention in present awareness is
    meditation.

For none of your actions whatsoever to be careless
And to maintain harmony with the Dharma is conduct.
To have one-pointed diligence in the practice of view, meditation,
    and conduct as described
Will lead to the manifest accomplishment of the result during
    your lifetime,
Tsultrim Ten-sung, my friend.

I, Yeshé Dorjé, who is neither a layperson nor a monk,
Wrote neither quickly nor slowly
This so-called heart advice that are not true or false,
Neither before nor after noon, but during the noon session break.

13. Realization of the empty nature of apparent existence

How amazing!

Realization of the empty nature of apparent existence,
All phenomena of samsara and enlightenment free from formulations
   like space, is the king of views.
Present awareness is uncontrived, primordially present dharmakaya.
To sustain the natural state without grasping is the supreme key to
   meditation.

To maintain a balance between view and conduct
And always to be careful regarding virtuous and negative actions is
   correct conduct.
Practice like this and your innate dharmakaya will become evident.
Seize this ultimate result!

I, Jñana, wrote this.

14. Without great incisive knowledge

Without great incisive knowledge's understanding that phenomenal existence, infinite purity, is the display of the wisdom deity's body, wisdom's magical gesture, even though you have practiced the doctrine's guardians, they will become graveyard demons and you will never accomplish the wisdom deities.

Without realization of profound emptiness, the view that samsara and enlightenment are no other than your own perception, your reliance on any wisdom deity, grasping it as solid and real, will only cause you to become *rudra*.

Without the capacity to transform meditative states' mentally created offerings, magical emanations of the sky treasury's symphony, into the myriad objects your guests desire, your meager array of material offerings will not delight the wisdom deities.

Without the vital instructions to transform and transfer all impure appearances of samsara into the display of the pure nature of phenomena, your mere recitation of words and repetition of mantras will not accomplish the wisdom deity.

Further, in deity practice, without the vital instructions for constant stability of appearances as the deity, accomplishing the wisdom of phenomenal existence's infinite purity is impossible.

Without the vital instructions for visualizations of lights shining and returning in any application of activity related to intensive mantra practice of approach and accomplishment, accomplishing any of the infinite activities you undertake is impossible.

Without first seeking understanding through listening to the meaning of practice, then using reflection to resolve misconceptions, and finally gaining confidence through realization born of meditation, eons of meditation on mere "blind" meditative techniques to settle the mind will not lead to enlightenment.

Without the vital instructions of the magic-like yoga—the mode of being in which hope and fear, acceptance and rejection, samsara and enlightenment, have been destroyed—keeping all major and minor prescribed tantric commitments is impossible.

With mere understanding but without practice's strength born of intense diligence, reaching the level of omniscient Buddhahood is impossible.

Without the profound vital instructions for the swift path of great secrets—Direct Vision (*thod rgal*)—accomplishing the state of enlightenment in one lifetime is impossible.

Without repeatedly bringing to mind the features of the pure lands of the Buddhas and a consuming will to be reborn there, accomplishing that rebirth with mere verbal recitation of prayers of aspirations is impossible.

Without recognition of this vast expanse of the dharmadhatu as primordially perfect within samsara and enlightenment's original ground, for it to manifest as other than that ground itself is impossible.

I, Jñana, wrote this.

15. This fresh state of present awareness, unspoiled

This fresh state of present awareness (*da lta'i shes pa*)
Unspoiled by dualistic thoughts,
Effortlessly sustained in the natural state,
Is Buddha Kuntu Zangpo's wisdom mind.

Do not hope or fear for good or bad outcomes.
Regardless of what formulation of thought occurs, they arise and
    are liberated simultaneously;
Their essential nature is empty awareness.
Reach that unmoving, unassailable state.

I, Jñana, spoke these words immediately
In response to Zangmo's supplication. May this be virtuous!

16. Externally, this age of conflict's chaos erupts

Externally, this age of conflict's chaos erupts;
Internally, exhaustion engulfs body and mind;
Secretly, vivid thoughts flood the conscious mind.
The practitioner who transcends these three
Keeps a happy mind and is oh, so joyful.

17. Rest at ease within the naturally settled state

Rest at ease within the naturally settled state.
In this fresh state of present awareness,
Unspoiled by mind's grasping to fixed points,
You will see the uncontrived nature of phenomena, your true nature,

Clarity without thoughts or anything that can be identified.
Within great exaltation, natural liberation of the six collections of
  consciousness,
The sun of happiness dawns from within.
You reach the unassailable state that is never joined or separated.

A la la! These words from my heart
Strike Orgyen Palzang's mind.
This is Yeshé Dorjé's nonsensical talk:
May it cause realization and liberation to happen simultaneously!

Jñana wrote this.

18. Rest at ease within the uncontrived nature of mind

Rest at ease within the uncontrived nature of mind.
By looking, nothing is seen;
Seeing nothing is actually to see naked awareness:
That itself is Buddha Kuntu Zangpo.

Jñana wrote this for Péma Wangmo.

19. All phenomena of existence, samsara and enlightenment

All phenomena of existence, samsara and enlightenment,
Are a groundless and rootless display.
Realize the all-inclusive natural state
In encompassing, pervasive space
Is inexpressible empty clarity.
This is Great Perfection's inconceivable view.

Do not spoil this present ordinary mind[64]
With grasping to meditation and its mental constructs.
Relax, let go,
Never leaving the stable naturally settled state without meditation.
This is meditation of natural liberation without fixation.

Relax yourself in the natural arising of the six collections of
    consciousness,
Have your conduct conform to the Dharma,
And let go in non-action, allowing things to occur of themselves:
Know this as the ultimate conduct.

When you energetically cultivate these experiences,
Do not search for results outside yourself;
You will surely find their natural dwelling place directly within you:
This is the pinnacle of the result.

20. Within the continuity of uncontrived present awareness

Within the continuity of uncontrived present awareness (*da lta'i rig pa*), do not spoil it with mental grasping to meditation, and do not slip into non-meditation's endless distractions. Settle, relaxing within the open natural state in this direct knowing free from reference points. This is called "Great Perfection's view and meditation."[65]

When settled in this state, recognize what thought arises from the aspect of awareness and do not prolong it. Gaze directly at thoughts' essence: they unravel without a trace. Relax in non-action. This spreading evenness in a state without grasping, in which thoughts naturally arise and are naturally liberated, is to reach dharmakaya directly. This is the practice of Cutting through Solidity, or *Trekchö* (*khregs chod*).

Now, to that practice add any suitable postures of the body and gates of perception and focus on the objective world. The radiance of awareness, the light of self-manifest incisive knowledge, will dawn in the forms of the expanse of outer clarity and chains of luminous spheres, appearing directly to the senses. This is the tantric practice of the path of Direct Vision, or *Tögal* (*thod rgal*). Regardless of what arises, have no grasping to its appearance, no attachment to its emptiness, and no hope or fear toward anything at all.

In brief, dwell directly in a state without even the most subtle atom's worth of a mentally created reference point, such as "This is it!" and deeply come to a final conclusion that this is the correct state. Trust this sincerely and keep it firmly in mind. We are Great Perfection's practitioners of space; our spiritual tradition has neither meditation nor distraction. Therefore, when we gain confidence in this, we cut through the empty core of samsara and enlightenment with a single stroke. Since the sun of a happy mind surely rises from the center of your heart, consider as supreme these pith instructions of knowing one thing that liberates everything, and take it to the level of the exhaustion of phenomena!

I, Jigdral Yeshé Dorjé, gave this advice from my heart to the fully ordained monk Longsal Dorjé, who is rich in holy faith.

21. Lord Lotus–Born, chief of a hundred Buddha families

Lord Lotus-Born, chief of a hundred Buddha families,[66]
You reside innate, never separate from me since the beginning,
As the essence of my awareness in the center of my heart.
Recognizing this, the view, to you I bow.

Gazing out at the field of external experiences,
Forms appear in myriad ways—I am amazed!
Appearances, they are the unobstructed nirmanakaya, skillful means;
Emptiness's magical display, they are ultimate incisive knowledge.
Appearance and emptiness in union, they are the wisdom deities' bodies,
Primordially existent, uncreated wisdom deities
That do not need to be accomplished with deliberate effort.
Attachment to them as substantial is delusion;
Settling without grasping is liberation.
Practitioners, let appearances go free.

Gazing inward at my own mind,
Its stillness and movement are inseparable, essentially empty.
The victorious ones of the three times' wisdom mind is complete
Within this ordinary awareness's fresh state:
In stillness, it abides in the continual nature of phenomena (*dharmata*).
When it moves, the movement arises as wisdom's play.
Settle in the fundamental nature, the natural state, unspoiled by clinging
  to meditation,
And see the dharmakaya.

When intellectual reference points collapse, joy arises.
Practitioners, settle in the natural liberation of consciousness's six
  collections.
The view inwardly resolved
Does not need to be illustrated with many wearisome terms or examples;
Its meaning, naked self-manifest wisdom,
Is the result spontaneously accomplished without action.
Proficient Great Perfection practitioners

Can resolve the three existences right now.
Even if this cosmos collapses there is nothing to fear:
What object of hope or fear is there?
Practitioners, recognize this royal city of the great exaltation of evenness

And attain that unassailable place!
I, the old father Dudjom, spoke these words for Péma Dégyal. Heed them!

22. In any virtue you accomplish, large and small

How amazing! Listen, woman diligent in virtue!
In any virtue you accomplish, large and small,
The key is to have the three excellences[67] guide you.
In generating compassion and the mind of awakening (*bodhicitta*)
   in your mind,
Stable mindfulness is important.
Within samsara and enlightenment's space-like nature,
Recognition of awareness's essential nature
As the unfabricated dharmakaya is the view.
To settle naturally in unfabricated present awareness is meditation.
Take as the key of conduct
That all your activity should accord with the sacred Dharma.
Practice diligently as I've described.

I, Jñana, spontaneously wrote this as a woman named Jñana requested.

23. You have the fortune to practice the sacred Dharma

How amazing! Listen, venerable nun!
You have the fortune to practice the sacred Dharma:
Be diligent in practicing them.
Train your mind in the mind of awakening,
The great path all the victorious ones' heirs tread.
Within the view, great emptiness,
Meditate, settling uncontrived and without grasping.
Conduct must accord with the Dharma.
Take these as the essential keys to practice.

I, Jñana, carelessly wrote this in response to Sang-ngak Chödron's request.

24. Now that your spiritual connection has been forged

Incomparable Lama, at your feet I pay homage.

Listen, fortunate one.
Now that your spiritual connection has been forged,
Achieve your eternal goals.
Strive on the sole path of all the victorious ones' heirs:
Generate compassion and the mind of awakening.

The view is the great emptiness of samsara and enlightenment;
Concluding that your own awareness is the unformulated dharmakaya
    is the sovereign view.
Meditation is to settle unconcerned
Within unfabricated present awareness,
Unfettered by grasping.
Take as the supreme kind of conduct
Not to fall under the negative influence of carelessness
But to have your acts accord with the Dharma.

Be diligent in undistracted practice.

I, a crazy, ragged tulku, wrote this spontaneously in response to Norbu Gyatso's request.

25. Listen! While practicing the sacred Dharma

Listen! While practicing the sacred Dharma,
Determination, renunciation, and faith
Are indispensable: Single-mindedly foster them.
Samsara and enlightenment's emptiness is the view;
Natural, uncontrived abiding within it is meditation.
Conduct's key is for your body, speech, and mind's acts to accord with the
    Dharma.
Keep these words in your heart!

I, with the title Dudjom Tulku, wrote this so as not to refuse your request.

26. Stable, unchanging devotion

How wonderful! Listen, fortunate woman!

These constitute the essence of the sacred teachings' practice:
Stable, unchanging devotion,
Unceasing compassion,
Forthright keeping of tantric commitments,
And resolute diligence.
Take these as the essence of what you should practice:
The view of the wheel of life and enlightenment's pervasive evenness;
The meditation of uncontrived settling in awareness itself;
And the conduct of your acts in accord with the Dharma.

I, Jigdral Yeshé Dorjé, wrote this in response to Könchok Lhamo's request.

27. Among methods to practice the sacred Dharma

Alas! Listen, friend!
Among methods to practice the sacred Dharma,
Three—faith, keeping tantric commitments, and diligence—
Are indispensable:
Always rely upon them in your heart.
Samsara and enlightenment's emptiness is the view.
Natural, uncontrived settling is meditation.
The body, speech, and mind's acts aligned with the Dharma is conduct:
These are the essence of practice,
Be sure to keep them in your heart!

I, Jñana, wrote this in response to a request by the one named Jampa.

28. Unfailing devotion to your Lama

How amazing! Listen, fortunate one!

These constitute the essence of what you should practice:
Unfailing devotion to your Lama,
Steady love and affection for your tantric companions,
Intense compassion for beings,
And inspiration based upon impermanence and renunciation.
Nurture diligence and determination in your practice of the Dharma.

Samsara and enlightenment's pervasive evenness is the view;
Within it, meditation is uncontrived settling in the natural state.
Conduct is to relax in non-activity.
Accept these as the keys of view, meditation, and conduct.

Make meaningful all activities guided with compassion and the mind of
    awakening.

Not possessing these in my own mind,
I am a celebrated lecturer of others,
Giving advice, like a deaf person playing music.
I don't think these words will be helpful to others,
Yet, merely not to refuse your earnest request,
I spoke a few verses,
And may even they ripen within your mind!

*I, the foolish, dull-minded Jigdral Yeshé Dorjé, who has three concerns
[eating, sleeping, defecating], wrote this in response to Jampa-la's request.
May it be virtuous!*

29. Inspire yourself with faith, devotion, and renunciation

How amazing! Listen, woman who practices the Dharma!
Inspire yourself with faith, devotion, and renunciation.
Diligence in spiritual life is important.
Guide the virtue you accomplish, great or small,
With the mind of awakening: That's the key!
The view is samsara and enlightenment's emptiness;
Within it, meditation is natural settling in awareness itself.
Conduct is acts that accord with the Dharma.
Take these three as the essential keys of practice.

I with the title Dudjom Tulku wrote this not to refuse an earnest request.

30. These are the heart jewels

O! O! Listen, woman diligent in virtue.
These are the heart jewels of all Buddhists:
Intense renunciation, faith, and devotion
Diligent in practicing the sacred Dharma
Without laziness or procrastination
And guarding the tantric commitments as you do your eyes.

Always cultivate compassion and the mind of awakening
For sentient beings who were our mothers,
And do what you can to help them:
This is the training of the Victorious One's heirs.

Realization that all phenomena of samsara and enlightenment are empty
And recognition of one's own awareness as dharmakaya
Constitutes the sovereign view.

To settle in this unfabricated present awareness's own ground
Without distraction, grasping, or thought
Is meditation.

Not to be careless in body, speech, and mind
And to align your behavior with the Dharma
Are the practical instructions for perfect conduct.

Take these instructions as your heart's essence.

I, youthful Jñana Vajra, wrote this in response to Déva Taré's request.

31. When you have a human body so difficult to achieve

Alas! Listen, intelligent woman!
When you have a human body so difficult to achieve,
Do not get involved in many distractions and busy-ness:
Achieve your lasting goals.

In whatever virtue you accomplish, great or small,
Three stages—preparation, main practice, and conclusion—
    must be complete.
At all times, compassionately accomplish
Whatever you can to help others.

To recognize samsara and enlightenment
As great emptiness
And one's own unformulated awareness as primordial wisdom:
These are the sovereign view.

To settle in this view evenly within the natural state
Is meditation.

Not to allow your actions and behavior to slip into carelessness
And to align them with the Dharma is the supreme form of conduct.

Place these instructions in the center of your heart.

I, Vajra Jñana, wrote this in response to Vakapasham's request.

32. Lodrö, sir, in practicing a teaching

Lodrö, sir, in practicing a teaching, you must associate diligence and faith. Guide any virtuous act you undertake with the preparation, cultivation of the mind of awakening; the main practice, non-fixation; and the conclusion, dedication prayers.

It is appropriate not to present yourself to others as someone with something to boast about, saying, "I have practiced a high teaching!" Make a continual effort to exert yourself in a noble altruistic mind. That itself is the teachings.

Study instruction manuals and listen to the Lama's oral instructions for other teachings, such as the Great Perfection, and practice exactly as they teach you.

It is certain that a humble person like me has no higher heart advice than this to teach. If this is a fault, I ask you not to be distressed with me.

I had no time to compose verses and thought you had waited long enough for this to come; please don't be upset. From Yeshé Dorjé.

33. Samsara and enlightenment's emptiness

Listen, faithful nun!
Samsara and enlightenment's emptiness is the view;
Settling your uncontrived awareness (*shes pa*) within this is meditation.
It is important for your conduct to accord with the Dharma.
These three lines are the essential keys.
Keep this practice in your heart.

I, careless Jñana, wrote this in a relaxed manner in response to Venerable Jamyang's request.

34. All that appears

All that appears is exalted Bodhisattva Great Compassion's body;
Resonant sounds are the six-syllable mantra's[68] wisdom speech;
All recollection and thoughts are clear light, the exalted Bodhisattva's
wisdom mind.
Yet, these are not newly fashioned:
Know that they exist self-manifest.
Sustain this knowledge within the natural state and you will be liberated.

I, Jñana, wrote this in response to a request.

35. To accomplish enlightenment during your lifetime

Lama, Buddha Vajradhara incarnate,
To you I pay sincere homage: Grant me your blessings!

To accomplish enlightenment during your lifetime,
Pray to your Lama with devotion;
Have love, affection, and veneration for tantric companions;
Inspire yourself with compassion and the mind of awakening toward
  beings
And with renunciation and the contemplation of impermanence.
Exert yourself without distraction in spiritual practice!

The view is samsara and enlightenment's all-pervasive evenness;
Meditation is to settle within it, in the uncontrived natural state.
Conduct is to live free of activity and effort.
Take these words as the essential keys to practice.
The result will awaken within you.

*I, by the name of Jñana, wrote this in response to Gyurmé Wangchuk's
request.*

36. This fresh state of present awareness transcends fabrication

This fresh state of present awareness
Transcends fabrication, transformation, suppression, or cultivation.
To sustain this in the relaxed natural state
Is to practice the Great Perfection.

In thinking, the thinker is empty in essence.
In stillness, the place of stillness has no root or ground.
What arises occurs within the continuity of naked empty awareness.
Never separated from this in primordial purity—how joyful!

I, Jñana, wrote this.

37. Relax without grasping in the natural state

Relax without grasping in the natural state,
This naked present awareness.
When delusion's dualistic perceptions are exhausted,
You reach the royal city of naturally liberated dharmakaya.

I, Jñana, wrote this.

38. This fresh fundamental nature of self–manifest awareness

This fresh fundamental nature of self-manifest awareness
That faults and stains have never tainted
Is the original lord, dharmakaya Lama.
He dwells together with you, never separate,
Yet dualistic grasping's power prevents you from recognizing this
   abiding nature.
Taking delusion's perceptions as real, how exhausting!
Searching for liberation's ground elsewhere, how wearisome!
How can you look at the insubstantial nature of phenomena?
Who meditates upon natural luminosity arising unceasingly?
What result is free from renunciation, attainment, and fixed location
   points?
Now, discard the naturally liberated six collections of consciousness[69]
   where you will.
Accomplish right now your aspiration for an open and happy mind.

I, Jigdral Yeshé Dorjé, spoke this directly to faithful Dawa.

39. The essence of Great Perfection practice

O sir, the essence of Great Perfection practice is this:
All phenomena of samsara and enlightenment are only your own mind's
     magical display.
Primordially, your mind's nature lacks substantiality;
It is unconditioned empty luminosity, the essential nature of awareness.
It dwells primordially and eternally as dharmakaya's essence.
Yet not recognizing your own nature, transitory dualistic clinging creates
     delusion,
Deceptive attachment to perceptions of happiness and suffering in
     samsara and enlightenment.
In fact, your mind's nature transcends the bounds of good and evil, hope
     and fear.
In this space of great emptiness, free from transition and change,
Self-manifest awareness is present knowing.
This relaxed settling in the uncontrived natural state is the view, and is
     also the key to meditation.
When meditating, as soon as thoughts arise from awareness's dynamic
     energy,
Use mindfulness to identify them:
Self-arising, self-liberating, like waves on water.
Recognize them as such and let them go without prolongation.
"Meditation" is just the meager term we use to designate this.
Continuously maintain boundless conduct free of action.
Discard the six collections of consciousness; leave them as they are,
     without fixation.
Do not hope for a result at a later date.
It is in the present itself: reaching the unassailable state, attainment of
     self-mastery.

I, Jigdral Yeshé Dorjé, wrote this, corresponding to the request
of Ngawang Zöpa.
May this virtue become the cause for simultaneous realization
and liberation!

40. To extract the essence from this life

For you, Kalden Dawa in Yanglésho,[70] diligent practitioner, who has taken
  oaths, and sincerely practices the Dharma,
I collect my heart's loving advice as follows:

To extract the essence from this life so difficult to find,
Yearn for freedom from samsara's seas of suffering,
Trust in the Triple Gems as your infallible source of refuge,
And flawlessly choose between the causes and effects of positive and
  negative acts..
The Dharma's four eternal jewels are especially indispensable:
Devotion and respect toward your root Lama;
Love and affection toward your spiritual companions who share the same
  tantric commitments;
Compassion and the mind of awakening toward all beings, who were
  your mothers;
And curtailing plans because the conditioned is impermanent.

The Lama and wisdom deity are inseparable from your own mind.
Meditate on the creation stage's empty appearances to be like the moon's
  reflection on water.
The extent of ritual repetitions and recitation is the empty sound of
  mantra.
Everything is the dance of the nature of phenomena, one's own
  awareness, alone.
In the expanse of the nature of phenomena, neither helpful nor
  harmful objects exist;
Samsara and enlightenment, hope and fear, are nothing but
  designations of terms.
When you are introduced to wisdom that resides in continual
  primordial presence,
You'll see that acts you have done reinforce delusion.

Within the state of non-action, reach the unassailable state of
  awareness itself.

Release your naked ordinary awareness:
"Settling" or "not settling" in evenness are nothing more than terms.
When thoughts arise, let them arise, and release them in natural
    liberation.
In stillness without thoughts arising, allow that stillness, and relax in the
    natural state.
When meditation's faults—drowsiness and agitation—occur, dispel them
    immediately.
When day and night become a circle of infinite luminosity, you will not
    hope for the result at a later date. how amazing!
Diligently practice as I've described.

I, Jigdral Yeshé Dorjé, wrote this and sent it off.

41. One's own awareness, fresh and uncontrived

One's own awareness, fresh and uncontrived,
Is the primordially present ultimate Lama
From whom you have not been separated for even an instant.
This meeting with the original abiding nature—how amazing!

I, Jñana, wrote this in response to Changchub Palmo's request.

42. Heart advice sufficient in itself

Heart advice sufficient in itself is this:

Pray to Guru Rinpoché, then settle within the state of your mind and the
   guru's mind inseparable.
In the relaxed openness of your mind's uncontrived state of naturalness,
Do not stop, cultivate, accept, or reject thoughts.

Relax without grasping; whatever arises will be self-liberated.
This is the ultimate guru. Abide in that natural state!
It is not a new attainment; it has never been separate from you.
Although not separate, you did not recognize it, which is delusion.

Now there is already endless delusion
So whatever thoughts arise, look directly at their essence.
When you look, you will not see it; cast the searcher aside.
The place where you cast it is dharmakaya's essential nature, all-
   pervasive emptiness.

In that place, where can you go or stay?
Understand this, realize its meaning, and sustain it in practice.
The result of this practice is to be without hope or fear.
Having attained confidence in this has made this old man satisfied.

A la la ho! Old man Dudjom wrote this.

43. This is the essence of practice

This is the essence of practice:

Pray to your Lama and, while praying, blend your mind inseparably with
    your Lama's wisdom mind.
Having merged inseparably, settle in the state of naturalness, the nature
    of mind.

To be settled in the state of naturalness, this fresh knowing
Uncontrived and unaltered, is luminous naked awareness.
When thoughts arise within that nature,
Recognize them on arising, and relax within that recognition.
Their arising and liberation occur simultaneously, like a drawing on the
    water's surface.

When thoughts do not arise, that is non-meditation free from thoughts.
Emptiness, beyond meditator and object of meditation,
Is called ultimate wisdom present from the beginning.
Give up hope and fear; hold to the natural state of awareness.

Thoughts are delusion; stop following after them.
Hope and fear are obstacles; don't go to greet them.
If you can rest within the nature that is beyond intellect and activity,
You will definitely discover the dharmakaya in your own heart.

I, Vajra Jñana, spontaneously wrote this for Kadak Lodrö Yeshé.

44. Faith opens the door to the Dharma

Faith opens the door to the Dharma.
Diligence forms their central pillar.
Practice is their final conclusion.
Who gathers these three is the best Buddhist practitioner.

This is old man Dudjom's foolish advice.

45. This fresh present knowing, unbound

Doctor Sherab Jorden:

This fresh present knowing,
Unbound by the intellect that clings to meditation,
Is naked unobstructed non-meditation.
Relax at ease
And settle in the state of naturalness.
This is the meaning of realization of meditation.

When thoughts move, let them.
Movement arises and is liberated without a trace.
When there is no movement, don't search for it.
This is empty luminosity, naked empty awareness.
Tantric practice without suppression or cultivation of thoughts
Brings the accomplishment of the destruction of hope and fear.

There is nothing more to add to this.
Madman Dudjom said this:
Let it remain like this in your heart.

I, Jñana, wrote this.

46. Faithful disciple, any thought at all can arise

Faithful disciple,
Any thought at all can arise,
Yet when thoughts of wrong views do,
Immediately recognize them.

If you sincerely acknowledge them, they will be purified.
At all times, train in pure vision
Toward your Lama and vajra brothers and sisters.
This is the profound vital point.

I, Dudjom, wrote this. May it prove virtuous!

Heart Gem for Fortunate Disciples:

Pointing-Out Instructions of the Great Perfection[71]

HOMAGE TO MY LAMA!

The Great Master from Oddiyana said:

> Do not cut to the root of phenomena, cut to the root of your mind.
> Cutting to the root of your mind, then knowing that one thing, liberates everything.
> Not cutting to the root of your mind, then knowing everything, you missed that one thing.

Therefore, when engaging in the actual practice on the ultimate truth of mind, straighten your body, let your breathing flow naturally, and look with your eyes half open at the space before you. Think to yourself that now for the benefit of all motherly sentient beings, I will look at awareness itself, the true face of Buddha Kuntu Zangpo. With devotion, fervently supplicate your root Lama who is inseparable from Orgyen Péma [Guru Rinpoché], and your mind finally united with his, rest in evenness.

When abiding in this way, your mind will not stay in this state of luminous empty awareness for long, but will become restless, agitated, and unsettled, moving about like a monkey. This is not the nature of mind. These are called thoughts. If you pursue them, there is not one thing that these thoughts won't think about recalling, think about needing, or think about doing.

In the past, this is exactly what has thrown you unconsciously into the ocean of samsara, and moreover, it will certainly throw you there again in the future. Right now, wouldn't it be better to limit the spread of these negative deluded thoughts?

You may ask, "When thinking is curtailed, what does awareness look like?" It is utterly empty, totally open, spacious, free, and resplendently blissful. It has never been established as having substantial characteristics. There are no phenomena in samsara or enlightenment that are not pervaded by it. From the beginning, it is naturally and spontaneously present and never separate from oneself. It lies beyond action, effort, and the mind's comprehension.

Now you may ask, "What is it like to recognize the natural face of awareness?" Even though you recognize awareness itself, you do not know how to describe it, like a mute person trying to describe his dream. You do not know how to distinguish the sustainer, yourself, from the awareness that is sustained.

Previously, you were unable to abide for even one moment, constantly thinking and doing everything: These thoughts, who are the old destroyer, have nothing to do now in the vast expanse of awareness, which is like a cloudless sky. The movement of thoughts dissolves, disperses, and falls away. All the power and strength of thought is lost in awareness. Then awareness, the wisdom of the naturally abiding dharmakaya, just abides clearly and nakedly.

Now you may ask, "Who introduces this awareness to you? What is decided upon? How is confidence established?" Initially, you are introduced to awareness by your Lama. Through that introduction, you know your own true face and directly recognize your true nature (*ngo rang thog tu 'phrod*).[72] However the phenomena of samsara and enlightenment appear, know that they are none other than the natural display of awareness. Thus, decide upon this single awareness (*thag rig pa gcig thog tu chod*). Just as the waves of the ocean subside back into the ocean, all thoughts that arise vanish directly into awareness. Thus, gain confidence in liberation (*gding grol thog tu bcas pa*). Therefore, it is beyond being an object of meditation, the act of meditating, and the mind that grasps on to meditation.

If that is so, you may say that it will be sufficient even if one does not meditate. It is not like that at all! Just by recognizing awareness one does not arrive at the state of liberation. During beginningless lifetimes, we have been confined within a structure of deluded habitual patterns. From then until now, we have spent our human existence as the servant of our worthless thoughts. At the time of death, we do not know where we will go, but we follow our karma and inevitably suffer. Therefore, now it is necessary to meditate, sustaining the continuity of awareness that was introduced.

The great omniscient Longchenpa said:

> Although you have been introduced to your nature, if you do not
> become familiar with it,
> You will be carried away by the enemy of thought like an infant in
> battle.

Generally, what is called meditation means resting in awareness without distraction or clinging and sustaining its continuity through original mindfulness[73] of the state of naturalness, thus becoming accustomed to the original essential nature. Furthermore, when you are meditating and thoughts arise, the way to become familiar with your nature is to let them arise. There is no need to view them as enemies. Relax naturally in their arising. If they do not arise, do not try to make it so. Just rest directly in its non-arising.

Also, when meditating, if a gross thought suddenly appears, it is easily recognized. But in regard to subtle thoughts, until a few have arisen, you are not aware of them. Therefore, they are called undercurrents of thought. Because these undercurrents of thought act as the sneaky thieves of meditation, it is very important to place the sentry of mindfulness on guard. If you can sustain the continuity of mindfulness in all situations, whether eating, sleeping, moving about, or sitting, in meditation or in post-meditation, that itself is enough.

The Great Master said:

> Although hundreds or thousands of explanations are given,
> There is only one thing to be understood:
> Know the one thing that liberates everything;
> Sustain awareness itself, your true nature.

The Great Master also said:

> If one does not meditate, confidence is not gained,
> But if one meditates, confidence will be gained.

What kind of confidence will be gained? By meditating with intensive diligence in this way, there will be signs that familiarity has been actualized, such as this: Concrete tight clinging and grasping to the solidity of dualistic perception gradually relaxes, and the many efforts associated with happiness and suffering, hope and fear will lessen. Your devotion toward your Lama will intensify and trust in your Lama's profound instructions will arise from your heart. After a time, the solid mind that clings to duality will disappear by itself. Then gold and rocks become equal. Food and excrement become equal. Gods and demons become equal. Virtuous actions and negative actions become equal. You will not have a preference between pure lands and hell realms.

Until this happens, to the face of dualistic mind, there will be virtue; there will be negative actions; there will be pure lands; there will be hell realms. There will be joy and sorrow, and action and its results are all undeniable.

This being so, the Great Master said:

> My view is higher than the sky;
> My attention toward karma and its consequences is finer than flour.[74]

For this reason, it is not acceptable to say, "We are Great Perfection practitioners," or "We are great meditators," while stinking from alcohol, farting, and sleeping. Instead, establish a foundation with pure faith, devotion, and tantric commitments, follow the main practice with an intense unrelenting diligence, and put aside all the activities of this meaningless life in order to meditate. The special quality of the profound path of the Great Perfection is that you will certainly reach the unassailable state in this very lifetime without relying on future lives.

My Lama said:[75]

> I am an old man, thinking of nothing other than my Lama, reciting nothing but supplication prayers, sustaining nothing but nonaction. Like this, I am at ease. Now I am happy, carefree, and at ease, without fixation.

I, Jñana, spoke this Heart Gem for the Fortunate *as direct instructions placed nakedly in the palm of your hands.*

For (la) the accomplishment of the *permanent (gtan)* goal of one's
   wishes *(bsam),*
The profound *instructions (gdams)* of the Great Perfection are alone
   enough.
These ('di) notes were arranged as *words (ngag)* easy to understand,
Were written by the crazy Dudjom, and were *given (sprad)* to you. [76]

May this prove to be virtuous!

Unspoiled by thoughts of past, present, or future

Unspoiled by thoughts of past, present, or future,
This stainless naked awareness
Is the essence of Buddha Kuntu Zangpo.
Sustain this in the relaxed state of naturalness.
The six avenues of consciousness will be self-liberated—great wisdom—
And you will reach the royal city of non-abiding dharmakaya.

I, Yeshé Dorjé, spoke this directly to the faithful Dawa.
May it prove to be virtuous!

≈§ II

Songs of Realization
and Songs of Tantric Gatherings

Fortunate vajra brothers and sisters gathered here,
Faith and devotion without doubt or hesitation guide your aspirations and acts;
Your conduct is fearless activity free from concepts concerned with purity and impurity:
Enjoy this festival of delight, the tantric feast-wheel of great exaltation![77]

Introduction:
Songs of Realization and
Songs of Tantric Gatherings (*mgur tshogs*)

T HIS SECTION OFFERS the reader a translation of the entire collection of songs of realization and of tantric gatherings (*mgur tshogs*), entitled *The Celebration of Fortunate Ones: A Compilation of the Cycle of Songs of Realization and Songs of Tantric Gatherings,* as found within the *Collected Works of His Holiness Dudjom Rinpoché,* volume *ah,* pp. 269–90. This collection comprises four songs of tantric gatherings and five songs of realization. In addition, I have added one profound and beautiful song of tantric gatherings from Dudjom Lingpa's Tröma cycle.

The first five songs are called *tsok lu* (*tshogs glu*), songs of tantric gatherings. These songs, which are written in verse and sung with beautiful melodies at tantric feast gatherings, are an expression of His Holiness's realization. They are usually sung when the feast is offered to the vajra master. The Tibetan word *tsok* literally means "gathering," and *lu* means "song." For the tantric feast ritual (*ganacakra*) different things are gathered. First, it refers to the gathering together of male and female practitioners, yogis and yoginis. Next, it refers to the gathering together of wisdom beings and guardians of the Dharma. Thirdly, it is the gathering of offerings that are pleasing to the senses, which must include meat and alcohol. Meat is the substance symbolic of skillful means that hooks spiritual attainment. Alcohol is the symbolic substance of wisdom, the luminous lamp of wakefulness. In the context of a tantric feast gathering it is held that spiritual attainment cannot occur without these two substances. Finally, "gathering" refers to the gathering of merit and wisdom through participation in this tantric feast.

For followers of Guru Rinpoché, the tantric feast-wheel ritual (*gana-*

cakra) is considered the highest, most extraordinary, and most effective practice. It is considered the most effective practice because it is a method that removes our mind's two obscurations through the accumulation of merit and wisdom; it is the most profound method to confess downfalls in our tantric commitments; it is the best means to remove obstacles; and it is through making the remainder aspect of the feast offering that all the worldly deities are satisfied.

Technically, a tantric feast ritual must include both male and female practitioners. If there are only male or female practitioners present, it is called just a "feast offering." To whom are the offerings made? They are made to the six guests who are gathered: the Lamas, wisdom deities, dakinis and guardians of the Dharma, male and female practitioners, worldly deities, and dakinis of the outer and inner twenty-one and thirty-two sacred places. These guests are pleased in different ways. The root and lineage Lamas are pleased with the offering of one's view; the wisdom deities are pleased by one's concentration during the creation stage of the ritual; the dakinis and protectors of the Dharma are pleased by keeping one's tantric commitments pure; male and female practitioners are pleased by the enjoyable qualities of the food and drink offered; the worldly deities are pleased with the remainder offering; and the dakinis of the outer and inner twenty-one and thirty-two places are pleased by the vajra songs chanted during the ritual.

The best occasions to perform a tantric feast ritual are on the eighth (Buddha day), tenth (Guru Rinpoché day), fifteenth (full moon day), and twenty-fifth (dakini day) days of the lunar moon; when beginning retreat; and upon conclusion of a retreat, to name a few instances. In the New Treasures tradition of Dudjom Rinpoché, on Guru Rinpoché day rituals are performed related to various manifestations of Guru Rinpoché, such as Lake Born Vajra and Dorjé Drolö. On dakini days, rituals are performed related to the dakini, such as Yeshé Tsogyal and the Black Wrathful Goddess (Tröma Nakmo).

The *tsok lu*, song of tantric gatherings, is a specific type of *gur*, or song of realization (Skt: *doha*). *Gurs* are songs that manifest the realization of a fully realized being, directly, spontaneously, without pre-meditation, carrying with them profound meaning using inspiring verse and melody. Songs of tantric gatherings are songs of realization that are sung specifically at a tantric feast gathering. Both songs of realization and songs of tantric gatherings can originate either as a spontaneously written work or as a song spontaneously sung. This section contains the songs of tantric gatherings that are the manifestation of Dudjom Rinpoché's realization. This song is then sung with an inspiring, beautiful melody as an offering of realization to the vajra master at the same time the symbolic substances of food and drink are offered.

The next four songs are called *gur*, songs of realization. The first song is called *The Wall Song* and was first sung by His Holiness while constructing the Great Copper-Colored Mountain Temple in his homeland of Kongpo, in Buchu, Tibet. This temple is modeled after the one of the same name in Guru Rinpoché's pure land. I can imagine the joy of everyone singing this inspiring verse as they built this sacred temple for the benefit of all sentient beings during happy times in southeastern Tibet before their exodus.

The next four are beautiful, simple songs of realization of a wandering yogi—Dudjom Rinpoché—using the natural poetic imagery drawn from Tibet's expressive landscape; they are rich in blessings from the practice and realization of countless fully enlightened male and female yogins. They remind me of the beautiful songs sung by the great yogin from the Repkong region of Tibet, Shabkar. I highly recommend reading his autobiography *The Life of Shabkar*, brimming with delicious songs of realization.[78]

The final song of realization, called *The Magical Play of the Original State: A Song and Dance of Sublime Aspiration*, is nothing short of an amazing, profound, poetic song of realization. It demonstrates the vast, limitless, pure view of the Great Perfection as it penetrates deep into our hearts. This song does not sing *about* the ultimate point of view, it *is* this view, brought directly home to us, triggering recognition of our own pure awareness.

To conclude this section I have added a song of tantric gathering written by Dudjom Lingpa—His Holiness's previous incarnation—that comes from the Black Wrathful Goddess (Tröma) cycle of revealed teachings. I could not resist including it. It is extremely beautiful. In practice it is accompanied by a melody that originated in the wisdom deity's pure land, and it is based upon the five perfections: the perfect time, place, teacher, retinue, and Dharma, as described in the song itself.

The Celebration of Fortunate Ones:

A Compilation of the Cycle of Songs of Realization and Songs of Tantric Gatherings

1. In the center of the palace

How amazing!

In the center of the palace on the highest Copper-Colored Mountain,
An assembly of awareness-holders, dakas, and dakinis gathered together;
Their hundred moods of great exaltation captivate with playful,
    charming grace.
Thinking of them, deep in my heart I recall my sole father, Lake Born
    Vajra.
The vivid splendor of your body in form, the *rupakaya*, arrayed with the
    major and minor marks of physical perfection, overwhelms other
    appearances in existence;
Your melodious speech of the great secret *nada* is a lute's sweet sound;
And your sublime mind has the nature of undefiled luminous wisdom.
What can rival this feast—seeing the guru's beaming face!

My hope to gaze again and again is unbearable—such a wonderful sight!
Sweet smiles, with loving side-long glances,
As I listen to dakinis' sweet secret words in symbolic songs
And they sway in swift dances.

Yet cataracts of dense stains of dualistic thought
Cover the young water-bubble eyes of this wretched child—
I have no chance to see this marvel! Despondent with regret, I call out in
    lament:
Lotus-Born! Do you hear me?

If you hear me, take your golden scalpel of wisdom and compassion
And remove the shell of the thick veil of my ignorance.
Actually take my forefinger
And please lead me to the realm of my sole father, a delightful pleasure
    grove!

If I am without the fortune to be led there immediately,
Send awareness-holders, dakas, and dakinis as companions to console me.

In joyful delight, I will participate in glorious festivals of untainted great
    exaltation
And gradually follow my father.

My body, a white eagle, swelling with the youth of threefold faith,
Has wings of the view and conduct in unison.
When the six powers of perfectly pure tantric commitments are
    complete,
The city of Lotus Light (Péma Ö) will not be so far away.

My male and female divine companions, a group who shares the same
    karma and good fortune,
Make prayers of aspiration to join the ranks of awareness-holders!
In an exultant mood, with joyful laughter,
Let us set out together, never separating, for the terrestrial pure land.

Thus, a song of yearning arises of itself in this young cuckoo's melodious
    voice,
Sung in my throat's energy center of rapture's playful display,
A messenger to invoke my Lama's wisdom mind.
Send down now the gentle nectar shower of your blessings!

*I, Jigdral Yeshé Dorjé, a fortunate child born in Péma Kö (Array of Lotus
Flower) region, spontaneously spoke this at the age of nineteen, on the
tenth day of the eleventh lunar month, in the Water Dog Year (1922).*

2. In the pollen heart of a blossoming eight-petalled blue lotus

In the pollen heart of a blossoming eight-petalled blue lotus,
You appeared, a self-manifest Buddha—
Lord of the Land of Snow, your rupakaya—enlightenment's form body—
  bedecked with the major and minor marks of physical perfection.
I recall my Lama, Lake Born Vajra.

I invoke you, crying out with a clamorous roar of yearning
In unison with instruments—the melodious sounds of skull drums and
  symbols.
When I invite you to this celebratory tantric feast of gathered tea,
  alcohol, and meat,
Come eagerly, your face as lovely as the full moon.

Now, from the center of Glorious Mountain's palace on Tail-Fan Island,[79]
Dakas and dakinis, including Tara and Mandarava,
Arrayed in myriad manifestations—separately or indivisible as one deity
  to subdue beings—
Come as the youthful awareness-holders' companions in play.

To please all the three roots, I send forth cloud offerings
In self-manifest holders of exaltation—vessels as white as Venus—
Uncontaminated enjoyments, limitless pleasures for the senses, are
  contained:
Samaya substances of outer, inner, and secret offerings of the *ganacakra*,
  the tantric feast-wheel.

Hosts of oath-bound spirits whose potent force
Protects all the amazing terrestrial pure lands, such as Tsaritra,[80]
And all my guests from sacred places and regions, illustrated by
  Jalandhara,[81]
Manifestly enjoy this tantric feast celebration.

Impure karma's wind as coarse as stinging nettles
Circulates within the indestructible central channel, which is not stiff,
    stale, or faulty.
Forceful binding of the karmic energy produces great exaltation's co-
    emergent wisdom,
Which I transform into the vajra performance of wondrous union.

In the essential nature of the naturally settled state, free from defiled
    transition and change,[82]
I have used the tantric practice of continuous luminosity, which is not
    merely sporadic,
To purify my flesh, blood, and essence into an indestructible rainbow
    body,
And I now set out on a journey to help beings, emptying the depths of
    the three realms.

I effortlessly raised my voice with confidence in the view
To sing this far-reaching sweet song of laughter, Ha He!
The profound essential points of the Vajra Essence Ati's excellent path.
A la la ho! This is the kindness of my sole father, Lotus-Born.

The teacher and circle of disciples, with complimentary good karma and
    prayers, are gathered here together as one.
I make the prayer that by the power of the truth of the auspicious
    connections of pure samaya,
We will meet, without separation,
In the gathering of the highest city, Lotus Light (Péma Ö).

To satisfy a request from the illuminator of the Ancient Translation's doc-
trine, Batrul Kunzang Ngédon Longdrol, I, indolent Jigdral Yeshé Dorjé,
wrote down whatever came to mind and offered it. Jayantu!

3. From the beginning, the essential original nature of luminosity

How amazing!

From the beginning, the essential original nature of luminosity,
Simplicity that is the spontaneous display of union's great exaltation,
Co-emergent Vajra Queen, consort of sublime secrets,
Come as a consoling companion, of all phenomena manifesting as
    dharmakaya.

In the realm of the essence, primordial purity, complete in the original
    ground of the nature of phenomena,
The unique vital sphere is realization of wisdom's immediacy.
I turn the wheel of the tantric feast gathering of impartial view:
Dharmakaya dakinis of empty awareness, enjoy this festival of delight!

In the realm of the nature, spontaneous presence, continual luminosity,
Wisdom's uncontrived naturally settled state transcends dualistic mind.
I turn the wheel of the tantric feast gathering of meditation, free from
    reference points:
Sambhogakaya dakinis of empty luminosity, enjoy this festival of
    delight!

In the realm of spontaneous and infinite wisdom's all-pervading
    compassion,
The fearless activity of non-action transcends keeping or releasing,
    coming or going.
I turn the wheel of the tantric feast gathering of conduct, free from
    accepting or rejecting:
Nirmanakaya dakinis of empty appearance, enjoy this festival of delight!

In the great essence of the six lights' enclosure of rainbow light,
The inner radiance of awareness is unobstructed—the assemblage of
    kayas and wisdoms.

I turn the wheel of the tantric feast gathering of luminosity's four
   visions:
Enjoy this festival of delight, the exhaustion of phenomena beyond
   mind!

The great sphere of profound clarity has no edge or boundary.
The four naturally manifest lights neither increase nor decrease.
Whatever appears is the wheel of wisdom—why strive or struggle in
   practice?
I now release my original knowing into openness.

All phenomena of dualistic delusion's perceptions are liberated within
   birthlessness;
Existence's and enlightenment's uncontrived all-pervasive equality is
   self-manifest Buddhahood.
I have found the original protector's kingdom within me;
The sun of spacious happiness has dawned in the center of my heart.

If we are Kuntu Zangpo's and Lotus-Born's lineage children,
Let us rely upon the swift path of the definite secret, the supreme
   vehicle's special features—
The vajra drama of the great transference rainbow body—
And depart to aid beings, emptying the very depths of existence's three
   realms.

Fortunate vajra brothers and sisters gathered here:
Faith and devotion without doubt or hesitation guide your aspirations
   and acts.
Your conduct is the fearless activity free from concepts concerned with
   purity and impurity.
Enjoy this festival of delight, the tantric feast-wheel of great exaltation!

I make this aspiration prayer:
May the power of our tantric feast and of the truth of the profound
   inconceivable nature of phenomena

Lead us together to take pleasure in the resplendent enjoyment of
    stainless indestructible great exaltation
Among the gathering in the Highest Pure Land's celestial city.

*When I was twenty-seven years old, I presented vast tantric feast offerings
to the gatherings of the three regions' dakinis on the tenth day of the waxing moon during the month of the constellation Shravana, Iron Horse Year
(1930), at Pawo—a special place among the amazing terrestrial pure
lands—where there is a mountain whose slope resembles a standing lion,
at its throat an extraordinary retreat hut which is pleasing to glorious
Vajra Yogini's host of deities. On that occasion, a spontaneous song arose
through the flute of my throat, which I, Jigdral Yeshé Dorjé, the awareness-
holders' offspring, have here transposed in part.*

4. Uncontrived luminosity, wisdom's music

How amazing!

Uncontrived luminosity, wisdom's music
And the unobstructed net of magical appearances are an inseparable
array.
Lord of all mandalas, Lake Born Vajra,[83]
Send down your supreme blessing—the realization that whatever
appears is dharmakaya!

Outwardly, the co-emergent gatherings in sacred places, regions, and
charnel grounds
Are inwardly divine hosts within the self-manifest vajra body's sacred
space.
In your intoxication with the youthful freshness of indestructible
stainless great exaltation,
Direct the play of the indestructible nada's melody.

Vajra brothers and sisters gathered together here, linked with good
karma and positive prayers, I offer this prayer:
Just as we now enjoy this tantric feast celebration of great exaltation's
pleasures,
May we accompany one another as a single group
Among the tantric feast assembly in Highest Lotus Light Pure Land's
palace.

I, Jñana, wrote this in response to Könchok Rabten's request.

5. The Wall Song: Sung While Constructing Glorious Copper-Colored Mountain Temple at Kongpo Buchu[84]

Lord, source of all blessings, Lotus-Born:

Precious master, you are the only focus your child needs.
If my devotion does not fluctuate,
Won't you escort me to the place of eternal exaltation?
Father, I've never thought that your compassion would deceive me.

With yearning in my heart and mind, I pray to you:
Bestow your blessings that your child will equal you.
In this happy land, the eastern wooded region of Kongpo,
At the sacred place of Buchu's secret grove,

We build Tail-Fan Pure Land's Glorious Copper-Colored Mountain
   Temple
To help sentient beings, all our mothers with whom we are connected.
Kind lord-protector, bestow your blessings
That we accomplish our goals without obstacles

And that we plant the Buddhist doctrine's victory banner.
May our friends, the dakas and dakinis, help us!
May the sacred Dharmas' protectors and guardians accomplish
   enlightened activity!

May this child's higher intention reach completion!
May I bring my lord guru's intentions to completion![85]
May the six realms of beings, our mothers, be placed in exaltation!
May joy and happiness come to this land!

6. The lofty snow mountains' upper summits

And also:
The lofty snow mountains' upper summits

Are where the white snow lion roams.
When the snow lion remains within his snowy haunts,
His turquoise mane becomes resplendent, indeed.
The lion roams in many places,
But you know that's where he majestically shakes his turquoise mane.

The southern lowlands' sandalwood forests
Are where the Bengal tiger roams.
When the tiger remains within these forests,
His myriad expressions flourish, indeed.
The tiger roams in many places,
But you know that's where he shows off his varied expressions.

The green turquoise lake at the valley's end
Is where the white-bellied golden fish swims.
If the golden fish remains within the lake,
His small bright golden eyes shine, indeed.
The golden fish swims in many places,
But you know that's where he best bobs and weaves.

The azure mid-heaven high above
Is where the white eagle soars.
If the eagle remains in the sky,
His wings demonstrate their three skills.
There are many ways to travel through the high heavens,
But you know that's where the eagle can spread his wings.

7. When the sun arrives at the center

And also:

When the sun
Arrives at the center of the blue mid-heaven,
The auspicious connections occur
For the earth's grove of lotus flowers to bloom.

When drops of honey rain
Arrive from the cluster of the sky's white clouds,
The auspicious connections occur
For the valley's flowers and fruits to ripen soon.

When awareness-holding practitioners
Arrive in regions of their directionless wandering,
The auspicious connections occur
For fortunate disciples' benefit and happiness to appear.

8. I, a roaring lion

A song I sang as I was about to depart from Kongpo[86] to wander aimlessly in central Tibet and other regions:

I, a roaring lion, do not need a palace:
My lion palace is the snow mountains' exalted heights.
I shake my excellent turquoise mane as I please
As I roam at will in delightful snow mountain ravines.

I, an eagle, do not need a fortress:
My white eagle fortress is the loftiest cliff.
I spread wide my excellent wings as I please
As I soar through the space of the vast blue heavens.

I, a tiger, do not need a castle:
My tiger castle is the densest jungle.
I show off my stripes as I please
As I set out to prowl in the best sandalwood forests.

I, a golden bee, do not need farmland:
My bee farmland is the finest lotus groves.
I sing beautiful melodious songs as I please
As I hover to take the sweetest tasting nectar.

I, a yogi, do not need a home:
My yogi home is good any place I roam.
I naturally achieve my two noble goals
As I set out to wander aimlessly as I please.

I, Dudjom, spoke this nonsense.

9. The Magical Play of the Original State: A Song and Dance of Sublime Aspiration

How amazing!

In the sacred place, Blissful Pure Land (Dewachen),
Abides the dharmakaya master, Buddha Amitabha, Limitless Light.[87]
Think of me, your child who prays to you, with compassion:
Grant me your blessings and supreme empowerment.

My awareness, empty clarity, beyond center or boundary—
Lord, isn't this your wisdom mind?
My abiding nature, ever without transition or change—
Buddha Amitabha, Unchanging Light, isn't this you?

I have never been apart from this, even for an instant;
Never apart, yet I was unaware of it.
Now that I recognize it,
Buddha Amitabha, Limitless Light, vanishes;
Blissful Pure Land disappears.

Unobstructed[88] within the unborn space of the nature of mind,
I exult within awareness, the play of empty exaltation.
When all experience arises as the pervasive manifestation of
  dharmakaya,
Clinging to pure lands is misleading;
The label "Buddha," the narrow path of attachment.
There is no Buddha Amitabha outside me: I look within.
I have discovered the dharmakaya within myself. How exhilarating!

This is never-ending happiness. How amazing!
This is the kindness of my holy Lama
And the blessing of the Lama's profound instructions.
I sing this joyous, exalted song
And dance upon reaching the summit of my aspirations.

How amazing!

In the sacred place, Potala Mountain's Pure Land,
Abides the sambhogakaya master, Bodhisattva Chenrezi, Great
    Compassion.
Think of me, your child who prays to you, with compassion:
Grant me your blessings and supreme empowerment.

My awareness, naturally clear, without covering veils—
Lord, isn't this your wisdom mind?
The display of my awareness, the spontaneous wisdom of love and
    supreme knowledge—
Chenrezi, Lord of Compassion, isn't this you?

I have never been apart from this, even for an instant;
Never apart, yet I was unaware of it.
Now that I recognize it,
Bodhisattva Great Compassion vanishes;
Potala Mountain disappears.

Unobstructed within the unborn space of the nature of mind,
I exult within awareness, the play of empty exaltation.
When all radiance has the nature of the sambhogakaya,
Clinging to pure lands is misleading;
The label "sacred Dharma," the narrow path of attachment.
There is no Bodhisattva Great Compassion outside me: I look within.
I have discovered the sambhogakaya within myself. How exhilarating!

This is never-ending happiness. How amazing!
This is the kindness of my holy Lama
And the blessing of the Lama's profound instructions.
I sing this joyous, exalted song
And dance upon reaching the summit of my aspirations.

How amazing!

In the sacred place of Tail-Fan, Glorious Copper-Colored Mountain's
  palace,
Abides the nirmanakaya master, Lotus-Born from Oddiyana.
Think of me, your child who prays to you, with compassion:
Grant me your blessings and supreme empowerment.

My awareness, unceasing self-liberation—
Lord, isn't this your wisdom mind?
My mind's nature, source of kayas and wisdoms—
Lotus-Born, isn't this you?

I have never been apart from this, even for an instant;
Never apart, yet I was unaware of it.
Now that I recognize it,
Lotus-Born vanishes;
Tail-Fan's Copper-Colored Mountain disappears.

Unobstructed within the unborn space of the nature of mind,
I exult within awareness, the play of empty exaltation.
When any appearance of the energy of awareness is nirmanakaya's
  display,
Clinging to pure lands is misleading;
The label "bodhisattva," the narrow path of attachment.
There is no Lotus-Born outside me: I look within.
I have discovered the nirmanakaya within myself. How exhilarating!

This is never-ending happiness. How amazing!
This is the kindness of my holy Lama
And the blessing of the Lama's profound instructions.
I sing this joyous, exalted song
And dance upon reaching the summit of my aspirations.

How amazing!

In the sacred place, the energy center of great exaltation at the crown of
    my head,
Abides the peerless lord-protector, my root Lama .
Think of me, your child who prays to you, with compassion:
Grant me your blessings and supreme empowerment.

My present awareness, the fourth aspect beyond the three times—
Lord, isn't this your wisdom mind?
My awareness, the foundation of all phenomena—
Root Lama, isn't this you?

I have never been apart from this, even for an instant;
Never apart, yet I was unaware of it.
Now that I recognize it,
My root Lama vanishes;
Designated pure lands disappear.

Unobstructed within the unborn space of the nature of mind,
I exult within awareness, the play of empty exaltation.
When all experience arises as the Lama's nature,
Clinging to pure lands is misleading;
The label "rupakaya," the narrow path of attachment.
There is no Lama outside me: I look within.
I have discovered enlightenment within myself. How exhilarating!

This is never-ending happiness. How amazing!
This is the kindness of my holy Lama
And the blessing of the Lama's profound instructions.
I sing this joyous, exalted song
And dance upon reaching the summit of my aspirations.

How amazing!

In the sacred place, Blazing Fire Mountain Pure Realm,
Abides the chief wisdom deity, great Héruka.
Think of me, your child who prays to you, with compassion:
Grant me your blessings and supreme attainment.

My own awareness, splendor of all existence and enlightenment—
Wisdom deity, isn't this your essential nature?
My realization's incisive knowledge of selflessness, a brave warrior—
Vajra Kumara, isn't this you?

I have never been apart from this, even for an instant;
Never apart, yet I was unaware of it.
Now that I recognize it,
The host of wisdom deities vanishes;
Blazing Fire Mountain disappears.

Unobstructed within the unborn space of the nature of mind,
I exult within awareness, the play of empty exaltation.
Phenomenal existence's purity is the wisdom deities' nature;
Clinging to pure lands as separate places is misleading;
The label "wisdom deity's body" as substantial, the narrow path of
    attachment.
There is no wisdom deity outside me: I look within.
I have discovered the supreme deity within myself. How exhilarating!

This is never-ending happiness. How amazing!
This is the kindness of my holy Lama
And the blessing of the Lama's profound instructions.
I sing this joyous, exalted song
And dance upon reaching the summit of my aspirations.

How amazing!

In the sacred place, the pure celestial land,
Abides the chief of all dakinis, Vajra Varahi.
Think of me, your child who prays to you, with compassion:
Grant me your blessings and remove obstacles.

My original basic nature, the vast uncontrived expanse—
Companion, isn't this your stainless space?
This wisdom of empty exaltation without coming together or
    separating—
Wisdom dakini, isn't this you?

I have never been apart from this, even for an instant;
Never apart, yet I was unaware of it.
Now that I recognize it,
Vajra Varahi vanishes;
The celestial pure land disappears.

Unobstructed within the unborn space of the nature of mind,
I exult in awareness, the play of empty exaltation.
When appearances, sounds, and incisive knowledge have the female
    Buddha's nature,
Clinging to pure lands is misleading;
The label "sublime mother," the narrow path of attachment.
There is no dakini outside me: I look within.
I have discovered the mother of the Victorious Ones within myself. How
    exhilarating!

This is never-ending happiness. How amazing!
This is the kindness of my holy Lama
And the blessings of the Lama's profound instructions.
I sing this joyous, exalted song;
I dance upon reaching the summit of my aspirations.

How amazing!

In unfixed locations, pure realms of charnel grounds,
Dwell seas of Dharma protectors, the oath-bound guardians.
Think of me, your child who prays to you, with compassion:
Grant me your blessings and accomplish my activity.

My awareness, in which all acts are primordially and effortlessly
    accomplished—
Seas of oath-bound ones, isn't this your life-essence?
This protection from the dualistic perceptions of existence and
    enlightenment—
Ultimate guardian, isn't this you?

I have never been apart from this, even for an instant;
Never apart, yet I was unaware of it.
Now that I recognize it,
The protectors and guardians vanish;
The charnel grounds and sacred places disappear.

Unobstructed within the unborn space of the nature of mind,
I exult within awareness, the play of empty exaltation.
In the protector's display, natural liberation of the mass of my thoughts,
Clinging to designated sacred places is misleading;
The label "guardians" as separate entities, the narrow path of attachment.
There is no guardian outside me: I look within.
I have discovered oath-bound protectors within myself. How exhilarating!

This is never-ending happiness. How amazing!
This is the kindness of my holy Lama
And the blessings of the Lama's profound instructions.
I sing this joyous, exalted song;
I dance upon reaching the summit of my aspirations.

*My vajra brother Lama Sönam Chöpel asked me, "Sing a song of what-
ever experience manifests from your realization." I examined my own*

mind and saw: My Lama is excellent: I have touched the feet of Lotus-Born incarnate; the teachings are profound: I have met Great Perfection, the pure essence of the dakinis' heart blood. I have nothing to boast about as hardship in meditation practice, in the style of staying in a mountain cave, the entrance sealed with mud. Nevertheless, I live never parted from the wisdom of the natural state of rest and thus have no need for many hopeful and fearful worries concerning anything whatsoever. Although this person has not actualized Great Perfection, I am happy with Great Perfection's spiritual tradition. I do not consider it unreasonable for me to sing this song of excellent aspiration, like a young donkey pleased with his own penis. I, the wanderer Jigdral Yeshé Dorjé, spoke this without shame on the shores of Tso Péma (Lotus Lake) in Zahor, India.

10. Dudjom Lingpa's Song of Tantric Gathering

How wonderful![89]

The perfect time is the evenness of primordial purity;
The perfect place, Highest Pure Land, the dharmadhatu, the stainless
space of phenomena;
The perfect teacher, dharmakaya Buddha Kuntu Zangpo;
The perfect retinue, the Victorious Ones of the five families;
The perfect teaching, Secret Mantra's vehicle.
Come to this tantric feast celebration, the display of all-encompassing
equal purity.

Next, the perfect time is in primordial purity's vast expanse;
The perfect place, Mount Malaya's peak;[90]
The perfect teacher, the powerful Lord Vajradhara (Dorjé Chang);
The perfect retinue, the assembly of nirmanakaya's magical displays;
The perfect sublime teaching, the direct path of primordially pure Great
Perfection.
Come to this tantric feast celebration to guide disciples.

Finally, in the time of the joyous fortunate age:
The perfect glorious place is Samyé and Lhasa;
The perfect teachers, Lotus-Born from Oddiyana and Vimalamitra;
The perfect retinue, the reincarnated king, subjects, scholars, and
accomplished masters;
The perfect teaching, the direct path of luminous Great Perfection.
Come to this tantric feast celebration of those fortunate in karma and
aspirations.

In the midst of this perfect present time of self-manifest reality,
The perfect teacher is the Lama who is one's own awareness;
The perfect retinue, the fortunate gathering;
The perfect sublime Dharma, the direct path of the Great Vehicle.
Come to this tantric feast celebration of realization of the natural state.

May the power of the interdependent links I have made singing this
   joyous song of experience
And the strength of profound wisdom's and skillful means' truth
Bring this feast's magical display of this teacher and gathering of the
   circle of disciples
To liberation together in the encompassing evenness of the immortal
   vase body endowed with the six special qualities.

I make this prayer to accomplish the rainbow body's great transference.

*I, Dudjom Lingpa [Jigdral Yeshé Dorjé's previous incarnation], wrote
this at yogi Karma Sönam's request. May this be virtuous!
May all be auspicious!*

[From Tröma volume, pp. 919–20]

≈§ III

Supplication Prayers

You turn me away from wrong paths of negative actions,
And connect me to virtue's correct path.
Guide on the path to liberation's permanent exaltation,
Wisdom master, think of me![91]

Introduction:
Supplication Prayers (*gsol 'debs*)

I HAVE CHOSEN to present the majority of the supplication prayers (*gsol 'debs*) section from His Holiness's *Collected Works*, volume *ah*, pages 1–105. The few prayers that I omitted are ones Dudjom Rinpoché wrote at the request of students for a supplication prayer to his or her Lama.

Faith and devotion are key prerequisites for the practice of the Vajrayana and Great Perfection. They are also the very foundation and path that naturally contain within them the result of full enlightenment. As the omniscient Longchenpa writes in *Resting in the Magical Display*:[92]

> In guru yoga, however, the path [of faith and devotion], by its very nature alone, awakens the realization of the natural state within one and brings liberation. For that reason guru yoga is the most profound of all paths.

Faith and devotion protect us from getting lost in the labyrinth of samsara. They enable the Dharma to penetrate our being so that our practice does not remain superficial, merely skin deep; and they rapidly and safely transport us along the noble path up to its final step, that step that can only be taken through direct recognition of our true nature that is always present, has always been present, and will always be present.

It is important to understand that our faith and devotion are not only directed to the "outer" Lama. There are three aspects to the guru: outer, inner, and secret. The outer guru is your master in the flesh before you. The inner guru is the Dharma received from the outer guru. The secret guru is your mind's true nature, pure awareness, fully enlightened Buddhahood. As Lama Tharchin Rinpoché explains in his commentary to the *Concise Preliminary Practices of the New Treasures of Dudjom Rinpoché*:

There are actually three gurus: the outer guru, the inner guru, and the secret guru. The outer guru [your guru] is the same as Guru Rinpoché who has taken form. The inner guru is the Dharma he has given that has arisen from his realization. These instructions can lead us to the discovery and unveiling of our own Buddha-potential. As practice is established and the fruition begins to materialize, the realization of the secret guru dawns as none other than our own all-knowing wisdom awareness mind. (p. 41)

The supplication prayers section contains three parts:

1. four prayers placed by His Holiness before the actual supplication prayers section: a prayer based upon the life and liberation of Dudjom Lingpa, His Holiness's past incarnation; a prayer in verse to His Holiness's teachers, containing a description in prose of the empowerments, textual transmissions, and empowerments received from each; a prayer based upon His Holiness's past incarnations; and a concise one-verse version of the previous prayer
2. prayers of the genre "Calling the Lama from Afar"
3. various supplication prayers to Dudjom Rinpoché that he himself wrote as requested by his students

The supplication prayers contained within this collection help engender faith and devotion toward your Lama, inspiration for our spiritual lives, and fortitude in the face of difficulties encountered in the ups and downs of our daily life.

The first prayer, based upon the life and liberation of Dudjom Lingpa, is part of an important genre of Tibetan literature—that of *namthar* (*rnam thar*) or accounts of the lives and liberation of realized Lamas—which are a crucial part of a disciple's training. These biographies trace the lives of realized masters and describe their travails (if any), trainings, spiritual experiences, and complete realization. Quite often these books also contain teachings in the form of songs of realization or of instructions sung for the local people that the Lamas would encounter. As Matthieu Ricard writes in the introduction to *The Life of Shabkar*:

Tibetan hagiographies are called *namthar*, which means "perfect, or complete, liberation." A *namthar* is not only the detailed account of a saintly person's life, but the description of his or her journey to liberation: a narrative and a teaching as well. More than any other teaching, in fact, a *namthar* leaves a deep impression on the reader's mind. Far from abstract considerations, it puts in our hands a chart to guide us on the journey, a testimony that the journey can be accomplished, and a powerful incentive to set out quickly on the path. *Namthars* of recent masters remind one that these accounts are not ancient fairy tales; they demonstrate that, even in our time, there are accomplished beings who are living examples of enlightenment.[93]

My Lamas highly recommend reading life stories of realized masters, and the following are available in English (see Bibliography for details):[94]

1. *Guru Rinpoché: His Life and Times*
2. *The Lady of the Lotus-Born* (Yeshé Tsogyal's life story of liberation)
3. *The Lives and Liberation of Princess Mandarava*
4. *The Life of Shabkar: The Autobiography of a Tibetan Yogin*
5. *The Life of Milarepa*
6. *The Autobiography of Jamgön Kongtrul*
7. *Masters of Meditation and Miracles* (of the Longchen Nyingtik tradition)
8. *The Divine Madman: The Sublime Life and Songs of Drukpa Kunley*

The prayer at hand, based on Dudjom Lingpa's life story, is a sub-genre—a prayer based upon these life stories of liberation—written in verse, inspiring us to attain that same realization and requesting blessings that we will attain it. Through reciting this prayer with genuine faith and devotion, the blessings of Dudjom Lingpa's wisdom mind are transmitted to our mind.

In the next work, Dudjom Rinpoché praises his teachers in verse and then lists in prose the teachings, textual transmissions, and empowerments he received from each one. I find that reading Dudjom Rinpoché's list of his teachers and their rich variety of instruction inspires faith and confidence in this amazing fully realized being. This text is also an important reference document to which I like to return periodically.

The third prayer is based upon Dudjom Rinpoché's past incarnations. This is an inspiring prayer that all followers of his New Treasures tradition recite before beginning meditation. The last prayer in this section is a concise version of this past incarnation prayer.

The second series of prayers belong to the genre "Calling the Lama from Afar." These are my favorite prayers. I can't count the number of times when in personal retreat I would begin my session with the prayer called "In the depth of my heart" only to notice at some point that hours had passed and I had not yet begun the main practice! I find these prayers powerful, pure conduits to direct all my energy and feeling, without the need to figure something out: One can just pray and sing from the heart. It is a very simple practice. My Lama always taught us that, in the privacy of our retreat cabin or practice place, we can sing and chant these devotional songs from the heart, in whatever melody we like, but *not* to do this in earshot of others as a way of boasting our faith or realization.

Supplication prayers such as these are actually a form of guru yoga, the essential element needed to attain full enlightenment in this lifetime. As Lama Tharchin Rinpoché writes:

> According to the Vajrayana view, guru yoga is the quintessential practice for attaining liberation. All Buddhas became enlightened by following their teacher's precious instructions. So the guru is considered even more important than the Buddha because without the guru there is no way to achieve Buddhahood. When the guru's instructions have penetrated the student's heart, this is the same as finding a precious wish-fulfilling jewel in your hand. Someone who has received the guru's mind transmission has no choice but to attain enlightenment, just as someone falling down a steep mountain totally out of control has no choice but to fall all the way to the bottom.
>
> The eighty-four mahasiddhas in India and Guru Rinpoché's twenty-five main disciples in Tibet, the treasure-finders, awareness-holders, and accomplished enlightened sublime beings, all became enlightened through the mind transmission of their gurus. This unbroken lineage has been passed from the primordial Buddha, Samantabhadra, to our own root Lama, who is the essence of all Buddhas of the ten directions and the three times.

All *siddhi*s [spiritual attainments] and blessings are carried and passed through this lineage. Because the path of guru yoga is so deeply profound, there is no doubt that if you practice it, you will become enlightened. (p. 38)

His Holiness gives the following instruction preceding the prayer called "Blessings Swiftly Received":

The principal task of those seeking to reach the state of omniscience in this lifetime is to see the master who grants you profound instructions that bring you to spiritual maturity and liberation as the Buddha incarnate, lord of all mandalas. Inspired with uncontrived intense yearning and devotion, pray in this way, as if calling out for help from afar.

An example of the devotional aspect of this genre of prayers can be found in the prayer "In the depth of my heart":

In the depth of my heart
At the center of my faith's blossoming thousand-petalled lotus,
You reside forever in delight
And always bless me.

Glorious lord Héruka,
Jigdral Yeshé Dorjé,
You are the essence of all the Victorious Ones..
Of this my heart is sure.

With intense, unbearable yearning,
I single-mindedly pray to you:
Bring me to maturity and liberation
With your nectar of blessing, empowerment, and attainments.

The unique aspect of these "Calling the Lama from Afar" prayers is that some prayers emphasize the ultimate Lama: our own enlightened mind. The prayer "In the depth of my heart" continues:

I cry out from afar
With overwhelming longing for you, my Lama,
Yet I cannot find you
Apart from this, my original mind.

When there is no one to hear my prayers
Nor anyone to voice them,
Why should I invent supplications
With forced, clinging contrivance?

Conceptionless naked empty awareness,
Vivid yet indefinable—
This I recognize as my ultimate Lama,
Indestructible wisdom (Yeshé Dorjé).[95]

In the original ground of the naturally settled state,
Supreme constant abiding in primordial presence,
I need not call my Lama from afar
Nor search for you nearby.

In the essential nature beyond my mind, all-inclusive awakening,
Delusion is unheard of,
Let alone transcendence of sorrow.
It is an endless expanse of evenness and exaltation.

Whatever arises is dharmakaya's pervasive manifestation,
Blessings beyond understanding.
Enter this yogin's heart—
How wonderful and amazing!

In the third part of this section there are a variety of supplication prayers to Dudjom Rinpoché, prayers to Guru Rinpoché, and a prayer based upon the series of names that Dudjom Rinpoché had in previous lives, all requested by his disciples.

Praying to the Lama in this way blesses us, accomplishing our goals and wishes in accord with the Dharma. Supplicating in this way is a very practical and direct approach to attain enlightenment in this very life. It protects us from a nihilistic attitude based upon mere intellectualism that will never accomplish our spiritual goals; will never protect us when the chips are down; and will never lead to realization in a million years. Therefore, these supplication prayers are the very bedrock of Vajrayana and Great Perfection practice. As Lama Tharchin Rinpoché writes :

> Have pure faith, devotion, and confidence in this [guru yoga] as a practice. This means genuinely feeling the guru's inconceivable qualities of kindness and wisdom. Direct instructions from the guru can reveal your own Buddha-nature, which has been obscured in samsara for countless lifetimes. Open your heart and trust in this. Thinking of the guru's qualities, how amazing and extraordinarily fortunate you are to have met a teacher like this, you may feel the hair on your body stand up or you may cry without control. Experiences will arise and suddenly your mind will change to pure awareness. All normal phenomena will cease. Meditation experiences will arise effortlessly and spontaneously. So when practicing, do not mouth the words mindlessly or without feeling but rather generate devotion, the heart essence of guru yoga. (p. 39)

The Chariot of Devotion

*A Prayer Based upon the Incarnate Supreme Treasure-
Revealer Traktung Dudjom Lingpa's Life and Liberation*

All Victorious Ones in a single form, Padmasambhava,
In these degenerate times, you manifested as an individual who tames
    beings.
Lord of a hundred Buddha families, supreme treasure-revealer, king of
    the Dharma,
Dudjom Lingpa, at your feet I pray.

From the beginning, even though you manifestly attained the nectar of
    peace
And completely rejected connections made with grasping and craving to
    elaborated characteristics,
You manifested infinite clouds of the four training methods' myriad
    magical apparitions.[96]
Display of hundreds of magical dances, to you I pray.

Especially now, during the doctrine of the fourth guide (Shakyamuni
    Buddha),[97]
Your lifetimes reflect our second teacher's (Guru Rinpoché) enlightened
    activity,
Including incarnations as arhat, awareness-holder, scholar, and
    accomplished meditation master in the Land of the Exalted [India] and
    in Tibet.
To the sweet series of your successive lives, to you I pray.[98]

The master who knows the three times
Came from Lotus Light Pure Land to enthrone you with his vajra
   command
As his sublime regent in these degenerate times.
You thereby intentionally took rebirth: to you I pray.

In an amazing place blessed by exalted bodhisattvas—
The Himalayan land of lower Amdo's Serlung,[99] region of medicinal
   herbs—
You considered taking rebirth in a pure family,
The Nub clan,[100] source of myriad scholars and accomplished masters: to
   you I pray.

Dakas and dakinis respectfully escorted you[101]
When you entered a qualified mother's womb.
Your mother and father's body and mind were blessed
With numerous wondrous and auspicious signs: to you I pray.

On the night of the tenth day of the Sheep Year's miracle month,
The lotus of your exquisite body's marks and signs blossomed.
A dome of rainbow lights, a sweet rain of flowers—
Boundless such good omens appeared: to you I pray.

At this time, numerous guides of sublime vision
Praised you fully as an unrivalled incarnation [nirmanakaya].
You received their infallible prophecy;
You were an individual who would accomplish limitless benefit for
   others: to you I pray.

Until your third year, a gathering of dakinis and protectors
Accompanied you with song and dance as guardians.
You sometimes saw them routing hostile *damsi* spirits' attacks.
Seer of many such visionary experiences, to you I pray.

On one occasion, you went to the northern pure land Lapis Light,
Where Transcendent Conqueror Unquestionable King
Honored and confirmed you as his regent.
You thereby recalled your former lives: to you I pray.

In the celestial pure land, the stainless space consort Yogini
Diffused hundreds of thousands of dakinis' life essence in the form of
     seed syllables, which dissolved into you;
You received the supreme empowerment of their blessings' transference.
Victor over the attacks of adverse circumstances, to you I pray.

From a young age, you perfected your innate capabilities;
You transcended common life, your sublime sacred inherent potential
     awakened.
With boundless clairvoyance and miraculous powers,
You inspired impartial faith: to you I pray.

In your ninth year, a wisdom dakini
Came with a gift of exaltation-sustaining nectar, according to prophesy.
You relied upon her as a sublime teacher
Who simultaneously opened hundreds of doors to hearing and
     reflecting's noble qualities: to you I pray.[102]

The sole deity of great love [Chenrezi], in an exquisite youthful white
     body,
Remained inseparably with you as a friend, carefully protecting you.
Lion of Speech [Manjushri] visibly accepted you as his disciple;
The energy of your incisive knowledge (*shes rab*) burst forth: to you I
     pray.

Beings of wisdom's magical body—bodhisattvas of the three families,[103]
     female Buddha Taré-ma,
Venerable Saraha, the Archer, the eight accomplished awareness-holders,
Longchenpa, and others—
Accepted you as their disciple and you received their blessings: to you I
     pray.

Especially, you went in waking life to the Glorious Copper-Colored
     Mountain in Tail-Fan.[104]
You transformed one day into twelve years
And received the nectar of ripening [empowerments] and liberating
     [instructions] from the lord guru [Guru Rinpoché].
You became his holy successor: to you I pray.

At your extremely subtle level, you saw inconceivable displays
Of incalculable Buddhas' lives and pure lands.
In every one of them, you sent endless emanated forms
To enter immeasurable gateways to the Dharma: to you I pray.

In brief, you did not depend upon training completed during this
    lifetime.
Your karmic propensity from past familiarization awakened,
Its splendor overwhelmed those renowned as scholars and accomplished
    masters.
You had the highest degree of wisdom and realization: to you I pray.

Gatherings of dakinis, such as Yeshé Tsogyal,
Nurtured you as their child and related concealed prophecies.
Oath-bound protectors and treasure guardians accompanied you like
    your shadow,
Honoring you as obedient servant messengers: to you I pray.

Not attached to the taste of inferior tainted bliss,
You dwelt in sublime unconditioned pure conduct.[105]
On the path of passion, you relinquished all faults, such as desire.
Ultimate virtuous practitioner, to you I pray.[106]

With extremely stable courage over eons of familiarization,
The intense power of love and compassion moved you.
You engaged in bodhisattvas' discipline; any connection with you became
    meaningful.
Great sublime being who tames sentient beings, to you I pray.[107]

Upon the swift path of the sublime secret great methods' first stage,
You perfected the deities' manifest forms
And perceived all appearances and sounds as the wheel of pure wisdom.[108]
Sublime lord of yogins, to you I pray.

You actualized the three forms of blazing primordial wisdom[109]
And gathers the three kinds of escorts like clouds.

Mastering the four activities and eight accomplishments,
You transformed your activity into whatever you desired: to you I
  pray.[110]

You applied amazing, forceful methods
To bind the sun and moon's movement in the *roma*[111] and *kyangma*
  channels[112] within the central channel's expanse.[113]
You thus overcame the defiled city's
Wheel of delusion of impure karmic subtle energy:[114] to you I pray.

The strength of supreme *chandali's* (*gtu mo*)[115] resplendent radiance
Intoxicated you with the taste of the sixteen changeless joys.
Your hundred dances of fearless conduct overwhelming phenomenal
  existence with brilliance
Inspired fortunate beings to great exaltation: to you I pray.

You attained the great secret, the secret of the pinnacle of the vajra view,
Much more secret than special secrets:
The naked essential nature—uncontrived, primordially pure, empty
  awareness—
Kuntu Zangpo's wisdom mind: to you I pray.[116]

In the natural state within the nature of phenomena free from activity or
  effort,
The genuine unimpeded unrestricted expanse, beyond mind,
You practiced the yoga of space within the continuity of no meditation,
  no distraction.
Your realization and liberation occurred simultaneously: to you I pray.

The spontaneously present inner luminosity, the pure radiance of the
  display of awareness,
Manifests as amazing phenomena—the path's appearances, the rupakaya.
You went as in a mirage to the level
Of the full measure of Clear Light Direct Vision's (*thod rgal*) noble
  qualities: to you I pray.[117]

The queen of space Gaga-dhu, embodiment of incisive knowledge who
    bestows exaltation,
Revealed to you Ati's vital points and entrusted you with the dakinis'
    secret trove.
Seeing that it would serve a vast and sublime purpose,
She encouraged you to open the door to the profound treasures: to you
    I pray.

In your vision of wisdom, of infinite pure appearances,
Inexhaustible mind treasures burst forth from the vast space of your
    realization,
And the profound earth treasures entrusted by the dakinis overflowed.
Universal monarch among treasure-revealers, to you I pray.

Your amazing treasures of teachings, a trove of jewels—
The trio of Lama, Great Perfection, and the Compassionate One;[118]
Meditations on the stages of generation, perfection, and Great Perfection,
Including their root, branches, activity rituals, and supplements—
Increase the festival of delight of your fortunate disciples: to you I pray.

In these late times, when spiritual vehicles based upon effort are not
    effective,
You kindled the light of the doctrine
Of the definitive secret essence, the Great Perfection Ati,
Following the exact truthful meaning the vajra scriptures extolled:
    to you I pray.

Your charming sublime body has impressive white robes and long hair.[119]
You gloriously sing fearless songs of realization (*doha*) (and) spiritual
    verse (*gur*).
Your realization's intense heat liberates the mindstream of karmically
    destined beings.
Unsurpassable Héruka, to you I pray.

You realized that all phenomena are unreal, like a magical display.
Your unobstructed awareness saw the true nature as it is;

Its force allowed you to pass through all material, substantial things
  that can be touched.
Master imbued with the power of miracles, to you I pray.

In degenerate times, your fury, power, and strength
Annihilate hordes of humans and non-humans, demons, savages,
  and invisible spirits
Who are very hostile to the doctrine and to beings.
Your activity triumphs in every direction: to you I pray.

On such occasions as empowerments, offering practice rituals,[120]
  and tantric feast gatherings,
Rainbow lights, rains of flowers, permeating fragrances,
And dakinis' symbolic songs
Awaken the wisdom of your fortunate disciples: to you I pray.

Seeing, hearing, remembering, or even your slight touch
Definitely bestows assurance of permanent exaltation.
Acclaim of your supreme noble qualities
Covers the surface of the wealth-bearing earth: to you I pray.

All those connected to you on the path of passion—
Five wisdom dakinis and fifty dakinis of
tantric commitments in hidden forms—
Were joined to fortune equal to yours, Héruka: to you I pray.

Your eight close sons[121] preserved your family line of bodhisattvas;
Thirteen sublime disciples accomplished a body of light;[122]
One thousand achieved the stage of awareness-holder.
With these and other disciples, you produced a royal lineage of
  accomplished masters: to you I pray.

Your aspirations' force ripened; the time had come for you to accept
  disciples.
By that power, you spread your profound treasures' activity
To Ngari, Ü, Tsang, the hidden land of Lomön,

Pu, Bo, Kongpo, Amdo, and Kham,[123] as well as India, China, and Nepal:
    to you I pray.

When you brought the actual activity to completion
And considered other great needs,
You departed with marvelous signs, including sounds and lights,
For Tail-Fan's Glorious Copper-Colored Mountain: to you I pray.

In pure lands such as Péma Kö, Lovely Lotus Array,
You displayed inconceivable dances of the moon reflected on water,
Offspring of the lotus family
To spread Padmasambhava's activity in hundreds of directions: to you
    I pray.

Protector, I respectfully remember your life, an ocean of noble qualities,
And supplicate you with yearning:
In your constant, compassionate kindness,
Nurture me as your disciple and may we never be apart, I pray!

Show your loving face and bestow your joyful sublime instruction
To us, your sincerely devoted lineage-holder heirs.
Grant your blessings with the empowerment of great indestructible
    wisdom
That we become indivisible from you.

May I travel the secret path to reach the primordial royal city.
May I spread the profound tradition throughout this world.
May clouds of my life stories of liberation, a wheel of inexhaustible
    ornaments,
Entirely pervade the stainless space of phenomena. May I become the
    same as you!

*Due to the request by numerous earnest seekers endowed with the wealth
of devotion, Jigdral Yeshé Dorjé spoke these words in his eloquent voice,
and I, Losal Trinlé Gyurmé, as if catching his words, wrote them down on
paper. Siddhi rastu!*

The Chariot of Devotion

Supplications to the Kind Lamas
to Swiftly Draw Their Blessings

Lotus-Born Master's supreme regent,
Display of Translator Bérotsana[124] and Dorjé Dudjom Tsal[125] in
 inseparable union,
Lord of ocean-like gatherings of scholars and accomplished masters,
 head of their family:
Zilnön Namkhé Dorjé, to you I pray.[126]

WHEN HE AUTHORIZED ME as the head of his teachings mentioned in
scriptures, he bestowed, like filling a vase, the entire range of
instructions for producing spiritual maturity [empowerments], liberation
[guidance], and support [transmission] from his own treasures' profound
teachings, such as the longevity practice, the Life Essence of Deathlessness.
In particular, he placed the abiding nature, Great Perfection's pith instructions (*man ngag*), in the palm of my hand. He gave me specific prophecies
and advice and granted his supreme confirmation that I would perform
activity to heal the Early Translation's doctrine. This illustrates how he was
the sole main cause of the gradual awakening of my positive karmic
propensity. Therefore, he is the Lama with whom I am karmically connected throughout my series of successive lives, the definite embodiment
of great exaltation, lord of all families, Padmasambhava.

Dance of Langdro Translator's[127] intentional rebirth;
Universal monarch among an ocean of scholars, accomplished masters, and awareness-holders;

> Lord of a secret trove of amazing sacred places and profound
>   treasures:
> Dudjom Namkhé Dorjé (also known as Trinlé Jampé Jungné),
>   to you I pray.

From him, I received the entire range of instructions for producing spiritual maturity [empowerments], liberation [guidance], and support [trans-
mission] for *The Treasury of Precious Instruction*,[128] which gathers in a
single collection the profound instruction from the eight great chariots of
the practice lineage. Further, I received a great amount of the nectar of
instruction from him, including full and wide-ranging guidance based on
the large commentary to *The Gradual Path of the Wisdom Essence*,[129] the
entire cycle of seal teachings from *The Great Treasury of Precious Rediscovered Treasures*,[130] and the cycle of his own profound treasures. The
mountain of his kindness in lovingly accepting me as his disciple exceeds
all measure.

> In former times, you were Buddha Supreme Doctor in Dense Array
>   Pure Land;
> In the future, you will be the fortunate eon's guide, Lion's Roar
>   (Sengé Dra);
> Now, you are a Héruka, Lord of Secrets, in person:
> Gyurmé Ngédon Wangpo, to you I pray![131]

From him, I received the entire range of instructions for producing spiritual maturity (empowerments), liberation (guidance), and support (transmission) for *The Great Treasury of Precious Rediscovered Treasures*,[132] *The
Wish-Granting Vase of Techniques of Accomplishment*,[133] the cycle of *Minling's New Treasures*,[134] Lord Khyentsé Wangpo's *Seven Transmissions*
cycle of teachings,[135] and the cycle of *The New Treasures of Dudjom*.[136] He
gave me very many kinds of transmission-instructions, including those for
all of Longchenpa's works for which the reading transmission still remains,
principally *The Seven Treasuries*;[137] the root texts and commentary to the
four medical tantras; and Patrul Rinpoché's *Collected Works*.[138] He gave me
personal guidance to establish me firmly in the practical procedures of vajra
masters' main activities, including drawing mandalas, giving empower-

ments, performing burnt offerings, and consecration. The mountain of his kindness in lovingly accepting me as his disciple passes beyond the sky's horizon.

> Outwardly, you maintain a life of scholarship, nobility, and excellence;
> Inwardly, you perfected the mastery of the two stages of tantric practices.[139]
> Secretly, you are the sublime regent of the unmatched sixth Buddha [Vajradhara]:[140]
> Gyurmé Pendé Öser, to you I pray.[141]

Beginning with giving me the complete vows of a layperson, he bestowed the entire cycle of the Early Translation's canon, principally the three central texts: *Sutra, Miracle,* and *Mind.*[142] He gave me the empowerments, with instruction and reading transmissions, for Nyang-ral's [Nyima Öser's] *Eightfold Gathering of Joyful Buddhas,*[143] Sangyé Lingpa's *Gathering of the Lamas' Intention, The Four Volumes of Great Perfection's Heart Essence Teachings,*[144] the cycle of *Minling's New Treasures* (*smin gling gter gsar*), Longsal Nyingpo's *Central Texts* (*klong chen snying thig rtsa pod*), and the tantric tradition of Dorjé Purba (*phur pa rgyud lugs*). He gave teaching on the king of tantra *Secret Essence,*[145] Longchenpa's *Seven Treasuries,*[146] *The Trilogy of Natural Rest,*[147] *Ascertaining the Three Vows,*[148] *The Treasury of Noble Qualities,*[149] and *The Treasury of Knowledge.*[150] Further, I received many other transmissions from him. The mountain of his kindness in lovingly accepting me as his disciple, such as according his supreme confirmation that I would perform activity for other's benefit, can never be measured.

> The three trainings' nectar filled your wisdom mind's excellent vase.
> You gained signs of accomplishment from your practice of the two stages.[151]
> The light of your teaching and practices illuminated the secret doctrine:
> Orgyen Namdrol Gyatso,[152] to you I bow.

He gave me many kinds of nectar of profound instructions from many central texts, such as the major empowerment and practice of *The Eightfold Gathering of Joyful Buddhas* and Guru Chöwang's[153] *Razor of Dorjé Purba, Further Gathering of the Great Compassionate One;*[154] most of the Nyingma tantras;[155] and the Middle Way's tradition of the bodhisattva vows. On the direct path of supreme great secrets, he bestowed detailed and wide-ranging transmissions, pith instructions, and practical procedures for the *Tantra of Noble Qualities' Nectar*. Such was the kindness I received from him.

> Cared for by the Lama and the high deities,
> You fully completed great power on the path of the two stages.
> Yogin of space, both learned and accomplished:
> Orgyen Chöjyor Gyatso, to you I pray.[156]

From him, I received the instructions for producing spiritual maturity [empowerments], liberation [guidance], and support [transmission] for most of the profound teachings of Karma Lingpa, Longsal Nyingpo, and Dudjom Lingpa. I received many teachings, including the ripening guidance of the preliminary practices. Moreover, he had me enter the gate to the teachings [taking refuge] and was the first to instill in me the incisive knowledge from hearing and contemplation. Hence, the breath of his kindness is beyond limits.

> Renunciation and the discipline of individual liberation was your
>   stable root;
> Bodhisattvas' conduct for others' benefit, your moving branches
>   and leaves;
> Secret Mantra's supreme techniques, the two stages, your fortune
>   of fruit:
> Jampal Tsultrim Drakpa, to you I pray.

He gave me many kinds of nectar of profound instructions, such as the entire range of instructions for producing spiritual maturity [empowerments], liberation [guidance], and support [transmission] for *The Treasury* of the *Kagyu Tantras of Marpa's Tradition*;[157] the major empowerment of Chokling's *Heart Practice that Dispels All Obstacles*;[158] and *The Essential Manual of Heart Advice*.[159] Such is the kindness I received from him.

> You received your root and lineage awareness-holding masters'
> essential realization,
> Unsurpassable lord of wisdom, realization, and capability.
> Kind master who extended the life of the teachings in the hidden
> land [Péma Kö],
> Péma Wangi Gyalpo, to you I pray.

From him, I received the instructions for producing spiritual maturity [empowerments], liberation [guidance], support [transmission], and extraordinary entrusting of profound instruction for Jatson Nyingpo's *Six Volumes of Profound Teachings*,[160] Rikdzin Dorjé Tokmé's[161] *Seven Profound Teachings*, Dorjé Drak Ngak's cycle of profound treasures, and Gampo Drodül Lingpa's[162] cycle of teachings on the wrathful form of Vajrapani [the Lord of Secrets]. Such was the kindness I received from him.

> In supreme incisive knowledge, you saw the abiding nature as it is;
> In supreme compassion, you strove solely for others' good;
> In supreme diligence, you raised the victory banner of learning and
> practice:
> Garwang Sangyé Dorjé, [163] to you I pray.

From him, I received the kindness of instructions for producing spiritual maturity [empowerments], liberation [guidance], support [transmission], and the entrusting of profound instruction for the entire cycle of Düdül Dorjé's[164] profound treasures in a lineage far superior to others, the extraordinary lineage of his spiritual heirs.

> You see everything that can be known in their entirety;
> You ascended the two stages' path to a high stage of
> accomplishment;
> Fearless renunciant, yogin of space,
> Ngawang Gendun Gyatso, [165] to you I pray.

From him, I received the vast kindness of instructions for producing spiritual maturity [empowerments], liberation [guidance], and support [transmission] for the entirety of the great treasure-revealer Péma Lingpa's[166] profound treasures, and such profound instruction as the entire *Hundred Thousand Nyingma Tantras*.

> For your own good, you reached the sublime stage of peace,
> Yet for other's benefit you used the magical means of attachment to existence
> To skillfully increase the doctrine and beings' well-being and happiness in supreme measure:
> Ngawang Jigmé Lodrö, to you I pray.[167]

When I received his reading transmission of the entire translation of the Victorious One's Word,[168] which he read with three qualities—clarity, precision, and pleasing sound—I felt I had the good fortune to have made my human life meaningful.

> Exalted magical display of the three bodhisattvas in a single form,
> Your activity brings anyone connected with you to the path of liberation.
> Place of refuge for beings in this degenerate time, master from Taklung:[169]
> Ngawang Palden Zangpo, to you I pray.[170]

From him I received the vows from two traditions[171] of development of the mind of awakening, and instructions for producing spiritual maturity [empowerments], liberation [guidance], and support [transmission] for many tantras of the Later Translation tradition, principally Cakrasamvara (Supreme Bliss), Hévajra (Vajra Creator of Delight), and Guhyasamaja (Matrix of Mystery).

> You attained the inner realization of the three lineages' awareness-holding Lamas

And hold the extraordinary wisdom dakini's secret treasure.
Renunciant, yogin of space, Héruka:
Jigmé Trogyal Dorjé,[172] to you I pray.

From him I received the kindness of the teaching transmission for various Early Translation tantras, transmissions, and pith instructions,[173] principally *A Collection of Explanations on Vajrakilaya*;[174] and most particularly, he gave me the entire range of instructions for producing spiritual maturity [empowerments], liberation [guidance], and support [transmission] for every profound treasure—mainly those of the Lama, the Great Perfection, and Great Compassion—discovered by the queen of treasure-revealers, Déchen Déwé Dorjé.[175]

Unrivalled holder of the teaching and family lineage
Of the great treasure-revealer, king of the teachings Chokling,[176]
You are an awareness-holding bodhisattva with whom any connection is meaningful:
Orgyen Tséwang Palbar,[177] to you I pray.

From him, I received well the kindness of his instructions for producing spiritual maturity [empowerments], liberation [guidance], and support [transmission] for the entire three classes of Great Perfection teaching—Mind, Vast Expanse, and Pith Instruction—from treasures not previously known.

Chökyi Jungné, lord of scholarship, nobility, and excellence, you received the lineages' blessings
And are the designated heir of the practices of Slayer of the Lord of Death; and
Ngédon Chökyi Gyatso,[178] master of superlative innate qualities,
Endowed with a vajra tongue: to you both I pray.

From the former, I received empowerments, instructions, and pith instructions including *Lord of Death Chief of Longevity: The Iron-like Iron Scorpion (gshin rje tshe bdag lcags 'dra lcags sdig)*, and the *Further Reversal [of*

Obstacles]: Razor of Fire (yang bzlog me'i spu gri). From the latter, I received profound treasures' empowerments and transmissions, including Ratna Lingpa's[179] *Four Cycles of Gathering*,[180] as well as much guidance, including direct guidance in the five stages.[181]

> Tantric practitioner Orgyen Tenpa Rabgyé,
> Preserver of accomplished masters' line and epitome of supreme
>   knowledge, realization, and power;
> Péma Könchok Rabten,[182] awareness-holder,
> Who has perfected the powers of hearing, reflection, and meditation:
>   to you both I pray.

From the former, I received *The Four Branches of Great Perfection's*[183] *Heart Essence Teachings*, the nine volumes of Jigmé Lingpa's[184] teachings, and other texts. From the latter, I received many cycles of fundamental texts,[185] such as *Entering the Conduct of Bodhisattvas*,[186] *Ascertaining the Three Vows*,[187] and *The Treasury of Noble Qualities*.[188] He also gave me detailed and extensive explanation and guidance in some domains of knowledge, including poetic composition, based on *The Mirror of Poetry*,[189] and prosody.

> Orgyen Gyurmé Tenpa Namgyal,
> Lord of supreme knowledge, love, and power from Kathok[190]
>   Monastery;
> Péma Trinlé Gyatso,
> Conveyance on the great secret doctrine's ocean: to you both
>   I pray.

From the former, I received detailed explanation and guidance in Rongzom Pandit[191] and Longchenpa's traditions for *The Magical Secret Essence Tantra (sgyu 'phrul)*. From the latter, I received detailed and extensive explanation and guidance in the Zur[192] tradition's own system of *The Secret Essence Mahayoga Tantra*.

Incomparable Ngawang Chökyi Gyaltsen,
Exalted lord bodhisattva, protector of beings;
Karma Lekshé Puntsok,[193] sublime designated inheritor
Of the lineage of blessing and practice: to you both I pray.

From the former, I received the empowerments and transmissions for some Drukpa Kagyu tantras, including the three special deities. From the latter, I received many ripening empowerments and liberating instructions from the Karma Kagyu's oral lineage, including Cakrasamvara (Supreme Bliss)[194] and Vajravarahi (Vajra Sow).[195]

Lotus-Born's awareness-holder, Ngawang Jamyang Lodrö Gyatso,[196]
You attained erudition and accomplishment;

Tséwang Tendzin Zangpo,[197] seer of the domains of phenomena,
Rich in sacred wealth: to you both I pray.

From the former, I received explanation and guidance in some New Translation tantras, such as *Two Sections of Vajra Creator of Delight's Tantra*.[198] From the latter, I received many [transmissions], including the collected works of Jamgön Kongtrul.[199]

Lord Rikdzin Péma Wangdrak,[200]
Keeper of the oral lineage's[201] nectar trove of pith instructions;
Orgyen Sang-ngak Tendzin,[202] the supreme designated heir
Of mantras' and tantras' infinite activity : to you both I pray.

From the former, I received the entire instructions for producing spiritual maturity [empowerments], liberation [guidance], and support [transmission] for Traktung Namkha Jikmé's[203] pure vision treasure, *The Life Force Practice of Awareness-holders*, and *The Vajra Essence: Clouds of Spontaneous Songs*. From the latter, I received many concealed teachings, extraordinary pith instructions for tantric activity, including *The Black Heart-nail Pith Instructions* and Jatson Hung-Nak's *Black Hung Vital Heart Essence Teachings*.

Great scholar Ngawang Khyentsé Norbu,
Seer of all phenomena, endowed with superlative scholarship,
    nobility, and excellence;
Gyurmé Gendun Rabgyé, [204] diligent in vows,
Trained in the mind of awakening, friend to beings: to you both
    I pray.

From the former, I received cycles of instruction in the domains of
knowledge, such as poetic composition, based on *The Mirror of Poetry*;
prosody, based on *The Source of Jewels*; and Indian and Chinese astrology.
From the latter, I received detailed and wide-ranging explanations and guidance in the main medical tantras and the outer tantras.

Gyalsé Jigmé Kunzang Dorjé, [205]
Renunciant leader of the learned, noble, and accomplished;

Péma Rinchen Norbu, [206] well-educated spiritual friend
Trained in the mind of awakening: to you both I pray.

From the former, I received many cycles of inner profound meaning,
including *Ascertaining the Three Vows*. [207] From the latter, I received explanation and guidance in *The Gradual Path of the Wisdom Essence*, [208] and
many kinds of reading transmissions, including biographies of Marpa,
Milarepa, and Dakpo Lhajé (Gampopa).

The Pearl Necklace

A Supplication to the Series of
Successive Lives of His Holiness Dudjom Rinpoché[209]

In changeless exaltation inseparable with emptiness, Buddha Kuntu
    Zangpo's sky, which is the stainless space of phenomena [dharmadhatu],
Billow an array of immeasurable wisdom clouds of knowledge supreme
    and love.
Skilled in bringing down showers of excellent compassion,
All-pervading lord, supreme master, to you I pray.

In this realm of an eon of illumination renowned as "fortunate,"
You are the crowning Buddha of the thousand guides.
You reveal yourself in the form of the supreme lord of yogins;
Powerful Vajradhara (Nüden Dorjé Chang), [210] to you I pray.

Other Victorious Ones abandoned beings in this age of conflict;[211]
Yet Friend of the Sun [Shakyamuni Buddha] accepted them as his own.
Inseparable from him as his disciple foremost in incisive knowledge,
Noble Shariputra, [212] to you I pray.

Intoxicated with indestructible and taintless youth, appearing in
    any form,
You sealed the three realms' animate and inanimate life
With the arrow of great exaltation.
Brahmin Saraha, [213] to you I pray.

Entrusted with the sash of authority by Indrabhuti, the destined unique
 divine ruler,
You proclaimed the king's edicts
In the presence of he who ruled for others' well-being and happiness.
Religious minister Krishnadhara, to you I pray.[214]

Glorious Héruka, your magical dance of great exaltation
Reveals supreme, unchanging wisdom.
Awareness-holder of wisdom mind who accomplished Yangdak Héruka,
Master Hungkara, to you I pray.[215]

In the presence of the second Buddha, Lotus-Born,
You gained accomplishment in tantric practice; your realization
 equaled his.
Your mere gaze summoned birds from the sky.
Translator Drokben Khyé'u Chung,[216] to you I pray.

Lion of Speech[217] overtly accepted you as a disciple;
You then saw all phenomena exactly as they are.
Great bodhisattva, your skillful acts liberated beings;
Lord Smriti Jñana,[218] to you I pray.

Your perfection in all ten sciences
Set the glorious sun of the Victorious One's doctrine ablaze.
Sublime scholar of the Land of Sal Trees [Tibet],[219]
Rongzom Chökyi Zangpo,[220] to you I pray.

The thousand-lights of magnificent enlightened activity
Rose fully from mighty Victorious One Lotus-Born's ocean
 of compassion.
Sun of the Early Translation's doctrines, founder of Kathok,
Venerable Dampa Deshek,[221] to you I pray.

Deshek Phakmo Trupa's heart-disciple,
You mastered realization on the inner path.
Héruka, Land of Snow's foremost accomplished master,
Illustrious Lingjé Répa,[222] to you I pray.

Your marvelous spreading manifold illumination of supreme knowledge
and love
Makes the Cool Land's [Tibet] lotus groves of beneficence and happiness
blossom.
Manjushri transformed into the divine ruler of human beings,
Drogön Chögyal Phakpa,[223] to you I pray.

Your sight of supreme ultimate truth, the nature of phenomena free
from elaborations as it is,
Freed you from the chains of existence.
You gained sovereignty over the kingdom of changeless dharmakaya.
Khar-nakpa of Drum,[224] to you I pray.

Your vast fearless conduct, prayers of aspiration, and accomplishment
Crushed the brains of wild beings difficult to subdue.
You drank the yogurt of power and strength, wielding a vajra weapon.
Venerable Hépa Chöjung,[225] to you I pray.

Supreme lord of a hundred amazing hidden treasures and sacred places,
Including hidden lands, teachings, wealth, and sacred substances,
Lord of awakening's ten stages, and universal monarch among
accomplished masters:
Traktung Düdül Dorjé,[226] to you I pray.

Holder of the teaching and family lineages
Of Longsal Nyingpo—Wrathful Lotus incarnate,[227]
You illuminated the tradition of the essential definitive truth.
Heir of the victorious ones, Sönam Déutsen,[228] to you I pray.

Your special deity nurtured and blessed you;
Your karmic connection led you to hold the dakinis' secret treasure
And to lead those connected with you in any way to Lotus Light Pure
Land (Péma Ö).
Düdül Rölpa Tsal,[229] to you I pray.

Self-manifest non-human being, you received the Teacher's [Buddha's]
full blessings;

Treasures of Buddha Kuntu Zangpo's wisdom mind overflowed into the
    vastness of your mind.
Yogin of space, Crazy Wrathful King incarnate,
Garwang Dudjom Pawo, [230] to you I pray.

The guru and his consort from the island of Tail-Fan[231]
Conferred upon you their realization's intense heat, and you received
    their confirmation of attainment.
You raise aloft everywhere the sublime secret doctrine's victory banner.
Jigdral Yeshé Dorjé, [232] to you I pray.

Furthermore, in accord with your disciples'
Different characters, faculties, wishes, and fortunes,
You appear in any way or any place that can tame them.
In infinite manifestations, to you I pray.

At the time when barbarians gain the upper hand over the Sage's
    doctrine,
You will take rebirth as a lineage-bearing king
Called Vajra Sharpness (Dorjé Nönpo)[233] in the land of Shambhala.
Defeater of foreign invaders, to you I pray.

In the future, you will be the fortunate eon's last guide,
Manifesting as the Joyous Buddha Infinite Light of Devotion (Möpa
    Tayé).[234]
You will tame beings using the four immeasurable methods[235]
To empty the depths of beings' realms: To you I pray.

By the power of my supplications sung with sincere whole-hearted
    respect,
May I never be separated from you, complete protector, throughout all
    my lifetimes.
Forever serving you, my crown jewel,
May I become a fortunate one who drinks the nectar of your wisdom
    speech.

In your infinite great love and overwhelming compassion,
You accepted me as your heart disciple.
May I awaken to my courageous and virtuous lineage,
Able to spread your activity in a hundred directions.

In Highest Pure Land's (Ogmin) Palace of Lotus Light,
May I attain manifest enlightenment,
My teacher's mind and his disciples, inseparable in a single flavor,
And may I be a sublime leader for sentient beings whose numbers
    pervade all space!

Several devoted and earnest people have insistently requested me on a number of occasions saying that I must compose a supplication to the series of my successive lives. Simply not to renege on my promise I, Jigdral Yeshé Dorjé, wrote this, using treasure transmissions and the speech of previous awareness-holders as my sources. May there be good fortune!

The Concise Pearl Necklace

In the past, you were awareness-holder Nüden Dorjé Tsal (Powerful
   Vajra Adept);[236]
In the future, you will be Sugata Möpa Tayé (Joyous Buddha Infinite
   Devotion);
In the present, you are Lotus-Born's regent, Drokben incarnate:
Jigdral Yeshé Dorjé, to you I pray.

*I [Jigdral Yeshé Dorjé] wrote this in response to my faithful
disciples' request.*
Sarva mangalam!

Great Clouds of Blessings' Nectar:

A Compilation of Prayers of Supplication

1. A Spontaneous Song of the Original State: A Prayer Calling the Master from Afar

Essence of awareness, changeless from the beginning, your fundamental
   nature free from elaboration
Abides as primordial purity, inner clarity, the youthful vase body.
Yeshé Dorjé, dharmakaya master, think of me;
Grant me your blessings that I gain great confidence in the view, I pray.

The nature of awareness, your unobstructed, integral union, an
   assemblage of light,
Abides as your display, the spontaneously present five certainties.
Déchen Dorjé, sambhogakaya master, think of me;
Grant me your blessings that I bring meditation's great display to
   completion.

Compassionate qualities, your impartial wisdom free from extremes
Abides in the naked essence of pervasive empty awareness.
Drodül Lingpa, nirmanakaya master, think of me;
Grant me your blessings that I accomplish the enhancement of conduct.

In the original ground of one's own awareness there is no movement or
   change.
Whatever arises is dharmakaya's display, neither good nor bad.
Since my present awareness is the actual Buddha,
I have discovered the open relaxed master in the center of my heart.

Now that I realize that my original mind has the nature of my Lama,
I have no need for painful contrived prayers made with grasping
   attachment.
I relax freely in the natural settled state, uncontrived awareness,
And receive the blessings of the self-liberation of whatever arises,
   without fixation.

Activity will never accomplish enlightenment.

My analytic, mentally created meditation is a tricky enemy.
Now, with a madman's abandon, I let my worldview collapse;
I will spend this human life within the nature of uninhibited naked rest.

Happy in whatever I do, a practitioner of the Great Perfection,
Joyful in any company, Lotus-Born's descendant,
My lord protector, you are unrivaled, a great master treasure-revealer.
These teachings are matchless, the heart essence of the dakinis.

My heart's gloom, great delusion, has lifted from where it lay
And clear light's encompassing sun shines and never sets.
This, my good fortune, comes from your kindness, Lama, my true father.
Your kindness is unrepayable. Master, I turn my thoughts to you.

In response to my foremost vajra disciple Tulku Jigmé Chöying Norbu Tamché Drubpé Dé, I, Jigdral Yeshé Dorjé, spoke this nonsense. May it prove virtuous!

2. Blessings Swiftly Received: A Prayer Calling the Master from Afar

Namo guru-yé

The principal task of those wishing to reach the state of omniscience in
this lifetime is to see the master who grants you profound instructions
that bring you to spiritual maturity and liberation as the Buddha incar-
nate, lord of all mandalas. Inspired with uncontrived intense yearning
and devotion, pray in this way, as if calling out for help from afar.

Lama, think of me!
Lama, think of me!
Lama, think of me!

Embodiment of all Buddhas,
Source of the teachings of scriptures and realization,
Sovereign of the exalted spiritual community,
Unsurpassable Lama, think of me!

In essence (*ngo bo*) you are primordially pure, dharmakaya;
Your nature (*rang bzhin*) is spontaneous presence, sambhogakaya;
Your compassionate qualities (*thugs rje*) are all-pervading, nirmanakaya.
Lama who unites them all, think of me!

Treasure trove of an ocean of blessing,
Source of jewels of accomplishment,
Your activity is as swift as lightning.
Noble Lama, think of me!

You turn me away from wrong paths of negative actions
And connect me to virtue's correct path.
Guide on the path to liberation's permanent exaltation,
Lama, think of me!

Captain who ferries me across the river of endless suffering
Of samsara's six classes of beings[237]
To the island of peace and happiness.
Lama, think of me!

You cultivate the fields of your disciples' minds
With the method of renunciation.
Sower of seeds of the mind of awakening's aspiration and application,[238]
Lama, think of me!

Your rains of the four empowerments that bring me to maturity[239]
Cleanse the stains of my four obscurations.[240]
You pour the four wisdom bodies' qualities into my mindstream.[241]
Lama, think of me!

Alas! Sentient beings like me are burdened with negative acts,
Yet your guiding compassion toward us
Exceeds that of other Buddhas.
Incomparable wisdom Lama, think of me!

Lama, whose kindness cannot be repaid,
From my heart, I remember you
And call out to you in prayer!
Please quickly look upon me with compassion!

The essence of leisures and opportunities has arrived;
Remembrance of impermanence arose in my mindstream,
And my attachment to samsara collapsed.
Kind Lama, think of me!
In your compassion, grant your blessings
That I be able to reject and undertake acts in relation to their causes
    and effects.

For irreversible faith,
To see my Lama as the Buddha incarnate;
For deep loving respect, such as I feel for my own brothers and sisters,

Toward my spiritual companions with the same tantric commitments;
For limitless love and compassion
Toward all sentient beings, my parents;
For stable vigilance and mindfulness
From considering death's unpredictability:
Kind Lama, think of me!
In your compassion, grant your blessings!

When I receive profound heart advice
From a holy qualified Lama
And have spurned laziness and procrastination,
Kind wisdom Lama, think of me!
In your compassion, grant your blessings
That I be able to persevere in practice.

My Lama is imbued with threefold kindness;[242]
May I not treat him as an equal or perceive him as a human being,
Nor have even a trace of doubt or wrong view!
Kind wisdom Lama, think of me!
In your compassion, grant your blessings
That I perfect pure vision.

In the conduct of the Victorious One's heirs [bodhisattvas], who work
    for other's good,
Adverse circumstances appear as an aid
And friends and foe are seen impartially.
Kind Lama, think of me!
In your compassion, grant your blessings
That the mind of awakening take birth in my mindstream.

To constantly remember my wisdom Lama,
For my acts and conduct in thought, word, and deed
To always change into the sacred Dharma,
Kind Lama, think of me!
In your compassion, grant your blessings
That I practice as long as I live.

Your blessings and empowerments brought me to maturity
And the stream of your realization flowed to my mind.
Kind Lama, think of me!
In your compassion, grant blessings
That I realize my mind's genuine, unimpeded nature
As the essence of my Lama.

The view is all-pervasive equality of samsara and enlightenment;
Meditation, the uncontrived natural state;
Conduct, freedom from action and effort.
Kind Lama, think of me!
In your compassion, grant your blessings
That I recognize the result as being my true nature.

Think of me, very kind Lama!
I have no place for hope other than you!
Wisdom Lama, grant your blessings
That our minds merge as one.

*Praying one-pointedly and sincerely, not just saying these words, have
no doubt that blessings will enter you.*

*I, Jigdral Yeshé Dorjé, holder of the great treasure-revealer Dudjom
Lingpa's blessed name, wrote this according to the wishes and aspirations of he with sublime faith, Gyurmé Palden. May this be the cause of
supreme virtue and excellence!*

3. My kind, precious root Lama

Lama, think of me!
My kind, precious root Lama, essence of all Buddhas in one, to you
I pray.

Bless my mindstream, I beseech you!
Grant your blessings that the essence of leisures and opportunities
remain.
Grant your blessings that I remember death and impermanence.
Grant your blessings that trust in karma arises.
Grant your blessings that my attachment to samsara collapses.
Grant your blessings that I see my Lama as Buddha.
Grant your blessings that my mind blends with the Dharma.
Grant your blessings that I become free from attachment to this life.
Grant your blessings that I have no unfinished business in my mind
at death.
Grant your blessings that I have no extreme pain at death.
Grant your blessings that I be adept in the profound path of transference.
Grant your blessings that I be liberated in the intermediate state's clear
light.
Grant your blessings that I recognize the nature of phenomena (*chos
nyid*).
Grant your blessings that delusion be liberated within itself.
Grant your blessings that I receive supreme assurance of rebirth in
the pure lands.
Grant your blessings that I awaken to my true nature, awareness itself.
Grant your blessings that I accomplish the immortal vase body.
Grant your blessings for the spontaneous completion of the two goals!

*I, Jigdral Yeshé Dorjé, wrote this in response to a request by the faithful
lady Déchen Tsö. May this prove virtuous!*

4. Essence of all Buddhas of the three times

Essence of all Buddhas of the three times, lord of oceans of Buddha
   families and mandalas, precious incomparably kind root Lama, think of
   me!
Bless my mindstream, I pray.
Grant your blessings that I recognize dreams as dreams.
Grant your blessings that I emanate and transform appearances in
   dreams.
Grant your blessings that dreams arise as clear light.
Grant your blessings that clear light blends with every aspect of life.

I, Jñana, wrote this.

5. All Buddhas' compassion combined into one

E ma ho!

All Buddhas' compassion combined into one,
Precious, sole refuge for me and my negative acts,
Lord, Lama, whose kindness I can never repay,
When I pray to you with heartfelt longing,
Never leave me, consider me with compassion, and bestow your
blessings!

Bless me that I may gain the essence of my human life's freedoms
and endowments.
Bless me that I recall impermanence and death.
Bless me that I see samsara's sufferings.
Bless me that I embrace virtue and abandon negative acts.
Bless me that I take the Triple Gems as my refuge.
Bless me that I train in the altruistic mind of awakening (*bodhicitta*).
Bless me that I purify the two obscurations and their habitual patterns.
Bless me that I complete the two accumulations of merit and wisdom.
Bless me that I attain your blessings, empowerments, and spiritual
attainments.
Bless me that I be able to keep my vows and tantric commitments.
Bless me that my practice remains firm and unpretentious.
Bless me that misfortunes arise as aids.
Bless me that I stabilize undistracted diligence.
Bless me that I reject ego-clinging.
Bless me that I dispel the darkness of ignorance.
Bless me that I realize the view of primordial purity.
Bless me that I directly see the nature of phenomena (*dharmata*).[243]
Bless me that visionary experiences increase.[244]
Bless me that awareness reaches full measure.[245]
Bless me that I arrive at the place of phenomena's exhaustion in the
nature of phenomena.[246]
Bless me that I gain liberation in the immortal vase body.

Bless me that I accomplish the rainbow body in this life.
Bless me that I may empty samsara to its depths!

I, Jigdral Yeshé Dorjé, wrote this in response to the insistent requests by Prince Tséring Wangchen, a person of virtuous mind dedicated to the profound path. Virtue!

6. Embodiment of the supreme knowledge and love

Embodiment of the supreme knowledge and love
Of all Buddhas of the three times,
Kind Lama, my sole source of refuge,
Jigdral Yeshé Dorjé,

You reside inseparably
At the crown of my head,
As an ornament of the *cakra* of great exaltation.
Always look upon me with compassion, I pray!

I do not search elsewhere with hope.
These are not mere mouthed words.
From the very bottom of my heart,
Again and again, I pray to you!

Sublime Lama,
Your blessings now enter all beings' mindstreams, including my own.
Infallible Lama, think of me
That I attain the result, your state,
In this very life.
Think of me, Lama, think of me!

I, Jigdral Yeshé Dorjé, wrote this, simply not to refuse responding to the earnest requests of the previous awareness-holder's attendant-disciple named Dampa Dzom. May there be virtue and excellence!

7. Essential embodiment of all Buddhas

Essential embodiment of all Buddhas,
Great treasure of supreme knowledge, love, and power,
Imbued with threefold incomparable kindnesses—
Dudjom Yeshé Dorjé, to you, I sincerely pray!
With constant vigilant compassion,
Bless my mindstream!
May I accomplish the rainbow body!

I, the nonsensical beggar [Jigdral Yeshé Dorjé], wrote this in response to the one diligent in spiritual practice, Jampa Chödzin.

8. Supplication based on Dudjom Rinpoché's names

This supplication is based upon my, Dudjom Tulku's, series of names.

When the sense faculties of your karmic body of habitual tendencies,
Cultivated from the very beginning, first awoke,
Lopön Ngak Chang,[247] learned in the tantric activities,[248]
Gave you the name Nyima Gyaltsen:[249] To you I pray.

A dakini told your venerable father,[250] member of the aristocracy,
    Jampal Norbu,[251]
"A son greater than his father will appear."
Known by the name foretold before your birth,
Yeshé Dorjé,[252] to you I pray.

In Godavari, the ultimate secret place of deathlessness,
Lotus-Born's regent, Namkhé Naljor,[253]
Gave you the crown of an empowerment name,
Jigdral Déchen Dorjé Drakpo. To you I pray.[254]

When you trained on the path of the conventional sciences
Under the foremost among the learned, noble, and excellent—
    the supreme lord scholar—
He called you the youth that delights Lotus-Born,
Tsojung Gyépé Ngonmé Dawa Sarpa: To you I pray.[255]

The epitome of compassion, called Manju,
Conferred upon your mind the layman's vows of individual liberation.
At the completion of the ceremony, you were renowned
As Gyurmé Délek Choklé Nampar Gyalwa: To you I pray.[256]

With the great bodhisattva, Ngawang Palden,[257]
You donned the armor of the supreme mind of awakening.
At that time he named you Gyalsé Lodrö Drimé Pendé Dawa
Ösel Palbar. To you I pray.[258]

Kind lord of the family, Ngédon Wangpo,
Had you enter Vajrayana's great mandala.
At the time of the empowerment as a close son,
You were known as Dorjé Dütsal: To you I pray.[259]

King and supreme guide, lord of the Dharma, Trulzhik [Rinpoché][260]
Had you gradually enter the pith instructions of the innermost secret
    heart essence.
When he entrusted you with the oral transmission lineage,
He called you Yanpa Lodé:[261] To you I pray.

Lotus Skull-garlanded Adept (Péma Tötreng Tsal)[262] with consort [Yeshé
    Tsogyal], who embodies all Buddha families,
Confirmed you as the great secret path's charioteer
Through his prophecy, aspiration, and great name,
Extolling you as Drodül Lingpa.[263] To you, I pray.

One bad person can possess many excellent names,
Yet whatever you call him, he's still a vile old man.
If I pray to you without hypocrisy,
Bless me that I accomplish your life story of liberation!

*I [Jigdral Yeshé Dorjé] wrote this in response to the faithful Tendzin
Chöpel's request,*
*"You must definitely write verses of supplication to your entire series of
names as a support for my faith."*

9. Héruka, dancer in indestructible great exaltation

Héruka, dancer in indestructible great exaltation,
Awareness-holder who tames beings,
Inseparable from Péma Tötreng-tsal, Lotus Skull-garlanded Adept, one
   who overwhelms phenomenal existence with splendor:[264]
Jigdral Yeshé Dorjé, to you I pray.

Bless me to see the primordially pure, original manifest natural state,
To reach the culmination of the wisdom of the four visions of
   spontaneous presence,
And with unobstructed, compassionate enlightened activity,
To empty the depths of samsara!

10. Dance of the accomplished translator

Dance of the accomplished translator Drokben,[265]
Light of the speech of the master of stainless space, Déchen Tsogyal,[266]
Supreme magical display of the powerful sovereign Lotus-Born's wisdom
   mind:
Jigdral Yeshé Dorjé, to you I pray.

Lord-protector, for as long as samsara keeps turning,
At the specific times your enlightened activity emanates in any suitable
   way for others' benefit,
May I also be born at each time, first among your circle of disciples,
And may I obtain the power to preserve your secret teachings!

*Tendzin Jungné—the attendant of Dorjé Radreng [regent of the
thirteenth Dalai Lama, recognizer of the fourteenth], who is Buddha
Vajradhara—who has a clear virtuous mind, requested a supplication.
To make his request meaningful, I [Jigdral Yeshé Dorjé] wrote and
offered this. Virtue!*

11. Lord of a hundred families without exception

Lord of a hundred families without exception, complete protector,
Dudjom Héruka, to you I pray.
When you gain complete, manifest enlightenment and turn the wheel of
    Dharma,
May I be reborn in your first circle of disciples!

I, Jigdral Yeshé Dorjé, wrote this in response to Namkha Dorjé.

12. Lord Lake Born Guru's heart son

Lord Lake Born Guru's heart son,
Chief of the three places'[267] gatherings of awareness-holders and dakinis,
Héruka, who accomplishes enlightened activity to subdue beings,
Jigdral Yeshé Dorjé, to you I pray.

I [Jigdral Yeshé Dorjé] wrote and offered this to fulfill the wish of the
ruler's268 supreme wisdom consort, Kunzang Déchen Tsomo. Virtue!

13. Supreme regent of Kuntu Zangpo, Lake Born Guru

Supreme regent of Kuntu Zangpo, Lake Born Guru,
Universal ruler of an ocean of awareness-holders who tame beings,
Yogin of the magical luminous vast expanse:
Jigdral Yeshé Dorjé, to you I pray.

From now on, throughout all my lifetimes,
May I never be apart from you, venerable lord of the enlightened family.
May your blessings transfer, our minds merging as one,
And may I attain enlightenment in the teacher and disciple's inseparable
   realization!

I [Jigdral Yeshé Dorjé] wrote this in response to the request of the ruler's
wisdom consort of noble family, Sönam Paldrön. Virtue!

14. Magical display's dance

Magical display's dance of indestructible great exaltation,
You magnificently bestow the sublime wisdom of non-dual exaltation
    and emptiness.
Heroic Dudjom Drodül Lingpa, to you I pray:
Never part from me and bestow your blessings!

I [Jigdral Yeshé Dorjé] wrote this in response to Kalzang Wangdrön's request.

15. Lotus Skull-garlanded Adept, the union of the three roots

Lotus Skull-garlanded Adept, the union of the three roots,[269]
Empowered you as his regent.
Awareness-holder, any connection with you is meaningful.
Jigdral Yeshé Dorjé, to you I pray.

Bless me that from the moment of my birth, your feet never leave the
   crown of my head,
That I complete every undertaking that pleases you,
And that I quickly become a sovereign of the Dharma
At the stage of the highest wisdom, spontaneously accomplishing the
   two goals.

*I [Jigdral Yeshé Dorjé] wrote this in response to the request of she who
puts the Dharma into practice, Péma Yang Shu-bham.*

16. You received the blessings of the Lake Born Guru's lineage

You received the blessings of the Lake Born Guru's lineage of
    transmission of wisdom mind;
The wisdom of the three blazes[270] manifested,
And you effortlessly accomplished the enlightened activity of the three
    gatherings.[271]
Jigdral Yeshé Dorjé, to you I pray!

I [Jigdral Yeshé Dorjé] wrote this in response to the request of he who puts the Dharma into practice, Shéja Rabsel.

17. The great master from Orgyen, knower of the three times

The great master from Orgyen, knower of the three times,
Blessed and empowered you as his regent.
Jigdral Yeshé Dorjé, to you I pray.
At all times, care for me and never leave, I pray.

Bless me that I realize the view of primordial purity, like the sky;
That meditation's spontaneous presence becomes continual clear light;
That conduct of equal taste enhances my experience on the path;
And that I reach the result—liberation in the original ground!

*I, Jigdral Yeshé Dorjé, wrote this in response to Kalzang Chönyi
Wangmo's request.*

18. The great master from Orgyen bestowed upon you

The great master from Orgyen bestowed upon you the empowerment of
   his aspirations,
Thereby, you remove the decline and darkness of the doctrine and beings
   in these degenerate times.
Jigdral Yeshé Dorjé, to you I pray: care for me and never leave.
May I spontaneously accomplish the two goals!

*I [Jigdral Yeshé Dorjé] wrote this in response to Tulku Shédrub Gyurmé's
request.*

19. Kind Lama who ripens through empowerment

Kind Lama who ripens through empowerment and liberates through
   instructions my mindstream,
Lord, complete protector, to you I pray.
Lovingly, care for me, and don't leave me for an instant;
May blessings of your mindstream be transferred to my heart!

Now that I have entered the profound gate to the very secret sublime
   vehicle,
May misfortunes and obstacles not arise on my path;
May I naturally meet with excellent fortunate and conducive
   circumstances in accord with the Dharma;
And may my life and spiritual practice reach their consummation!

For my own benefit, may my spiritual experiences, realization, and noble
   qualities increase.
For others' benefit, may I spontaneously accomplish the bodhisattvas'
   conduct.
May I give all beings with whom I am connected assurance of supreme
   freedom;
May we attain manifest enlightenment together!

I, Vajra Jñana, wrote this in response to Lama Yeshé Rabsel's request.

20. Lotus–Born's regent, lord of all Buddha families

Lotus-Born's regent, lord of all Buddha families, complete protector,
Jigdral Yeshé Dorjé, to you I pray.
May you live for hundreds of eons and your enlightened activity reach
  consummation.
May our minds merge as one, and may I spontaneously accomplish the
  two goals!

*I [Jigdral Yeshé Dorjé] wrote this in response to Kalzang Gendun
Gyatso's request.*

21. Light of supreme knowledge and love

Namo guru-yé!

Light of supreme knowledge and love of infinite Victorious Ones with
their spiritual heirs
United in you, sublime guide protector of beings in these degenerate
times,
Lord imbued with the threefold kindness, you reveal the pith instructions
with ease:
Jigdral Yeshé Dorjé, to you I pray.

Bless me with your shower of compassion to ripen my mindstream fully;
Have me gain confidence in the view, perfect meditation's great force,
Reap enrichment in conduct, and actualize the result.
May I accomplish the rainbow body in this life!

*I, Jigdral Yeshé Dorjé, wrote this in response to the request made by the
faithful nun Tsultrim Wangmo.*

22. The supreme knowledge of Sun of Speech dawns

The supreme knowledge of Sun of Speech dawns in your heart;
You take the form of Treasure of Compassion's enlightened activity;
You have mastered Lord of Secrets' [Vajrapani's] skill and ability in
    conquering hordes of demons:
Jigdral Yeshé Dorjé, to you I pray.[272]

In all my lifetimes, may the holy Lama care for me;
May I drink empowerments' and instructions' glorious nectar.
In the highest pure land of Lotus Light,
On the level without return, may I become a Buddha.

*I, with the title of Dudjom Tulku, wrote this in response to the nun
Kunzang Chödzom's request. May this prove to be virtuous!*

23. You obtained the blessings of the Lama

You obtained the blessings of the Lama, the second Buddha
  [Padmasambhava],
And uphold the yogic practice of self-manifest self-liberated awareness.
Jigdral Déchen Yeshé Dorjé,
I pray to you from the bottom of my heart: Grant me your blessings!

*I [Jigdral Yeshé Dorjé] wrote this in response to the requests made by
both Gomchen Drakpa and Drag-go Lama.*[273] *May this prove to be
virtuous!*

24. Unborn awareness is
Buddha Kuntu Zangpo's essential nature

Unborn awareness is Buddha Kuntu Zangpo's essential nature.
Unobstructed luminosity dawns as vajra clouds of union.
Lama of the mind of awakening liberated in the ground,
In the genuine naturally settled state, to you I continually pray.
May all phenomena of existence and enlightenment be exhausted in the
    primordial ground,
And may my self-manifest awareness ripen in a body of light!

I, Jigdral Yeshé Dorjé, wrote this in response to Yönten's request.

25. Lotus-Born's regent, great treasure-revealer

Lotus-Born's regent, great treasure-revealer Dudjom Lingpa,
Intentionally took rebirth to subdue beings.
Jigdral Déchen Yeshé Dorjé, to you I pray!
Grant your blessings and never be apart from me!

*I [Jigdral Yeshé Dorjé] wrote this in response to the request by Sem-nyi
Dorjé, a disciple of my previous incarnation.*

26. Supreme epitome of excellent supreme knowledge

Supreme epitome of excellent supreme knowledge, love, and power,
Sublime guide who delivers beings in these degenerate times,
Héruka, regent of all Buddha families in one, lotus born:
Jigdral Yeshé Dorjé, to you I pray.

Lama, chief of the Buddha families, bless me that in my series of lives
    you do not leave me.
Once I gain entrance to the path of profound meaning,
May I fully achieve my own goal and spontaneously accomplish others'
    goals,
And be able to empty samsara from its depths!

*I, Jigdral Yeshé Dorjé, wrote this in response to the request of the nun
Péma Zangmo.*

27. The great master from Orgyen, overwhelming phenomenal existence

The great master from Orgyen, overwhelming phenomenal existence
   with splendor,
Through his aspiration prayer confirmed and empowered you as his
   representative.
During these degenerate times, you hoisted the profound secret
   teachings' victory banner:
Dudjom Jigdral Yeshé Dorjé, to you I pray!

*I [Jigdral Yeshé Dorjé] wrote and offered this in response to a request
from Zhokpa Tulku Lungtok Rabgyé.*[274]

28. Magical dance of Lake Born Guru's wisdom

Magical dance of Lake Born Guru's *wisdom* (Yeshé),[275]
Powerful Buddha *Vajra* (Dorjé) Bearer, complete protector:
Care for me and never leave.
Bring my mind to spiritual maturity and liberation, and may
    I spontaneously accomplish the two goals!

I, Jigdral Yeshé Dorjé, wrote this in response to a request from the tantric monk rich in devotion, Péma Dorjé.

29. The second Buddha, Lotus Skull-garlanded Adept

The second Buddha, Péma Tötreng-tsal, Lotus Skull-garlanded Adept,
Empowered you as his regent to subdue beings.
Dudjom Jigdral Pawo, to you I pray.
Bless me that our minds merge as one!

I [Jigdral Yeshé Dorjé] wrote this in response to Kyab Lama's request.

30. Renunciation arose in your mind

Namo guru-yé!

Renunciation arose in your mind; you rejected harming others, along
   with its basis [that is, negative thoughts].
You trained in the mind of awakening and accomplished others' good,
   along with its basis.
You immersed yourself in the two stages, performer of Guru Rinpoché's
   activity.
Jigdral Yeshé Dorjé, to you I pray.

May the glorious Lama's blessings enter my heart.
May I realize the Great Perfection's abiding nature as it is.
In this life may I reach the consummation of the four visions'
   cultivation,
And may I reach the everlasting kingdom of the immortal vase body!

*I, Jigdral Yeshé Dorjé, wrote this in response to Tsultrim Tharchin's
request.*

31. Original lord–protector, root Lama

É ma ho!

Original lord-protector, root Lama.
From the primordially pure realm of indefinite location
Spontaneously present great exaltation of the union of awareness and
    emptiness.
In the continual natural state without clinging, I pray to you.

Bless me with liberation from the confines of hope and fear in the view
    of the natural state,
That the stainless sun of clear light dawns from deep within me,
That I traverse like a mirage the four visions' paths and levels,
And that I accomplish the great transference rainbow body!

*I, the carefree crazy Jñana, wrote this in response to a request from the
tantric practitioner Namkha Tsho, who trains her mind on natural Great
Perfection's path.*

32. Calling the Lama from Afar: In the depth of my heart

In the depth of my heart
At the center of my faith's blossoming thousand-petalled lotus,
You dwell forever in delight
And always bless me.

Glorious lord Héruka,
Jigdral Yeshé Dorjé,
You are all the Victorious Ones' essence:
Of this my heart is sure.

With intense, unbearable yearning,
I single-mindedly pray to you:
Bring me to spiritual maturity and liberation
With your nectar of blessing, empowerment, and accomplishments.

I cry out from afar
With overwhelming longing for you, my Lama,
Yet I cannot find you
Apart from this, my original mind.

When there is no one to hear my prayers
Nor anyone to voice them,
Why should I invent supplications
With forced, clinging contrivance?

Conceptionless naked empty awareness,
Vivid yet indefinable—
This I recognize as my ultimate Lama,
Indestructible wisdom (Yeshé Dorjé).

In the original ground of the naturally settled state,
Supreme constant abiding in primordial presence,
I need not call my Lama from afar
Nor search for you nearby.

In the essential nature beyond my mind,
All-inclusive awakening, delusion is unheard of,
Let alone transcendence of sorrow.
It is an endless expanse of evenness and exaltation.

Whatever arises is dharmakaya's pervasive manifestation.
Blessings beyond understanding
Enter this yogin's heart.
How wonderful and amazing!

I, Jigdral Yeshé Dorjé, spontaneously wrote this according to the wishes of the noble lady Déchen Chödron, whose virtuous mind is openly devoted to me. She repeatedly made requests saying, "I need this kind of supplication to call my Lama from afar." When it had slipped my mind, Yédrok Tulku Rinpoché recently renewed that request. May it prove to be virtuous!

33. Requesting Your Vital Heart Promise

The embodied essence of infinite Victorious Ones,
Sole infallible and eternal refuge, complete protector,
Remembering you eases my longing.
Buddha Vajradhara (Dorjé Chang) from Orgyen,
With unwavering compassion, lovingly think of me now.

Alas! We've reached the depths of these dark degenerate times;
The merit of the Snowy Land's beings is exhausted.
Demons and starving spirits possess people's minds;
They misunderstand cause and effect, what they should do and what
    they must not;
And they accumulate the negative act of forsaking the Dharma.

Their selfishness blazes; they've rid themselves of modesty and shame.
The five degenerations spread; secular and religious laws are broken.
People cast aside the Triple Gems, place their trust in demons,
And hold unsuitable trash as dear as life itself.

They scorn vows and tantric commitments and fill themselves with
    deceitful pledges.
The land's vitality deteriorates; protective wisdom deities become
    inattentive.
Central Tibetan *damsi* spirits will befriend the border Chinese demons.
The nine brother starving spirits rule Tibet and Kham.
Barbarian armies at our borders point their weapons at Tibet;
They tear down the wheel of the Victorious One's teachings and raze it
    to its foundations.
Enemies plunder and carry away our accumulated wealth;
They kill or enslave this body and life we hold so dear but are powerless
    to protect.

They expel the doctrine-holders, members of the spiritual community,
    and noble people.
Wrong-doers' wrong views rage like massive brush fires.

Even those who wish to escape to the freedom of hidden lands
Are uncertain where to go, like sentient beings in the intermediate state.

The Tibetan people's unbearable sufferings are the hells—it's sure!
Negative karma has ripened into these ill-fated bodies—what a pity!
"This will happen at the future final time":
Knower of the past, present, and future, you foretold this.

And you said, "My special intention and activity during those times
Assure that my compassion responds faster than that of other Buddhas.
Pray to me; I will do as I say.
King and subjects, if I have deceived you, then Lotus-Born is not I but
    someone else."

You bestowed your loving final testament in those words,
Yet most people have entered the mire of wrong views.
Those who know your words to be true are lost in powerlessness or
    laziness;
They implement practice procedures ineffectively and lapse into chaos.

At the present time, like a moth entering a flame,
The lightning of what we abhor strikes; the wide lake of our bad karma
    overflows.
Now, wretched and unlucky beings, including myself,
Have no hope to turn to, no support or friend, except for you.

I have no refuge other than you—of that I'm sure!
From the depths of my heart, distraught, I pray to you ardently.
When I cry out to you,
Do your loving ears heed me, Guru Rinpoché?

Does your clairvoyant wisdom mind think of me, skull-garlanded
    master?
Does your compassion not care for me, Lotus-Born?

Protect me from these sufferings right now
With your enlightened activity's miraculous powers as swift as lightning!

Send away these malevolent times' intricate array of turbulence and
    disturbance.
Destroy all classes of malevolent demons and spirits.
Praise the positive protectors' states to the skies.
May the assembly of doctrine-holders be victorious over the onslaught
    of obstacles.

May the doctrine's life—the teaching and practice of sutras and tantras—
    be firmly established.
Bring the splendor of well-being and happiness to the country.
In brief, do not abandon your disciples, including me,
To the sway of karmic misfortunes.

Pacify all our outer and inner obstacles in this life
And spontaneously accomplish all our wishes in harmony with the
    Dharma.
In our next life, instantly lead us to Tail-Fan Island's Glorious
    Mountain[276]
And show us the fortress of permanent exaltation.

Bless me that I master evenness—
My body, speech, and mind inseparable from the noble qualities of
    Lotus-Born's three secrets—
And that the force of my enlightened activity to liberate all beings
    filling space
Equals, lord, your own!

I, Jigdral Yeshé Dorjé, spontaneously wrote this due to my sadness at
the present state of affairs, the principal cause for this composition,
and Kathok Öntrul Rinpoché's request, a contributing circumstance.
I composed it at Lotus Lake [Tso Péma, India] on the tenth day of
the waxing moon, during the first month [the month of miracles]
of the Iron Mouse Year (1960).

34. The Victorious Ones and their heirs' enlightened activity

Namo ratna guru-yé.

The Victorious Ones and their heirs' enlightened activity is joined
    in you.
Fearless (Jigdral) toward the four types of demons of ignorance,
You are ablaze with the energy of the *wisdom* (Yeshé) of twofold
    supreme knowledge,[277] powerful sublime *vajra-* (Dorjé)[278] holder.
Venerable Lama, at your feet I pray!

From your youth, your noble habitual tendencies awakened.
Perfect faith, incisive knowledge, and intelligence unfolded.
Love and compassion purified your mind.
Youthful noble being, to you, I pray!

You relied upon many holy and especially exalted Lamas
And received without satiation their nectar of teachings that ripen
    and liberate.
You preserve as your heart all the tantric commitments and
    bodhisattva trainings.
Lord of yogins, to you, I pray!

You see the view of the abiding nature as it is, Cutting through
    Solidity;
You perfect the great power of meditation, emptiness, and
    compassion;
You have the fearless conduct of undistracted benevolent conduct.
Sole sublime protector of beings in these degenerate times, to you
    I pray!

By the blessings of this supplication,
Bless me that your empowerments ripen my mindstream, that I keep my
    commitments pure,

That I train in faith, devotion, renunciation, compassion, and the mind
  of awakening,
And that I practice for as long as I live!

*The faithful Chöying Wangmo settled in the perception of this clump of
earth as gold and asked me, "Write a supplication." Merely not to refuse
her request, I, Jigdral Yeshé Dorjé, have written this tribute to myself
although I am without any noble qualities.*

35. Infallible lasting sole refuge

Infallible lasting sole refuge, complete protector,
Embodiment of all Buddhas, Vajradhara from Orgyen
   (Orgyen Dorjé Chang),[279]
I, a wretched being, have no hope other than you;
With compassion as swift as lightning, now take heed.

We have reached the depths of malevolent, degenerate times.
The nine brother *damsi* spirits with foul aspirations are becoming
   widespread,
And starving spirits possess most people's minds.
Whose compassion would never abandon Tibet's people

And has a loving presence? That's you.
Yet shameless persons enter malevolent paths
And view you, the guru, your doctrine,
And your followers as portents of doom.

They thunder with contemptuous wrong views, scorning your kindness;
They turn their minds to wild starving spirits for support.
They create disruption[280] and disastrous agitation, leading to ruin;
Bias and jealousy rises even among the humble.

They use deceit to burden even the honest with serious faults;
Their unfounded accusations and misfortunes swirl like tornadoes.
They act malevolentlylly, then say these are malevolent times.
Whatever I think about makes my heart sick.[281]

I am deeply distressed and distraught;
The time has come when I must cry out in pained grieving.
If I do not call out to you, my only father, whom should I call?
You have great love; if you do not see me, who will?

I exhort your vital heart promise, Tötreng-tsal, Skull-garlanded Adept!
Move your wisdom mind from stainless space, Drowolö![282]

The time has come to unleash the force of your power, strength, and
    ability;
Swiftly free me from these unwelcome misfortunes!

Repel demons' and obstructers' massive armies!
Bring hostile beings and my circulating energy,
Mind, and perception under my control!
Transform beings' minds into benevolent virtue!

In short, for all your disciples, including me,
Do not abandon us to our karmic misfortunes;
Dispel the unwanted mass of our outer and inner faults into stainless
    space!
Bless me that all my aims and desires are effortlessly fulfilled,

That your tradition spread throughout this world,
That I spontaneously accomplish the two goals,
That I be triumphant in all domains,
And that once I have become equal with you, my guru,
I be able to empty samsara from its depths!

*During a time of sadness, when many outer and inner misfortunes made
me distressed, these cries of lamentation and yearning surged forth, and
I, Jigdral Yeshé Dorjé, wrote them down.*

36. Calling the Lama from Afar:
Embodied essence of all Buddhas

Embodied essence of all Buddhas,
Source of the scriptures and realization of the sacred Dharma,
Crown ornament of the spiritual community's noble assembly:
Root Lama, think of me!

Highest king among Lamas,
Common glory of an ocean of wisdom deities (*yidam*),[283]
Leader of the three locations' gatherings of dakinis:
Lord Lama, think of me!

The nectar of your secret profound advice
Ripens and liberates my mindstream;
Your kindness cannot be repaid.
Vajra Lama, think of me!

Fervently remembering you, my Lama,
I pray with intense longing.
Your compassion knows no distance.
Grant me empowerment, blessing, and accomplishment.

The master on a relative level, the appearing aspect,
Is ultimately the magical display of awareness itself.
There, the master, self-manifest empty awareness,
Abides primordially together with me.

Now, when I recognize my true nature,
The "I" clung to as real
Vanishes by itself without a trace.
I have no object of attachment, hope, or fear.

Now, I harbor no hopes
For conventional prayers, positive delusory appearances.

I release my mind, this knowing, self-liberated and without grasping,
Into open all-encompassing evenness.

If there is cause for delusion, let there be delusion;
Deluded phenomena are traceless in empty movement.
If there is cause for liberation, let there be liberation;
The ground of liberation is baseless, without foundation.

I have reached the self-manifest Lama's
Exalted kingdom
Beyond the ordinary mind's reference points—
O how wonderful!

I, Jigdral Yeshé Dorjé, wrote this in response to the diligent practitioner Péma Gyurmé's requests, which he made over a long period of time.

37. Vajra speech, crown ornament of all Victorious Ones

Vajra speech, crown ornament of all victorious ones,
Enlightenment's self-manifest emanation as a tantric master,
Kind sole friend who protects Tibet,
Second Buddha from Orgyen, to you I pray![284]

Powerful lord who holds the secrets of all victorious ones;
The Teacher's[285] regent, observer of monastic precepts, who appears as a
    spiritual friend;
Kind first object of worship in the Cool Land [Tibet]:
Great scholar Bodhisattva, to you I pray![286]

Wisdom of all victorious ones' supreme knowledge, Manjushri,
Intentionally was reborn in this realm a king who protects the Buddha's
    teachings.
Kind charioteer of the doctrine in the Land of Snow,
Sovereign Trisong Déutsen,[287] to you I pray!

Myself and others *one*-pointedly remember you in our hearts.
May we acquire mastery over the *two* accumulations' treasury of noble
    qualities;
May the tradition you *three* began, the stainless Ancient Translation
    school,
Always increase and flourish throughout the *four* continents![288]

*In response to my son Thinley Norbu's entreaty, I, Jigdral Yeshé Dorjé,
wrote this in glorious Samyé's Changeless Spontaneously Accomplished
Temple. May this be completely virtuous!*

38. The Concise Pearl Necklace

In the past, you were awareness-holder Nüden Dorjé Tsal (Powerful
  Vajra Adept);[289]
In the future, you will be Sugata Möpa Tayé (Joyous Buddha Infinite
  Devotion);[290]
In the present, you are Lotus-Born's regent, Drokben incarnate:
Jigdral Yeshé Dorjé, to you I pray.

I [Jigdral Yeshé Dorjé] wrote this in response to those who have faith.

39. A Supplication to the Guru: To Dispel All Obstacles and for the Swift Fulfillment of Wishes

How wonderful!

Embodiment of all Buddhas' compassion,
Sole infallible and everlasting refuge, Lotus-Born,
To you I pray: Swiftly turn your loving attention to me, your child,
And bestow your blessings, empowerment, and accomplishment right
   now!

Although I know the degree of your liberation, noble qualities, and
   kindness
Is greater than other Buddhas,
During joyful times, guru, I did not remember you.
When I prayed, I merely recited the words.

Now, when the five degenerations' spreading decline has harmed me,[291]
When the lightening of unwanted suffering has struck,
I remember you, lord, from the bottom of my heart.
Lovingly heed this, my cries in longing and lament!

Dispel outer obstacles of the elements' turmoil without,
Such as earthquakes, fires, enemies, windstorms, droughts, and floods.
Dispel inner obstacles of the combination of humors' turmoil within,
Such as diseases of heat, cold, wind, bile, phlegm, and their
   combinations.[292]

Dispel into stainless space secret obstacles of mental turmoil,
The five unrestrained poisons, desire, anger, hope, fear, and demons.
When this world's beings' lake of suffering overflows,
Assure them of peace and happiness, Lotus-Born!

When the weapons of war rise in the central and outlying regions,
Repel the armies of these chaotic times, Lotus-Born!

When defilements, demons, contagious diseases, and malevolent beings
   torment me,
Eradicate demons and disease, Lotus-Born!

When I suffer from poverty, as the world and its beings' prosperity fades,
Open treasures of food and wealth, Lotus-Born!

When the time comes to aid beings with wealth, teachings, and sacred
   substances,
Give the father's inheritance to your children, Lotus-Born!

When I wander in hidden lands, solitary places, and mountain valleys,
Lead me to the right path, Lotus-Born!

When vicious fierce wild animals threaten me,
Drive away these malevolent beings, Lotus-Born!

When the four elements' volatility is about to destroy my illusory body,
Pacify the elements in their own place, Lotus-Born!

When wild men, bandits, and thieves harm me,
Destroy their malice and hostility, Lotus-Born!

When murderers' and hateful enemies' weapons torment me,
Place me within your vajra tent, Lotus-Born!

When my life ends and the time of death has come,
Lead me to the pure land of Great Exaltation, Lotus-Born!

When sufferings of the intermediate state's deluded perceptions arise,
Cast off delusion in self-liberation, Lotus-Born!

When I mistakenly stray into the karmic wheel of existence,
Show me the path to liberation, Lotus-Born!

At all times—in this life, the next, and in the intermediate state—
I have no other hope than you, Lotus-Born!

In short, never leave me; place your lotus feet forever
In the center of my heart devoted to you.
Bless me that all suffering of impure delusion be cleansed
And that I reach the unassailable state of permanent happiness!

*I, Jigdral Yeshé Dorjé, composed this supplication for the accomplish-
ment of my wishes when many outer and inner misfortunes troubled
my body and mind. For all persons connected to this supplication as well,
may it cause their outer and inner obstacles to be pacified and for their
hopes and wishes to be fulfilled.*

❧ IV

Aspiration Prayers

These intellectual judgements, deceptive illusions,
Can be right or wrong—it doesn't really matter.
Tossing away the eight worldly concerns I carry—
    useless as grass—
May I persevere in my practice of the sublime Dharma![293]

Introduction:
Aspiration Prayers (*smon lam*)

I HAVE CHOSEN to present here seven aspiration prayers (*smon lam*) that I feel are important among the works of Dudjom Rinpoché. These prayers come from the aspiration prayers section called *The Ship of Entirely Pure Benefit and Happiness: A Compilation of Aspiration Prayers* from Dudjom Rinpoché's *Collected Works*, vol. *ah*, pp. 427–79.

Aspiration prayers are often a teaching together with the aspiration for its attainment. For instance, in the introductory verse above, we are taught that our ordinary mind does not see things truly because it is like a "deceptive illusion." If one is having an hallucination—the invention of a reality—then it doesn't really matter what we decide upon as right or wrong because it is simply the deceptive, fabricated world we created. Therefore, it is unnecessary to involve ourselves with the eight worldly concerns that are related to our hallucination: gain and loss; praise and blame; pleasure and pain; fame and infamy. The world we take to be real is merely a fabrication of our intellect. The final line, "May I persevere in my practice of the sublime Dharma," is the aspiration to practice hard in order to realize the truth revealed in the preceding lines.

Aspiration prayers are extremely important in the context of Buddhism, because through reciting them from the heart, fired by faith and devotion, the blessings of these wisdom words of sublime beings enter us and touch our very being. These aspirations draw the object of our prayers toward us, or perhaps it is more accurate to say that these prayers draw the ultimate goal—the realization of our true nature, Buddha—out of us.

Often I wish I could move beyond just "understanding" the teachings, for the teachings and experiences gained to become part of me, only to find that when difficult circumstances arise, I suffer like a person who doesn't practice at all. Aspiration prayers remedy this. When recited genuinely and purely, without ulterior motives, these teachings penetrate deeply, and the attainment of the goal of one's aspiration is not a matter of if, but when. This is why my Lamas emphasize repeatedly the utmost importance of faith, devotion, and the recitation of genuine prayers of aspiration and supplication for all Vajrayana and Great Perfection practitioners. One's practice then becomes genuine, very juicy, as opposed to intellectual and very dry, like a kind of hobby or form of entertainment.

The first two writings are exquisite prayers to be reborn in the pure land of Guru Rinpoché, the Glorious Copper-Colored Mountain. The first was written by Dudjom Rinpoché following a visionary experience in which he actually went to the Glorious Copper-Colored Mountain on the dakini day of the second lunar month. I hope the translation can transmit some of the beauty and profound meaning of the original text.

The third work included in this section—"The Sublime Quintessence: An Aspiration Prayer of the Vital Points of Instruction"—is one of my favorite writings of His Holiness. He states in the colophon that he wrote this prayer for himself by synthesizing the heart advice of past wisdom masters. It really goes to the heart of the matter in poignant poetic verse, such as:

> Without seeing awareness, like a stainless crystal,
> Meditation with grasping and effort will not collapse.
> Not seeking this constant companion elsewhere,
> May I persevere in my practice of the sublime Dharma!

When times are tough, this prayer never fails to help me through difficulties in my life or in my practice. When all is well, it invariably uplifts and inspires me, laying bare what is meaningful and authentic, as the superficial things I take so seriously naturally fade away...

I included the fourth selection because it is a powerful, inspiring, and beautiful aspiration prayer that I wanted to make available. The sixth, "An Aspiration Prayer Related to Bringing the Intermediate State into the Path," is a very important prayer, especially for those of us in the West who tend to avoid anything related to death. We banish sickness, old age, and death to nursing homes, out of our sight and mind, to the point that even aging must be hidden behind the mask of cosmetic surgery.

This prayer is both a teaching on the intermediate state that awaits us all and also a practical prayer that can be recited as our own death nears or at the impending death of a loved one. It is a concise and practical teaching on the death process and the intermediate state leading to rebirth, and a very powerful aspiration prayer that guarantees to a faithful individual liberation or a favorable rebirth in the next life.

The seventh and final selection is an important and useful prayer, beautifully written in verse—as are all of His Holiness's writings—that is an aid to one's daily practice.

The Ship of Entirely Pure Benefit and Happiness:

A Compilation of Aspiration Prayers

1. The Awareness-holders' Sublime Path of Exaltation: A Prayer to Be Reborn in Tail-Fan Island's Glorious Copper-Colored Mountain[294]

How amazing!

Throughout the pervasive expansive stainless space of phenomena,
Wisdom's boundless appearances extend to infinity;
Their union creates clouds of vajra music.
May I be reborn in the Glorious Copper-Colored Mountain.

To the southwest [from Tibet] lies the cannibal demons' Tail-Fan Island,
Where many terrifying cities
Surround a majestic ruby mountain, lofty and resplendent.
May I be reborn in the Glorious Copper-Colored Mountain.

Upon its peak, spacious, vast, and flat,
Stands a marvelous great celestial mansion, glorious and beautiful,
Made from manifold magical jewels.
May I be reborn in the Glorious Copper-Colored Mountain.

The mansion's four corners, eight facets, and exquisite roof
Gleam with radiant light
From gems—crystal, lapis, ruby, and sapphire.
May I be reborn in the Glorious Copper-Colored Mountain.

The palace has three stories, balconies,
Skylights, windows, and wide gates,
Topped with fourfold gateways, Dharma wheels, parasols, and deer.
The doors' coral bolts are decorated with zi and agate.
May I be reborn in the Glorious Copper-Colored Mountain.

In the center, a three-tiered pagoda roof rises,
Made of turquoise, emeralds, rubies, diamonds, and other gems,
Embellished with an overhang and balconies.

An all-illuminating magical crowning gem shines brightly.
May I be reborn in the Glorious Copper-Colored Mountain.

Multi-colored jewels, half-netted and flowing ornaments are arranged;
Half-moons, vajras, silk scarves, and fans sway.
Bells and tiny bells ring with teachings' natural resonance.
May I be reborn in the Glorious Copper-Colored Mountain.

Gem clouds of bodhisattvas' aspirations gather from all quarters.
Captivating young gods and goddesses
Fill the spaces between the sky's billowing clouds.
May I be reborn in the Glorious Copper-Colored Mountain.

All raise fine parasols, victory banners, and flags,
Play sweet music, and sing songs of praise.
They pour scented bath water from immaculate crystal vases.
May I be reborn in the Glorious Copper-Colored Mountain.

Dense garlands of rainbow light from all directions and quadrants form
    tents
Where soft rains of flowers swirl in exquisite pavilions.
Gentle breezes carry sweet fragrances everywhere.
May I be reborn in the Glorious Copper-Colored Mountain.

Hosts of offering goddesses appear upon platforms.
With infinite expressions of charm, laughter, song, and dance,
They exude fathomless clouds of offerings, the treasury of space.
May I be reborn in the Glorious Copper-Colored Mountain.

Hosts of Buddhas, bodhisattvas, awareness-holders, and dakinis from
    other self-appearing realms
Come to pay their respects and
Gather in that realm, as numerous as dust in sunlight.
May I be reborn in the Glorious Copper-Colored Mountain.

Seven rings encircle the structure's perimeter:
Barriers, starting from the outermost,

Made from skulls, iron, copper, silver, gold, and five-colored lights.
May I be reborn in the Glorious Copper-Colored Mountain.

Within, in order, swans adorn bathing ponds;
Wild animals play in flower pastures, relaxed;
And rivers of nectar flow through meadows of medicinal herbs.
May I be reborn in the Glorious Copper-Colored Mountain.

Golden sands line the riverbanks;
Jeweled trees are bent with their leaves and fruit.
A flock of emanated birds sing sweet pleasant songs of the teachings.
May I be reborn in the Glorious Copper-Colored Mountain.

At the outermost ring, streams of blood cascade;
Chunks of human corpses toss in the churning waves;
Myriad fierce birds and wild animals rage as the wind.
May I be reborn in the Glorious Copper-Colored Mountain.

In gloomy canyons outside, groups of cannibal demons and gate
     protectors
Howl with piercing laughter and bear frightening weapons,
Denying masses of unfortunate beings the chance to travel past them.
May I be reborn in the Glorious Copper-Colored Mountain.

In the center of the palace of spontaneous qualities,
The sun and moon's spheres, method and wisdom, suffuse light
Upon a thousand-petalled lotus's pollen bed atop a jeweled lion throne.
May I be reborn in the Glorious Copper-Colored Mountain.

There sits my marvelous guide, embodiment of all refuges,
Buddha's manifestation,
Lotus-Born Master whose splendor overpowers apparent existence.
May I be reborn in the Glorious Copper-Colored Mountain.

He engages in fearless conduct;
His rainbow vajra body blazes with the glory of physical perfection's
     marks and signs.

He smiles in pleasure with a bright expression;
His loving, wide-open eyes gaze straight ahead.
May I be reborn in the Glorious Copper-Colored Mountain.

His supreme speech, inexpressible and unceasing,
Has all sixty aspects of Brahma's melodious voice.
This lion's roar resounds clearly with the sound of the teachings'
    profound and pervasive nectar.
May I be reborn in the Glorious Copper-Colored Mountain.

His non-conceptual mind, free from elaborations,
Encompasses depth, clarity, and the essence of non-dual wisdom.
He nurtures all beings like his own child with omniscience, compassion,
    and capability.
May I be reborn in the Glorious Copper-Colored Mountain.

Like the sun and its rays, an array of his magical forms
That can guide beings in any circumstance encircle the chief,
Such as the five facets of Skull-garlanded Adept and the Guru's eight
    forms.
May I be reborn in the Glorious Copper-Colored Mountain.

Hosts of Indian and Tibetan awareness-holders in the right front row
Sing melodious vajra songs and perform fearless conduct of union and
    liberation
Within realization's wide expanse beyond activity and effort.
May I be reborn in the Glorious Copper-Colored Mountain.

From supreme omniscient translators and panditas in the left row,
Distinct voices rise without dissonance,
Vividly heralding dialogue, translation, explanation, teaching, and
    listening.
May I be reborn in the Glorious Copper-Colored Mountain.

The treasure-discoverers' hosts of accomplished masters to the right
    of the right row

Perform the wondrous magical drama of revealing the mind lineage's
  meaning
And of deciphering the yellow parchment's word lineage.
May I be reborn in the Glorious Copper-Colored Mountain.

Hosts of mantric awareness-holders to the left of the right row
Battle hexes and redirect evil activity's arrows,
Grinding into powder hindrances, demons, enemies, and negative spirits.
May I be reborn in the Glorious Copper-Colored Mountain.

Hosts of Indian and Nepalese dakinis to the right of the left row
With radiant blissful expressions and the fullness of youth's elixir
Bestow sense pleasures of the supreme secret's great exaltation.
May I be reborn in the Glorious Copper-Colored Mountain.

Hosts of Mön and Tibetan dakinis to the left of the left row,
Glorious yoginis, perform vajra dances
And enjoy the tantric feast gathering of exaltation and emptiness.
May I be reborn in the Glorious Copper-Colored Mountain.

Master of the expanse, the consort Yeshé Tsogyal in front of the central
  sublime chief
Emanates offering clouds of great exaltation with an expression of
  complete veneration.
She nurtures fortunate disciples and reveals the four empowerments'
  symbolic teachings.
May I be reborn in the Glorious Copper-Colored Mountain.

Containers of texts, the expanse of the supreme vehicle's essence,
Are stacked behind, within dense nets of five-colored light.
They resound with the natural sound of the sutras, tantras, and pith
  instructions' teachings.
May I be reborn in the Glorious Copper-Colored Mountain.

Verandas hold spirits who wander in sacred places—
Glorious messengers, *gingkara*, Goddess of Lanka, Blazing Mouth, *tramen*.

They expel tantric commitment-violators and guard the oath-keepers as
   their children.
May I be reborn in the Glorious Copper-Colored Mountain.

At the four gates, the four great kings with their attendants
And armies of virtuous protectors gather in a crowd.
They prevent obstacles and send forth billowing clouds of offerings.
May I be reborn in the Glorious Copper-Colored Mountain.

Outside, the eight emanated great sovereign cannibal spirits
Use their law's symbols that distinguish good from evil
To bring the legion of flesh-eaters to the teachings.
May I be reborn in the Glorious Copper-Colored Mountain.

In a pavilion of dense five-colored light on the second story
Dwells the lord of compassion, Avalokiteshvara, Lotus-eyed One, the
   sambhogakaya.
Infinite numbers of the three roots, as many as atoms in all realms.
May I be reborn in the Glorious Copper-Colored Mountain.

At the center of the realm of emptiness and clarity's wisdom on the
   upper story
Dwells the primordial lord dharmakaya, Buddha Amitabha, Changeless
   Light.
A sea-like retinue, the display of his natural manifest display, surrounds
   him.
May I be reborn in the Glorious Copper-Colored Mountain.

The array of qualities and perfect glory
Of every pure land of the Victorious Ones' three kayas
Merge as one within this marvelous emanated realm.
May I be reborn in the Glorious Copper-Colored Mountain.

When I die,
May I be free from mortal suffering and physical pain.
May I not see delusion's perceptions in the intermediate state
But leave my body with immeasurable exaltation, joy, and happiness.

With silk roads of rainbows and lights, gentle rains of flowers,
Flags, parasols, victory banners, and manifold sounds of music,
May hosts of spiritual warriors and dakinis holding various kinds of
    desirable offerings
Approach to greet me.

May Mother Tsogyal, blazing with blue light,
Say, "My only child, let us go now to the Glorious Mountain,"
Visibly take me by the wrist,
And lead me to the Lotus Light Pure Land.

With courageous confidence without hesitation
Toward fearsome gate guards, dangerous passages, and so forth,
May I arrive there instantly, in the blink of an eye,
To see the supreme face of the guru, my true father.

May I have the power to draw from my jewel-mind, the treasure trove of
    space,
Whatever I wish—Bodhisattva Kuntu Zangpo's offerings
In clouds, filling all realms richly—and to dispatch them,
Creating pleasure among the host of deities.

May I enjoy the festival of the supreme vehicle's nectar
With the ranks of spiritual heroes and dakinis at their tantric feast,
Passing without difficulty to the state of awareness-holder
And gaining awakening within the vast expanse of Lotus-Born's wisdom
    mind.

May I employ manifold techniques of infinite enlightened activity,
The magical net's dance capable of guiding beings in any circumstances,
To lead every being, whose numbers equal the bounds of space,
To Tail-Fan Island's glorious mountain city.

May all beings who see, hear, remember, or are touched by me
Swiftly gain the excellent fortune
Of Buddha Lotus-Born's loving acceptance as his extraordinary disciple
And of his bestowal of ripening and liberating instructions.

May oceans of the Triple Gems and three roots' blessings
And the infallible truths of phenomena and of their nature
Ensure that my pure aspirations made with good intentions
Be crowned with auspicious unhindered accomplishment.

I, Jigdral Yeshe Dorjé, a new offshoot among awareness-holders, have
had the good fortune to be Lake Born Lotus's servant in all my lifetimes.
I wrote this as wishful words of prayer following a devotional vision
during the offering on the tenth day of the waxing second lunar month.
May this be the cause for all sentient beings, and those close to me, to
gain great liberation in the city of Lotus Light.

2. The Chariot of Joy and Good Fortune: An Aspiration to Journey to the Glorious Copper-Colored Mountain

Self-manifested purity, vajra space of supreme exaltation,
Spontaneous Highest Pure Land, the dance of interwoven magical
  display,
Most excellent among infinite oceans of realms of Victorious Ones:
May I be reborn in the Glorious Copper-Colored Mountain.

At the summit of the captivating imperial ruby mountain
Stands a tiered palace with a jeweled dome,
Superb and wondrous in its beautiful design.
May I be reborn in the Glorious Copper-Colored Mountain.

Amid pastures and sandalwood forests, fresh grassy regions of turquoise
Exhibit multi-colored lotus blossoms with smiling glowing pollen
  hearts
That flaunt their youthful laughter.
May I be reborn in the Glorious Copper-Colored Mountain.

Rivers of nectar moistened with camphor-scented water
Cascade delightfully and swirl into surrounding pools—
Youthful dancers who frolic and undulate.
May I be reborn in the Glorious Copper-Colored Mountain.

From the lattice openings of the rainbow pavilion,
Sprinkling rains of flowers fall like garlands of mist drops—
Great heroes who sport in dances of exaltation.
May I be reborn in the Glorious Copper-Colored Mountain.

Magnificent sense pleasures in great number
Provide exquisite adornments to the entire scene;
Clouds of dakinis spread endlessly into the sky's upper reaches.
May I be reborn in the Glorious Copper-Colored Mountain.

At the center of the gathered awareness-holders' ranks,
Lord of the victorious ones, Lotus-Born Master,
Universally proclaims his impressive lion's roar of profound secrets.
May I be reborn in the Glorious Copper-Colored Mountain.

"I am the essence of all Buddhas," he proclaims.
With the incomparable force of his wisdom of love and omniscience,
He takes forms equal to his unlimited number of disciples' characters.
May I be reborn in the Glorious Copper-Colored Mountain.

Merely to recall this limitless treasury of the [Lotus-Born Master] and
　　his oceans of noble qualities
Provides assurance of rebirth in that realm;
Such is the splendor and blessings of his wheel of wondrous activity.
May I be reborn in the Glorious Copper-Colored Mountain.

At this very moment, may I travel forcefully
To this celestial pure land, the beautiful city of Lotus Light,
And replicate your life story of liberation, wish-fulfilling
　　accomplishment of success for yourself and others.
May I become as you, incomparable guru!

*I, an elderly father, Jigdral Yeshé Dorjé, wrote this prayer of aspiration
with deep sadness and longing as helpful provision for the daughter of
the Buddha's family, Dékyong Yeshé Wangmo, on her journey to the
pure realm of Lotus Light. May this prove virtuous!*

3. The Sublime Quintessence: An Aspiration Prayer of the Vital Points of Instruction

Infallible and eternal sole refuge, lord of the mandala, precious,
   most kind root Lama,
I do not think of death but instead waste the leisures and
   opportunities[295]
I could use for spiritual life.
Please compassionately accept me as your disciple.

This fleeting, dream-like human life
Can be joyful or sorrowful—it doesn't really matter.
Not aspiring for joy or sorrow,
May I persevere in my practice of the sublime Dharma!

This human life, a butter lamp in a breeze,
Can be long lasting or short—it doesn't really matter.
So, while not letting ego-clinging tighten further,
May I persevere in my practice of the sublime Dharma!

These intellectual judgements, deceptive illusions,
Can be right or wrong—it doesn't really matter.
Tossing away the eight worldly concerns I carry—useless as grass[296]—
May I persevere in my practice of the sublime Dharma!

These friends and helpers, like birds flocked in a tree,
Can be with me or not—it doesn't really matter.
Keeping my own counsel,[297]
May I persevere in my practice of the sublime Dharma!

This illusory body, like a hundred-year-old decrepit house,
Can last or collapse—it doesn't really matter.
Not ensnared by effort to acquire food, clothing, or medicine,
May I persevere in my practice of the sublime Dharma!

Religious rank—what a child's game!
To keep it or lose it—it doesn't really matter.
Not fooling myself with all these trifles,
May I persevere in my practice of the sublime Dharma!

These gods and demons, like a mirror's reflections,
Can be helpful or harmful—it doesn't really matter.
Not taking my hallucinations as enemies,
May I persevere in my practice of the sublime Dharma!

These thoughtless conversations, fleeting as an echo,
Can be pleasant or not—it doesn't really matter.
Taking the Triple Gems and my own mind as witness,
May I persevere in my practice of the sublime Dharma!

The fields of science are unhelpful at the time of need, like a deer's
    antlers.[298]
If I have intellectual knowledge or not, it doesn't really matter.
Not placing my trust in mere studies,
May I persevere in my practice of the sublime Dharma!

These undeserved offerings, deadly poison—
If I receive them or not, it doesn't really matter.
Not spending my human life engaged in wrong livelihood,
May I persevere in my practice of the sublime Dharma!

This high social standing, like dog excrement wrapped in silk
    brocade—
If I have it or not, it doesn't really matter.
Smelling the rot between my own ears,
May I persevere in my practice of the sublime Dharma!

These close ties, as temporary as those among crowds on market day,[299]
Be they loving or hostile—it doesn't really matter.
Sincerely cutting the bonds of clinging,
May I persevere in my practice of the sublime Dharma!

These possessions, riches in a dream—
If I have them or not, it doesn't really matter.
Not using seeming conformity or flattery to deceive others,
May I persevere in my practice of the sublime Dharma!

This status, like a tiny bird alighting upon a tree,[300]
Can be high or low—it doesn't really matter.
So, not wishing for situations that will make me suffer,
May I persevere in my practice of the sublime Dharma!

Practice of black magic, like a weapon,
Can be successful or not—it doesn't really matter.
Not purchasing a razor to commit suicide,
May I persevere in my practice of the sublime Dharma!

Reciting prayers, like a parrot repeating OM MANI PEMÉ HUNG—
If I do it or not, it doesn't really matter.
Not keeping score of all I have done,
May I persevere in my practice of the sublime Dharma!

Irrelevant teachings, like cascading mountain streams—
If I am learned in them or not, it doesn't really matter.
Not meditating on ideas cleverly expressed as the teachings,
May I persevere in my practice of the sublime Dharma!

The keen analytical mind, like a pig's snout,
Can be sharp or dull—it doesn't really matter.
Not foraging in the debris of pointless desire and anger,
May I persevere in my practice of the sublime Dharma!

Experiences in meditation, like an Indian summer's
    water spring,[301]
Can increase or fade—it doesn't really matter.
Not chasing rainbows like a child,
May I persevere in my practice of the sublime Dharma!

This visionary experience, like rain upon a mountain peak,[302]
Can occur or not—it doesn't really matter.
Not taking my delusion as real,[303]
May I persevere in my practice of the sublime Dharma!

Without these leisures and attainments, wish-fulfilling jewels,
Accomplishing the sublime Dharma is impossible.
Not squandering them while they are mine,
May I persevere in my practice of the sublime Dharma!

Without having met my glorious Lama, the light of liberation's path,
Realization of the abiding nature is impossible.
Not falling off a cliff when I know the way to go,
May I persevere in my practice of the sublime Dharma!

Without listening to the sublime Dharma, healing medicine,
Knowing what to reject and what to accept is impossible.
Not swallowing deadly poison when I can tell help from harm,
May I persevere in my practice of the sublime Dharma!

Without noticing joy and sorrow's fluctuations, like summer
    alternating with winter,
Renunciation is impossible.
Concluding that suffering will return to me,
May I persevere in my practice of the sublime Dharma!

Without casting out now my immersion in samsara, a stone at the
    river bottom,
A later escape will be impossible.
Seizing the Triple Gems' lifeline of compassion,
May I persevere in my practice of the sublime Dharma!

Without knowing freedom's noble qualities, an island of jewels,
Cultivation of diligence is impossible.
Seeing the gain of lasting victory,
May I persevere in my practice of the sublime Dharma!

Without encountering these sublime stories of liberation, nectar's
   essence,
Fostering trust is impossible.
Not harming myself when I can tell the difference between success
   and failure,
May I persevere in my practice of the sublime Dharma!

Without nurturing the mind of awakening, a fertile field,
Enlightenment is impossible.
Not lapsing into complacency toward that very meaningful
   accomplishment,
May I persevere in my practice of the sublime Dharma!

Without tending to my own mind, a ridiculous monkey,
Renunciation of the passions is impossible.
Not imitating a madman by doing whatever I please,
May I persevere in my practice of the sublime Dharma!

Without relinquishing this ego-clinging, my ever-present shadow,
Reaching exaltation's land is impossible.
Not treating my captive enemy as a friend,
May I persevere in my practice of the sublime Dharma!

Without extinguishing these five poisons, embers under ashes,
Abiding in mind's genuine nature is impossible.
Not feeding venomous baby snakes in my home,
May I persevere in my practice of the sublime Dharma!

Without softening my own mindstream, as stiff as a leather
   butter-sack,[304]
Merging my mind with the Dharma is impossible.
Not spoiling the child born in me,
May I persevere in my practice of the sublime Dharma!

Without stopping these bad habits, a constant stream,
Freedom from conduct contrary to the Dharma is impossible.

Not putting weapons in the hands of my enemies,
May I persevere in my practice of the sublime Dharma!

Without giving up these distractions, ceaseless ripples on water,
Achieving stability is impossible.
Not creating samsara when I have a choice,
May I persevere in my practice of the sublime Dharma!

Without my Lama's blessings—like earth, water, and warmth [necessary
    for seeds to grow]—having entered me,
Recognition of my true nature is impossible.
Now that I've come to the direct path, not taking the long way around,
May I persevere in my practice of the sublime Dharma!

Without staying in this remote retreat, like a lush summer region of
    medicinal plants,
Noble qualities cannot grow.
When staying in the mountains, not wandering among bustling c
    rowds,
May I persevere in my practice of the sublime Dharma!

Without freedom from desire for comfort, like possession by
    a craving spirit,[305]
To stop energetically creating suffering is impossible.
Not making offerings to starving demons as my personal deity,
May I persevere in my practice of the sublime Dharma!

Without relying upon mindfulness, a castle's sealed gate,
Delusion's traffic will not stop.
Not leaving the gate unlocked when thieves come,
May I persevere in my practice of the sublime Dharma!

Without realizing the abiding nature, like the changeless sky,
I will not ascertain the view's basis.
Not tying myself up,
May I persevere in my practice of the sublime Dharma!

Without seeing awareness, like a stainless crystal,
Meditation with grasping and effort will not collapse.
Not seeking this constant companion elsewhere,
May I persevere in my practice of the sublime Dharma!

Without recognition of natural mind's face, like that of an old friend,
All that I do will mislead me.
Not closing my eyes to what I have in my hand,
May I persevere in my practice of the sublime Dharma!

In short, if I do not give up this life's activities,
Accomplishing the sublime Dharma for the next life is impossible.
Giving myself this, the kindest advice,
May all that I do turn into the sublime Dharma!

May my attainment of accomplishments have no impediment, such as
Wrong views toward my Lama when he gives instruction consistent
    with the Dharma,
Disappointment with the wisdom deity during upheavals of negative
    karma,
Or postponing spiritual practice if adverse circumstances occur.

All that I've done amounts to meaningless circling of an empty place;
All my efforts have caused my mind to become rigid.
All my thinking has reinforced my delusion.
All ordinary individuals' conceited spiritual activity causes our bondage.

So much done without having produced a single result,
So much thinking without the slightest lasting conclusion,
So many "needs" without time to fulfill them.
Giving up these activities, may I be able to meditate upon the profound
    instructions!

When I think, "I intend to do this," may the Victorious One's speech
    be my witness.
When I think, "I am doing [what I intend]," may my mind blend with
    the Dharma.

When I think, "I am putting [the Dharma] into practice," may I look to
   previous masters' lives of liberation.

To myself I say, "Spoiled one, why do anything else?"
Lama, grant your blessings that I assume a humble position,
Enrich myself with contentment's wealth,
Loosen my ties to the eight worldly concerns,
Apply myself with an unyielding will,
That my Lama's blessings enter me, that my realization equal the sky's
   breadth,
And that I enter Buddha Kuntu Zangpo's exalted succession!

*I, Jigdral Yeshé Dorjé, synthesized the meaning of the holy past masters'
vajra speech in their oral instructions to compose this for my own recitation practice.*

4. Those who have gone and those who remain

Those who have gone and those who remain in the ten directions and
   the four times—
Lamas, Triple Gems, Victorious Ones and your spiritual heirs,
Awareness-holders, seers, and those who can make words come true—
Witness the fulfillment of my prayer of aspiration, I beseech you!

From now until I attain enlightenment,
Throughout all my successive rebirths,
May I never be reborn in such places as the three lower realms' fearful
   cities of suffering,
Where leisure is unknown.

Once born in an excellent family aligned with the sacred Dharma,
Laden with every noble quality of leisure and attainment—
A supreme physical support superior to that of the gods—
May my previous propensity for virtue awaken!

May I be a worthy recipient for the Great Vehicle's path of Secret Mantra:
Imbued with faith, diligence, incisive knowledge, and compassion,
Humble, mentally stable, peaceful, and gentle,
Open-minded, of excellent character, able to keep secrets, and good
   natured.

May harmful disharmony, from such misfortune as illness, suffering,
   and poverty,
Never oppress me;
May I gain control over conditions conducive to the Dharma,
Such as longevity, merit, prosperity, and acclaim.

May I not meet companions who lead me down the wrong path,
But encounter true virtuous friends
Who show me the perfect and excellent path that delights the
   victorious ones;
And may I have the good fortune to correctly rely upon them!

May the seeds of freedom in my mindstream
Not be consumed in the fires of the negative act of forsaking the
    Dharma,
Such as when possessed by the demons of bias and pride,
To slander any other teaching or individual.

May my devotion and pure vision increase in every way.
May I respect the codes of conduct. May I reach the bounds of my
    hearing, reflection, and meditation.
Based upon my teaching and practice in the traditions of scriptures and
    realization,
May I be able to steer the Victorious One's doctrine to greater heights!

May all sentient beings who have a connection with me through positive
    or negative acts—
Be it through sight, hearing, or thought of me,
Praise, blame, or hate—
Not be turned back on the path to liberation!

May I realize that all phenomena are free from extremes, the great
    Middle Way,[306]
Cultivate the deeply uncontrived mind of supreme awakening,
And do nothing beyond the conduct that aids others.
May I be able to shoulder the great burden of guiding all beings!

Especially, on the supreme secret Vajrayana path,
May the four empowerments bestowed in the four sacred mandalas bring
    my mindstream to maturity.
May I keep my commitments purely, reach the limits of the stages of
    creation and completion,
And tread on the level of the four types of awareness-holders!

The always-noble evenness of samsara and enlightenment, the original
    essential nature,
Is self-manifest and effortless, the natural state of naked empty
    awareness,

Which merges into the vast expanse of inconceivable exaltation.
May I actualize this realization without renunciation or attainment.

May I pacify concepts' limitations and restrictions into the great
  luminous sphere;
May my material body ripen into a body of rainbow light;
And may the unobstructed outer radiance, in clouds of magical nets,
Employ the four types of liberation to empty the depths of beings'
  realms!

*The Ngapö Vajra Master Orgyen Sang-ngak Tendzin, who strives
diligently in his unassailable dedication to steering the Early
Translation doctrine to greater heights, asked, "Please compose a prayer
of aspiration for the fulfillment of my wishes, verses to recite in the
presence of the precious Jo Shakya statue in Lhasa." In response to
his request, I, Jigdral Yeshé Dorjé, a lazy village mantra practitioner
of the dark age, wrote down whatever came to mind and offered it.
May it prove meaningful!*

5. An Aspiration Prayer
Related to Bringing the Intermediate State onto the Path[307]

Glorious Lama, embodiment of all Buddhas,
My kindest only lasting refuge, lord of the mandala,
Stay forever on a lotus in the center of my heart.
Lovingly accept me as your disciple and grant your reassuring blessings,
    I pray!

Your excellent propensity led you to Great Perfection's path.
You used profound pith instructions to mentally resolve misconceptions.
With undistracted diligence, you understood the oral instructions.
Your familiarization with the direct crucial instructions left its mark

Not hoping for results at only a later date,
You forcefully purified impure delusion's stains.
May you traverse the four visions' paths and stages in the blink of an
    eye
And achieve rainbow body's supreme transference in this lifetime!

Although you are endowed with a mind that trusts the path,
You did not apply yourself to the utmost in the essential experiential
    cultivation
Or pursue the exhaustion of phenomena, the limit of accomplishment,
    during your lifetime.
When the time comes to die, to discard this body of ripened karma,
Your acquired certainty that all phenomena are magic-like
And knowledge of the crucial meaning of the creation, abiding, and
    destruction of the five elements' aggregates
Will prevent your panic at death.
May you revel in reaching the unassailable deathless state!

The reversal of the karmic circulating energies breaks knots at your
    body's five centers.[308]

The fire-equalizing circulating energy reverses: Your body's heat is
    damaged and you cannot digest food.
The life-sustaining circulating energy reverses: Your consciousness
    becomes completely unclear.
The downward-expelling circulating energy reverses: Your body's main
    fluids are unbound and escape.
The upward-moving circulating energy reverses: You cannot keep
    food down.
The pervasive circulating energy reverses: Your limbs become hard a
    nd stiff.
Breathing shortens, channels become dull (*rtsa rtul*), and you fall
    on your death bed.
May you then have no attachment to the existence that appears here.

The dissolution of the earth element into water destroys the navel's
    channel center.
As its outer sign, the body becomes heavy; as its inner sign, mind
    sinks into dullness;
As its secret sign, mirages of the clear light appear.
When these occur, may your mind grasp the dharmakaya Lama
    at the level of your heart!

The dissolution of the water element into fire destroys the heart's
    channel center.
As its outer sign, your mouth and nose become dry; as its inner sign,
    your mind becomes extremely agitated;
As its secret sign, smoke appears.
When these occurs, may your mind grasp the essential Lama of the
    wisdom body (*svabhavikakaya*) at the level of your navel!

The dissolution of the fire element into wind destroys the throat's
    channel center.

As its outer sign, you lose warmth; as its inner sign, your mind becomes
    confused and you cannot recognize others;
As its secret sign, firefly-like light arises.
When these occur, may your mind grasp the nirmanakaya Lama at the
    level of your forehead!

The dissolution of the wind element into consciousness destroys the
    secret channel center.
As its outer sign, breathing becomes labored; as its inner sign, you see
    many visions;
As its secret sign, lamp-like luminosity dawns.
When these occur, may your mind grasp the sambhogakaya Lama at the
    level of your secret place!

Consciousness dissolves into space, blocking the five senses.
Blood gathers in the life-sustaining channel, and strikes the heart:
    outwardly, your breathing stops.
The locations of the white and red elements move:
As they flow along the central channel, brilliant white and red lights
    appear.

When the two drops of bodhicitta meet, the consciousness between them
    is extinguished.
A field of black appears and the eighty innate thought patterns cease.

Space dissolves into luminosity:
The original ground's luminosity dawns like an autumn's cloudless sky.
May you instantly recognize this, and gain your own ground,
And be liberated in the vast expanse of the primordially pure
    dharmakaya!

Nevertheless, if you cannot gain liberation within that state,
When the inner breath stops, use the pith instructions for the moment
    of death
To send awareness, a pure drop, through Brahma's gate like a shooting
    star,

To move it to the Lama's heart.
May you awake as from a dream, travel to the celestial realms,
And there complete the stages and paths' noble qualities!

If you did not identify luminosity before death ends,
You will see the intermediate state of the nature of phenomena.
Luminosity dissolves into union:
Sounds, lights, and hosts of peaceful and wrathful deities fill the realms
   of the three thousand-fold universe.

When phenomenal existence appears in bodies of light,
May you use the key teaching of settling into natural meditation:
Recognize [the appearances] as your own perception, have confidence
   in that,
And gain liberation in the spontaneously present sambhogakaya
   pure land!

For those of the lowest degree of acuity, the overpowering force of
   delusion's patterns
Prevents recognition of the nature of phenomena, and its [appearances]
   naturally fade.
When entering the intermediate state of existence,
May you not see the intermediate state's suffering of deluded
   perceptions,
Such as terrifying sounds and a dreadful abyss.

May you not enter another rebirth,
But travel instantly to Lotus Light (Péma Ö),
And there receive the lord Guru [Rinpoché's] empowerments and
   prophecies.
There, may you finish training in what remains of your path
And obtain the glory of the spontaneous accomplishment of your goals
   for yourself and others!

May the power and blessings of infinite oceans of refuge,
The force of the two truths—natural and undeniable—

And the truth of my lofty pure intention
Bring this prayer of aspiration I make to certain full fruition!

---

*I, Jigdral Yeshé Dorjé, wrote this in response to the tantric monk Lodrö
Zangpo's request, "I need a prayer of aspiration like this for bringing the
intermediate state into the path."*

6. Glorious Lama, the original protector

Namo ratna trayaya.

Glorious Lama, the original protector,
Essence of an ocean of the kayas and wisdoms
Of all Victorious Ones and their spiritual heirs, whose numbers fill space,
To you I pray: May my aspiration prayers be completely accomplished.

Seeing the six kinds of beings' cities like a watermill's rim,
In constant movement, a land of suffering,
Like a city of cannibals or a forest of razors—
May sincere renunciation arise from within me!

Knowing this dream-like wheel of life's entire glory and wealth
To be fake and untrue, like an illusion,
May I never undertake these activities,
Like ephemeral rainbows in space!

May I never have the slightest trace of a sense of equality as friends
Toward the glorious Lama imbued with the threefold kindness.[309]
May I constantly supplicate him without distraction
With respect and devotion toward him as the Buddha incarnate!

When I consider all sentient beings, my mothers of the past whose
    numbers fill space,
May the precious sublime mind of awakening arise in my mindstream
Without the negative intent to accomplish my own benefit,
And may I strive for beings' benefit!

Once I enter the door of the supreme Secret Mantra Vehicle,
May the force of my fervent prayers of acknowledgment purify my
    mindstream
Of any serious obstacles that conflict with the path—
All obscurations that result from damage, violations, and transgressions
    of the tantric commitments!

Never separate from my Lama, a vast treasury of blessings and
  empowerments,
And meditating that he sits at the crown of my head,
May my supplications' strength blend his mind and mine as one,
And may the sun of realization dawn within me!

All phenomena of samsara and enlightenment, existence as it is,
My own perceptions, are unborn the moment they appear.
May I gain confidence in the view of recognizing awareness without
  elaboration,
Enlightenment's four bodies and five wisdoms, as my own nature.

When I sustain the naturally settled state without distraction or clinging
In the uncreated state of present, empty, and clear awareness,
Unfettered by the characteristics of mental frameworks,
May I perfect the great dynamic energy of meditation on the abiding
  nature!

Not favoring either the view or conduct,
May my body, speech, and mind act in harmony with the correct
  teachings.
Immersed without distraction or activity in magic-like tantric practice,
May the luminosity of night and day become an unbroken circle!

When the time to die arrives,
May I be free from clinging to the things of this life,
Not experience mortal pain,
And recognize all the death-process experiences of appearance, increase,
  and attainment!

During the intermediate state of the death process,
May my Lama's profound instructions come clearly to mind, like the
  Goddess of Charm gazing at her own likeness.
May the luminosity of the basis be apparent,
And may I gain liberation within the expanse of primordially pure
  dharmakaya!

However, if I do not grasp the luminosity of the original ground,
As soon as the peaceful and wrathful deities appear in the intermediate
state,
May I recognize them as my own, like a child comfortable in his
mother's lap,
And be liberated in the stainless space of spontaneously present
sambhogakaya!

If I do not gain liberation in the intermediate state of the nature of
phenomena,
Due to faint familiarity with practice,
May my karmic propensity continue, like connecting a water pipe.
May the entrances to the lower realms be blocked, and may I search for
an excellent support for my rebirth!

May I obtain an excellent, free, and fully endowed human body, have
independence,
Meet with a qualified Lama and the secret mantra teachings,
And have the fortune to practice—
May such a supreme body be mine!

Throughout all my lifetimes, may I keep my tantric commitments
purely,
Complete tantric meditation's two stages, and accomplish the two goals,
for myself and others.
May I swiftly attain the dharmakaya, Buddha Kuntu Zangpo,
Then empty the depths of samsara's three realms!

*I, Jigdral Yeshé Dorjé, wrote this in response to a request from both Doc-
tor Chönyi Gyatso and Yeshé Chödron. May this prove virtuous and
excellent!*

Appendices

Appendix 1
An Explanation of the Nine Vehicles

Buddhism didn't arrive on our Western shores in an organized way and, due to numerous factors, many of us do not have the basic training and foundation that would normally precede Vajrayana and Great Perfection practice. Therefore, I would like to take the time to explore these nine vehicles of Buddhism as taught by Dudjom Rinpoché in order to nourish trust and appreciation, so they may blossom into faith and devotion. This will inspire uncontrived confidence in the profundity of the Great Perfection pith instruction class.

I hope your seeing the pith instructions in the context of the nine vehicles will have the same effect on you that it does on me. Upon seeing that these teachings are the very essence of all Buddhist teachings, I am inspired, and faith, trust, and confidence in the teachings naturally grow. Reading these teachings inspired by faith, trust, and confidence protects from dry intellectualism and allows their juicy nectar to be absorbed in our heart. I include this explanation of the nine vehicles based on His Holiness's teachings with the hope that seeing the pith instructions within this context will have this effect on the reader.

The Nine Vehicles
According to the Nyingma Tradition

In the text translated in the Heart Advice section of this book, *Essential Advice for Solitary Meditation Practice*, His Holiness teaches the innermost secret Great Perfection, the summit of all vehicles. Let's see how this and His Holiness's other heart advice teachings fit into the world of Buddhist teachings. The Nyingma tradition classifies all Buddhist teachings into nine vehicles, based on the capacity of individual students:

Three causal vehicles:
- the Hearer Vehicle (Shravakayana)
- the Solitary Sage Vehicle (Pratyekabuddhayana)
- the Bodhisattva Vehicle (Bodhisattvayana)

Three resultant vehicles of Vajrayana, divided into six sections:
Three lower tantras:

+ Kriyatantra
+ Upatantra (also referred to as Caryatantra)
+ Yogatantra

Three higher tantras:

+ Mahayoga
+ Anuyoga
+ Atiyoga

There are three classes of Atiyoga:

+ Mind Class (*sems sde*)
+ Vast Expanse Class (*klong sde*)
+ Pith Instruction (*upadesha*) Class (*man snag sde*)

It is not that the Pith Instruction Class is considered to be the "best" teachings as opposed to the many "inferior" teachings found in the lower vehicles. All of Buddha's teachings are considered sublime, rich in special qualities that lead us away from life's sufferings and away from the inevitable suffering one experiences going from one life to the next and lead to higher and higher vehicles until full liberation is realized through Great Perfection. The Pith Instruction Class is the most sublime of the always sublime teachings of Buddha.

In order to see where his Holiness's heart advice teachings fit into the world of Buddhist teachings, we will briefly review in four sections the distinguishing features of these nine vehicles:

1. First, I will give a concise summary based upon a variety of sources, including my own teachers and the writings of Tulku Thondup.
2. Second, there will be a detailed review of Vajrayana's resultant vehicle based upon extensive translations and paraphrase of Dudjom Rinpoché's explanation of the nine vehicles called *The Festival of Delight in Which the Expression of Eloquent Teachings Manifest: A Concise Detailed Classification of the Nyingmapa Teachings, the Ancient Translation School of Secret Mantra.*[310]
3. Third, I will set forth Dudjom Rinpoché's review of the outer and inner tantras.

4. Fourth, a concise review of the three highest Vajrayana vehicles—Mahayoga, Anuyoga, and Atiyoga—will be given as found in this same text, which highlights important aspects not discussed in sections 1, 2, and 3 above.[311]

CONCISE SUMMARY OF THE NINE VEHICLES

To begin, the nine vehicles can be succinctly understood in terms of their:
  1. view
  2. meditation
  3. conduct
  4. result

The Causal Vehicles

Hearers

According to the vehicle of the Hearers, the view is the egolessness of self leading to complete purification of the passions. They also hold to the belief that phenomena are made of indivisible particles, so they do not believe in the egolessness of phenomena. Their practice includes meditation on the nine disgusting things and the sixteen impermanences. Their conduct consists of observing the two hundred and fifty monastic vows of the Vinaya. The result is attainment of the state of an arhat, or foe destroyer.

Solitary Sages

According to the vehicle of the Solitary Sages, the view is the egolessness of the self, and partial realization of the egolessness of phenomena since they believe that phenomena have no inherent nature, though they still believe phenomena are made of indivisible particles. Their practice is to meditate in reverse order on the twelve interdependent links of causation. Their conduct is similar to that of the Hearers. The result is attainment of the state of a Solitary Sage (*pratyekabuddha*).

Bodhisattvas

According to the vehicle of the Bodhisattvas, the view is the egolessness of self and phenomena. As a manifestation of this, one practices the six or ten perfections[312] and the four means of positively influencing others. One also practices meditation on the thirty-seven aspects of enlightenment during the four paths of learning.[313] The thirty-seven aspects consist of meditation on the four essential recollections,[314] the four aspects of correct renunciation,[315] the four aspects of miraculous power,[316] the five faculties,[317] the five powers,[318] the seven branches of enlightenment,[319] and the eightfold path.[320] The conduct of the bodhisattva is to act for the benefit of sentient beings out of compassion and loving-kindness. The result is the attainment of the two *kayas*.[321]

Vajrayana

As we have seen, there are six vehicles within the category of Vajrayana. Three outer tantras:

1. Kriyatantra
2. Upatantra (also referred to as Caryatantra)
3. Yogatantra

And three inner tantras:

1. Mahayoga
2. Anuyoga
3. Atiyoga

Outer Tantras

KRIYATANTRA

According to Kriyatantra, the view is that all phenomena are without essence. The activity is to keep very clean and utilize the three whites and three sweets.[322] The practice involves self-visualization as the commitment being (*dam tshig pa*), while visualizing the wisdom being (*ye shes pa*) in the sky in front. The relationship is like that of a subject to a king. One then receives blessings and spiritual attainments from the king-like wisdom deity in front. The path involves making offerings to the wisdom deity. The result is to attain the state of Vajradhara in sixteen lifetimes.

UPATANTRA

According to Upatantra, the view is to realize incisive knowledge (*shes rab*) without essence. The practice is basically the same as in Kriyatantra, self-visualization of oneself as the commitment being and visualization of the wisdom being in front. The relationship is like that of a friend or sibling. One receives blessings and spiritual attainments in this way. The result is attainment of the state of Vajradhara of the four families[323] in seven lifetimes.

YOGATANTRA

According to Yogatantra, the ultimate view is that all phenomena are completely free of elaborated characteristics and are empty luminosity. While all phenomena are in essence the nature of phenomena (*dharmata*), from the perspective of relative truth they are the mandalas of deities. The activity is not primarily concerned with cleanliness, as with the Kriyatantra and Upatantra. The focus is more upon the practice of meditation on the generation and completion stages, in which practitioners visualize themselves as the commitment being and invoke the wisdom being in front, which then dissolves into themselves. This is like water being poured into water. The result is attainment of the state of Vajradhara in three lifetimes.

DISTINCTION BETWEEN OUTER AND INNER TANTRAS

Tulku Thondup, in *Buddhist Civilization in Tibet*, clearly and concisely explains the difference between the outer and inner tantras:

> In the outer tantras the distinction between the Two Truths is maintained, divinities are not visualized with their female consorts, the five meats are not taken, and one does not attain the final result in this lifetime. In the inner tantras the Two Truths are held to be inseparable, all phenomena are equal, the five meats and five nectars are taken, the divinities are visualized with their consorts, and the final result can be attained in this life. The tantras of these three yanas are the special and distinctive Nyingmapa practices[324]

Inner Tantras

MAHAYOGA

According to Mahayoga, the view is the inseparability of appearances and emptiness. The method is to meditate on all appearances as being the mandala of the wisdom deity. The activity is the equality of pure and impure through the use of the five meats and five nectars. The result is the attainment of enlightenment in one lifetime or in the intermediate state (*bardo*).

ANUYOGA

According to Anuyoga, the view is to establish the three mandalas: the unborn mandala of the female consort Buddha Kuntu Zangmo, the wisdom mandala of the male consort Buddha Kuntu Zangpo, and the offspring of their inseparable union, the mandala of Great Exaltation. The conduct is to abide in evenness. The practice is that of the path of liberation and the path of skillful means, which includes working with channels (*rtsa*), vital energy (*rlung*), and essence (*thig le*). The result is the attainment of enlightenment in one lifetime.

ATIYOGA

According to Atiyoga, the Great Perfection, the view is that all phenomena are primordially and spontaneously enlightened. The conduct is to be without acceptance or rejection, since all phenomena are the display of dharmakaya. The practice is that of Cutting through Solidity (*khregs chod*), which is related to primordial purity (*ka dag*); and Direct Vision of Reality (*thod rgal*), which is related to spontaneous presence (*lhun grub*).

DETAILED REVIEW OF THE RESULTANT VEHICLES OF VAJRAYANA

As the writings of Dudjom Rinpoché relate mostly to the resultant vehicle of Vajrayana, it may be helpful to take a detailed look at these six Vajrayana vehicles. This detailed review is entirely based upon Dudjom Rinpoché's work *The Festival of Delight in Which the Expression of Eloquent Teachings Manifest*,[325] through the use of direct quotations and paraphrasing from the original Tibetan text.

There are six vehicles within the category of Vajrayana. The main attribute that makes these vehicles superior to even the Bodhisattva Vehicle is that the Bodhisattva Vehicle takes the cause of enlightenment—inherent Buddha-nature—as the path, whereas Vajrayana's sublime quality is to take the result as the path. His Holiness writes:

Therefore, in the vehicle of characteristics [that is, the vehicle of discourses, or Sutrayana] the nature of mind is simply known as the cause of enlightenment. Since it is held that enlightenment is attained through the condition of the increase of the two accumulations, and since the qualities manifested through purification (that cause enlightenment) are made into the path, it is called the causal vehicle (*rgyu'i theg pa*). Therefore, it is accepted that cause and result occur sequentially.

According to the vehicle of tantra (*sngags kyi theg pa*), the nature of mind primordially and naturally abides as the essence of the result, the embodiment of the wisdom bodies and wisdoms. Therefore, the nature of mind is established as the ground that exists within oneself in this present moment as the object to be attained. Entering into the realization of reality, as it is, removes temporary incidental stains. The nature of mind is established as the path from the perspective of recognition. It is established as the result from the perspective of actualizing the ground itself. In fact, since one does not distinguish a sequence in which a preceding cause is followed by a result, it is called the Resultant Vehicle (*'bras bu'i theg pa*) and Vajrayana (*rdo rje theg pa*). It is said in the *Secret Essence* (*gsang snying*):

> In any of the four times and ten directions
> The perfect Buddha will not be found.
> The nature of mind is the perfect Buddha.
> Do not search for Buddha anywhere else.

And,

> The most secret definitive result
> Constitutes the path.

Dudjom Rinpoché writes that in general, the extraordinary vehicles—those of Mantrayana[326]—are explained according to their:
1. essence (*ngo bo*)
2. definition of terms (*nges tshig*)
3. classification (*dbye ba*)

Explanation of the Tantric Vehicles
According to Their Essence

Regarding the explanation of the tantric vehicles from the perspective of essence, Dudjom Rinpoché writes:

> The teacher, Dorjé Chang, who taught the collection of teachings (*sde snod*) of the great vehicle of mantra, observed that cause and result are inseparable and spontaneously accomplished, manifesting as the nature of the truth of origination, which is the truth of the path; and as the nature of the truth of suffering, which is the truth of cessation. Therefore, with respect to action (*byed las*), the result is swiftly accomplished by practicing without accepting or rejecting anything within the natural state (*gnas lugs*) of the original ground (*gzhi*).

Explanation of the Tantric Vehicles
According to the Definition of Terms

Definition of Mantra

Regarding the explanation of the tantric vehicles from the perspective of defining the terms, what we in the West usually refer to as tantric or Vajrayana Buddhism is usually referred to in Tibetan as Secret Mantra (*gsangs sngag*), and in Sanskrit as the path of Mantrayana. This is why Dudjom Rinpoché now gives an explanation of the Sanskrit word *mantra*:

> The [Sanskrit word] *mana*, meaning "mind" [*yid*], and *traya*, meaning "protection" [*skyob*], become mantra, by combining the syllables, and from these words comes "protecting the mind" [*yid skyob* in Tibetan].

Definition of Collection of the Awareness-holders

The collection of Buddha's Word (*bka'*) related to the Mantrayana is called the Collection (*sde snod; pitaka*) of the Awareness-holders (*rig 'dzin; vidyadhara*) and also the Collection of the Vajrayana (*rdo rje theg pa*). According to Dudjom Rinpoché, *dé-nö* (*sde snod*) is the Tibetan translation of the Sanskrit *pitaka*, meaning "basket," or "container." It has been translated above as "collection." It is said that the collections of the three lower vehicles—of the hearers, solitary sages, and bodhisattvas—are gathered and perfected within the Awareness-holder, or Vajrayana, Collection. To support this assertion, Dudjom Rinpoché cites the *Tantra of the Extensive Version of the Magical Net (sgyu 'phrul drwa ba rgyas pa)*:

> As for the King of Awareness itself, which realizes the meaning of
> evenness:
> Just as all rivers flow into the vast ocean,
> In these vast skillful means that realize the unexcelled ultimate
> meaning,
> The inconceivable vehicles of liberation are all gathered.

The term "awareness-holder" (*rig 'dzin*) has many different meanings. According to Dudjom Rinpoché, in the context of the Mahayoga, awareness-holders are classified as four kinds:

1. awareness-holder of complete maturity (*rnam smin rig 'dzin*)
2. awareness-holder with the power over longevity (*tshe dbang ba'i rig 'dzin*)
3. awareness-holder of Mahamudra (*phyag chen po'i rig 'dzin*)
4. awareness-holder of spontaneous presence (*lhun grub rig 'dzin*)

Dudjom Rinpoché explains why the collection of Buddha's Word (*bka'*) related to the Mantrayana is called the *Collection of Awareness-holders* (*rig pa 'dzin pa'i sde snod*) as follows:

> It is called the "collection of awareness-holders" either because it
> is the basis of what an awareness-holder should study, or because
> they who enter this vehicle come to attain these common and
> supreme accomplishments.

Definition of Vajrayana

These six vehicles of Mantrayana are sometimes referred to as the Vajrayana, a name with which many Western practitioners are familiar. Dudjom Rinpoché defines the Sanskrit word *vajrayana* based on its Tibetan translation, *dorjé tekpa (rdo rje theg pa)*. *Dorjé* is understood to mean "indivisible" (*mi phyed pa*) and "indestructible" (*mi shigs pa*). That which is indivisible never moves from the nature of mind, which is the natural state (*gnas lugs*), no matter how samsara or enlightenment displays itself (*snang tshul*).

Dudjom Rinpoché explains the meaning of the word "indestructible" as follows:

> The mind of all Buddhas is indestructible because it is the essence of the nature of phenomena, which cannot be destroyed by any spiritual teaching based upon characteristics (*mtshan mar gyur pa'i chos*). Since it is similar to a dorjé, the wisdom mind of all Buddhas is called "dorjé" [indivisible and indestructible] and abides as the essence of mantra, as previously explained. The term *tekpa*, "vehicle," is used both literally and metaphorically, because it is either the support for the attainment of the mind of all Buddhas, or else the path traversed.

Definition of Tantra

Another term frequently used to refer to the Vajrayana is the Sanskrit word *tantra*, and its Tibetan translation *gyü* (*rgyud*), which according to Dudjom Rinpoché conveys the meaning of mind protection (*sems skyob*). *Tantra* has both the meaning of protecting the mind as well as of continuity. Dudjom Rinpoché explains the meaning of this important term as follows. Tantra means "mind protection" as it comes from two Sanskrit words, *cetana* and *traya*. *Cetana* is related to mind, while *traya* means "protection."

Dudjom Rinpoché cites the *Commentary on Difficult Points Entitled Endowed with Wisdom*:

> It is called "tantra" (*rgyud*) because it protects (*skyob*) the mind from thoughts. It is called the "tantric collection" (*rgyud sde*) because they form the collection (*tshogs*) or class (*rigs*) of the tantras (*rgyud*).

Tantra also refers to continuity, and is likened to the continuity of the strings of a lute (*pi wam*). Dudjom Rinpoché writes:

> It is also called "tantra" because it contains the naturally pure nature of phenomena of the mind from sentient beings to Bud-

dha, through the ground, path, and result, continuously abiding without interruption.

To give this scriptural support, Dudjom Rinpoché quotes from the *Matrix of Mystery* (*Guhyasamaja-tantra; gsang ba 'dus pa*):

> Tantra (*rgyud*) is called a continuity.
> There are three aspects of tantra:
> It is classified as ground, that ground's nature,
> And that which cannot be taken away.
> The aspect of the ground's nature (*rang bzhin*) is the cause.
> The ground is what is called skillful means (*thabs*) [that is, the path].
> Likewise, that which cannot be taken away is the result.
> The meaning of tantra (*rgyud*) is subsumed within these three.

Explanation of the Tantric Vehicles According to Classification

There are numerous ways to classify the tantric vehicles. Dudjom Rinpoché states that he uses the system that classifies the tantras into Kriyatantra, Caryatantra, Yogatantra, and Highest Yogatantra because this classification system presents these paths as methods for practitioners of different levels of ability. Dudjom Rinpoché quotes from the *Vajra Tent* (*Vajrapanjara-tantra; gur*):

> Kriyatantra (*bya ba'i rgyud*) is for those of lowest faculties; Caryatantra (*spyod pa'i rgyud*), for those who are superior; Yogatantra (*rnal 'byor rgyud*), for the supreme among sentient beings; and Highest Yogatantra (*rnal 'byor bla med*), for the highest.

Kriyatantra

Kriya means action since it mainly teaches the activity of body and speech. Dudjom Rinpoché writes:

> Its view is that ultimately, there are noble qualities through which one's very nature is realized to be pure and without conceptual elaborations of the four extremes,[327] and besides that, relatively, appearances are viewed as having the characteristics of

an utterly pure wisdom deity. One thereby uses the skillful
means of aspiring and striving toward spiritual attainment, which
is externally bestowed by the deity.

The key aspect of meditation in this context is for the practitioner to see
the external deity as master and the practitioner as servant. Dudjom Rinpoché quotes from the *Tantra of Self-Manifest Awareness* (*rig pa rang shar gyi rgyud*):

> Wisdom deity and pure practitioner
> are seen as master and servant, respectively.

Conduct, the activity of the Kriyatantra practitioner, is to please the deity
through offerings, cleanliness, fasting, and other austerities. The result is
the attainment of the state of a vajra-holder in sixteen lifetimes.

Dudjom Rinpoché lists some of the texts that set forth the practices of
Kriyatantra: *Tantra of the Dialogue with Subahu* (*dpung bzang*); *Tantra of
the Emergence of Tara* (*sgrol ma 'byung ba*); *King of the Three Commitments* (*dam tshig gsum rgyal*); and the *Subjugation of Demons* (*'byung po
'dul byed*).

Caryatantra

The key feature of Caryatantra (also known as Upatantra) is that it is practiced with the view of Yogatantra and the conduct of Kriyatantra. To support this point, Dudjom Rinpoché again quotes from the *Tantra of
Self-Manifest Awareness* (*rig pa rang shar gyi rgyud*):

> Upatantra is as follows:
> The view is that of Yogatantra,
> And the conduct is that of Kriyatantra.
> Therefore, it is known as the tantra of both.

In Upatantra, one practices meditation with characteristics by meditating on and one-pointedly joining one's mind to the syllables, mudras, and
forms of the deities. Through this process, samadhi is stabilized. The
Upatantra practitioner also engages in yoga without characteristics by placing the mind within ultimate reality. As the practitioner becomes accus-

tomed to this, many provisional results occur, such as the attainment of
the form of an awareness-holder. Ultimately, one actualizes the result of a
vajra-holder belonging to the four Buddha families (*rigs bzhi rdo rje*) either
in five lifetimes or after one or three eons.

According to Dudjom Rinpoché:

> The collections in which Upatantra is taught include the *Mani-
> fest Enlightenment of Vairocana* (*rnam par snang mdzad mngon
> par byang chub pa*), the *Empowerment of Vajrapani* (*phyang na
> rdo rje dbang bskur ba*), and so forth.

Yogatantra

Yogatantra emphasizes meditation, so it is called *yoga* tantra. To support
this with scripture, Dudjom Rinpoché quotes from *Synopsis of the Illumination of Suchness* (*de kho na nyid snang ba'i don bsdus*):

> This tantra is called "yogatantra" because it principally teaches
> samadhi meditation.

According to Dudjom Rinpoché, the view of Yogatantra is that the wisdom blessing—ultimate realization of the nature of all phenomena free
from elaborations as luminous emptiness—is seen relatively as the deity of
indestructible stainless space. The result is accomplished by endeavoring in
the acceptance of positive ideas and rejection of negative ones in relation to
that deity.

In the approach of Yogatantra, one meditates on oneself as the deity and
uses supporting conduct similar to that of Kriyatantra and Upatantra, such
as their emphasis on cleanliness. There are many provisional results associated with Yogatantra, such as becoming an awareness-holder of the Celestial Pure Land (*mkha' spyod rig pa 'dzin pa*). The ultimate result is the
attainment of Mahamudra in three or sixteen lifetimes. Afterward, Buddhahood is gradually attained on the level of the five Buddha families' pure
land of Dense Array (*rigs lnga stug po bkod*). Dudjom Rinpoché quotes
from *All-Creating King* (*kun byed rgyal po*):

> One who desires Yogatantra's pure land of Dense Array
> Is held to be liberated in three human lifetimes.

Dudjom Rinpoché writes that the collections in which these are taught include the *Embodiment of Suchness* (*de kho na nyid 'dus pa*) and the *Hundred and Fifty Verses on the Modes of Incisive Knowledge* (*shes rab tshul brgya lnga bcu pa*).

Tantras of Unsurpassable Union: Mahayoga, Anuyoga, Atiyoga

Dudjom Rinpoché explains that the Tantras of Unsurpassable Union (*rnal 'byor bla na med pa*) are superior to the three outer tantras of Kriya, Upa, and Yoga because these lower tantras are still similar to the vehicles of defining characteristics (for example, the Bodhisattva Vehicle) in that they are fettered by the dualistic perception of phenomena as being pure and defiled, thereby becoming involved in accepting what is pure and rejecting what is impure. In this way, they separate skillful means and wisdom because they are ignorant regarding the natural state (*gnas lugs*) of supreme exaltation. The Tantras of Unsurpassable Union are known as the "close path" (*nye ba'i lam*) and the "tantra of skillful means" (*thabs kyi rgyud*). When one enters this path, one is then connected with the result.

Therefore, on the path of the Tantras of Unsurpassable Union, the three poisons are not renounced as in the previous vehicles; instead, they are brought onto the path. Dudjom Rinpoché writes:

> In other vehicles the three poisons are renounced; here, by having driven in the nail of the non-conceptual view, the three poisons are brought into the path without being rejected—desire as the essence of empty exaltation, anger as the essence of empty luminosity, and ignorance as the essence of empty awareness. In this way, the skillful means by which the extraordinary level of oneness is accomplished in a single lifetime is amazing!

The Tantras of Unsurpassable Union are also superior to the other vehicles in that they teach the male and female deities in union as the inseparability of skillful means and wisdom.

Dudjom Rinpoché mentions that there are various classifications for the Tantras of Unsurpassable Union, and according to the Nyingma tradition they can all be subsumed within three subdivisions:

1. creation stage Mahayoga

2. perfection stage Anuyoga

3. Great Perfection stage Atiyoga

CREATION STAGE MAHAYOGA

VIEW

Mahayoga (*rnal 'byor chen po*) is called the creation stage of tantra. Dudjom Rinpoché defines Mahayoga as follows:

> Mahayoga, *naljor chenpo* [in Tibetan], is said to be far superior
> (*chenpo*) to outer Yogatantra because it connects (*jor*) the intellect to the meaning of non-duality [that is, genuineness (*nal*)].

Within Mahayoga, although there are numerous classes of both the tantra collection and the *sadhana* collection, Dudjom Rinpoché says that in this exposition he will explain Mahayoga based upon the explanations as found in the general tantra of the *Magical Net* (*sgyu 'phrul drwa ba*).[328] The natural state itself—the ground tantra (*gzhi rgyud*)—is established as the view to be realized. Dudjom Rinpoché explains:

> This view is not established through nominal, theoretical dialectics, but rather, it is established by three kinds of universally valid cognition and must be realized through direct perception of awareness itself.

PATH

The path of Mahayoga comprises two stages: skillful means and liberation.

PATH OF SKILLFUL MEANS

Through skillful means the practitioner brings the three poisons into the path and attains liberation. Dudjom Rinpoché describes this and gives a warning:

> Principally, the unique quality of skillful means is that one engages in the fearless conduct of practice directly subjugating the three poisons without rejecting them, and when one practices endowed with confidence in the view, not only is one not fettered,

one instead swiftly attains the result of liberation. On the other hand, if one cannot practice in this way, not only will liberation not be attained, instead there will be the great danger of falling into the lower realms. Therefore, there is great danger, as when preparing mercury.

PATH OF LIBERATION
The path of liberation is principally established through the three incisive knowledges: the wisdoms of study, reflection, and meditation.

VIEW ON THE PATH OF LIBERATION
The view is that through realization, the mind's fetters are purified and liberated within the vast expanse of the nature of phenomena. There is not the unique quality of speed as in the path of skillful means, the danger is less, but there is no difference in the result.

Dudjom Rinpoché describes the path of liberation as consisting of three aspects:

> The path of liberation has three aspects:
> The view characterized as knowing is the cause;
> The samadhi characterized as entering the path is the condition;
> The result brought about by the path is that of an awareness-holder.

The first has been described above. The second aspect of the path of liberation is samadhi. This includes devotional meditation and definitive perfection. The former [devotional meditation] is meditation as it brings into the path some aspects of mental images [of the deity] and devotion toward that deity. The latter refers to training until the five experiences of samadhi of both the creation and perfection stages are brought to completion.

Dudjom Rinpoché quotes from Vimalamitra's *Commentary on Meditation in Mudra:*[329]

> Agitation, attainment, familiarity, stability, and culmination
> are the five ways in which meditation arises.

MEDITATION ON THE PATH OF LIBERATION
As for meditation on the path of liberation, Dudjom Rinpoché cites the *Secret Essence Tantra (gsang ba'i snying po):*

Through their maturation during the stages of coming into
existence,
The aspects of the entrance are established to be five:
Because all that is substantial is awareness,
Death is [the moment of] the ultimate truth,
The intermediate state before rebirth is relative truth,
And the three stages of rebirth are non-dual truth.

Dudjom Rinpoché explains how Mahayoga perfectly shows the path that purifies at one and the same time death, the intermediate state, and the three stages of rebirth, and then describes the paths that correspond to this process. The path that is in accord with death's clear light is great emptiness. The path that is in accord with the intermediate state is great compassion. The paths that are in accord with the three stages of rebirth are, respectively, the sole mudra, the elaborate mudra, and the accomplishment of the assembled mandala [of deities].

TWO MODES OF PURIFICATION:
THE COARSE CREATION STAGE AND THE SUBTLE PERFECTION STAGE

In relation to meditation in Mahayoga, there are two modes of purification:

+ purification through the coarse creation stage (bskyed rim)
+ purification through the subtle perfection stage (*rdzogs rim*)

The Coarse Creation Stage. Dudjom Rinpoché explains that at the moment of death, the inner radiance of the dharmakaya manifests. In order to bring this into the path, one meditates upon the samadhi of ultimate reality— dharmakaya free from conceptual elaborations. If the clear light is not recognized, then one engages in the all-pervasive meditation on great compassion, the essence of the samadhi of all appearances, which are non-conceptual, that purifies temporary habits of the magic-like mental body during the intermediate state.

If one is not liberated during the intermediate state, then there are the coarse and subtle aspects of the sole mudra that purifies habitual tendencies from the time of conception in the womb until the moment of birth.

The samadhi of the causal basis—training in the seed syllables—is the essence of the process of purification of the intermediate state of taking existence. This is done by training in the seed syllables of the wisdom deities. From the time of entering the bardo of the union of the father's sperm and mother's egg until the moment the mental body awakens to the external sense objects at rebirth, one trains in the wisdom deity's body.

Next, there are four aspects for training in the elaborate seal that purifies habitual tendencies from birth to the time of becoming a mature adult—by emanation of mandalas, emanation of the assemblage of deities, emanation of numbers of wisdom deities (*grangs*), and emanation of the faces and arms of the wisdom deities.

Then the accomplishment of the gathered assemblage purifies the habitual tendencies from the time of becoming a mature adult to old age. This section has three aspects: apprehending the ground of accomplishment by the five aspects of excellence; doing the main practice with the four branches of approach and accomplishment; and demonstrating the time of accomplishing the result of an awareness-holder.

The Subtle Perfection Stage of Mahayoga. Dudjom Rinpoché describes five corresponding ways of purification according to the subtle perfection stage.

The first mode of purification is training that brings the previously mentioned five experiences to completion through meditation. This is done through two methods of resting:

1. resting in the immediacy of awareness, and
2. resting after insight.

Training in the immediacy of awareness means to have the key point related to the body, which is to abide in awareness so that while in meditation one will not even feel the prick of a thorn, since one rests in the fresh state of uncontrived awareness.

Resting after insight is to rest in the state of awareness after recalling the view that one has studied and reflected upon.

The second mode of purification is stamping the seal by not clinging to the forms of emptiness nor to whatever clear light phenomena appear at night.

The third mode of purification is stamping whatever phenomena arise with the sole seal of the wisdom deity's body. This is related to the melting bliss arising from the samadhi of beneficial great compassion that is impartial toward all phenomena.

The fourth mode of purification is through the vast increase of wisdom deity phenomena, to become accustomed to the deity's body, perfectly and distinctly—the main deity, retinue, and assembly—that is indivisible with all phenomena.

The fifth mode of purification relies on any mandala cluster in harmony with the creation stage—elaborated or unelaborated—in which male and female yogins and the male and female central deities in union are assembled; or the extremely unelaborated stage in which there is the inseparable union of the changeless great exaltation of the male wisdom consort and the emptiness endowed with all supreme aspects of the female wisdom consort.

RESULT

The third aspect of the path of liberation is the result: to become an awareness-holder. Dudjom Rinpoché explains that through meditating on the path of Mahayoga as previously described, the four kinds of awareness-holders included in the three untainted paths—of insight, meditation, and conclusion—are made manifest. The four kinds of awareness-holders are:

+ awareness-holder of maturation (rnam smin rig 'dzin)
+ awareness-holder with power over longevity (tshe dbang rig 'dzin)
+ awareness-holder of Mahamudra (phyag rgya rig 'dzin)
+ awareness-holder of spontaneous presence (lhun grub rig 'dzin)

Dudjom Rinpoché also mentions five kinds of awareness-holders of Mahamudra:

+ awareness-holder of indestructibility (*rdo rje rig 'dzin*)
+ awareness-holder of the wheel (*'khor lo rig 'dzin*)
+ awareness-holder of precious gems (*rin po che rig 'dzin*)
+ awareness-holder of the lotus (*pad ma'i rig 'dzin*)
+ awareness-holder of the sword (*ral gri'i rig 'dzin*)

Dudjom Rinpoché explains that the awareness-holder of spontaneous presence—such as the Lord of Secrets, Vajrapani—is superior over all others and is the spontaneous presence of the five kayas.

The final result includes the five kinds of wisdom body; the five kinds of wisdom speech; the five kinds of wisdom mind; the five kinds of noble qualities; and the five kinds of enlightened activity. The five kinds of wisdom body are:

1. dharmakaya
2. sambhogakaya
3. nirmanakaya
4. vajrakaya
5. manifest enlightenment kaya

The five kinds of wisdom speech are:
1. non-arising meaning
2. symbolic meaning
3. spoken word
4. inseparable indestructibility
5. of awareness's blessings

The five kinds of wisdom mind are:
1. wisdom of the dharmadhatu
2. wisdom of evenness
3. all-accomplishing wisdom
4. discerning wisdom
5. mirror-like wisdom

The five noble qualities are:
1. completely pure realm
2. dimensionless celestial palace
3. luminous and pure light rays
4. exalted throne
5. rapture of acting as desired

The five Buddha activities are:
   + pacification of suffering and its causes
   + expanding the excellent provisions
   + overpowering those who require training
   + annihilating those who are difficult to train
   + spontaneously accomplishing whatever occurs without effort

COLLECTIONS OF MAHAYOGA TEXTS
Dudjom Rinpoché writes that these teachings are found in two collections:
1. tantra collection (*rgyud sde*)
2. sadhana collection (means for accomplishment, *sgrub sde*)

The tantra collection includes the eight sections of the *Magical Net* (*sgyu 'phrul sde brgyad*), such as the *Tantra of the Magical Net of Vajrasattva* (*rdo rje sems dpa'i sgyu 'phrul drwa ba*).

The sadhana collection includes the eight general and specific sadhanas:
+ body: Manjushri (*'jam dpal sku*)
+ speech: the Lotus (*Hayagriva; rta mgrin*)
+ mind: Yangdak Héruka (*yang dak thugs*)
+ noble qualities: Vajra Nectar (*Vajra-amrita; bdud rtsi yon tan*);
+ enlightened activity: Vajrakilaya (*phur pa phrin las*)
+ liberating sorcery of Mamo (*ma mo rbod gtong*)
+ offering and praise to worldly deities (*'jig rten mchod bstod*)
+ mantras for the power activity of subjugation (*dmod pa drag sngags*).

TRANSMISSION ANUYOGA OF THE PERFECTION STAGE

Dudjom Rinpoché defines the Sanskrit word *anuyoga* as *jé su naljor* (*rjes su rnal 'byor*) in Tibetan, which can be translated into English as "conjunction yoga." Anuyoga is the connection between the creation stage of Mahayoga and the complete perfection stage of Atiyoga.

VIEW

The view of Anuyoga, as explained by Dudjom Rinpoché, is that all phenomena are, primordially and originally, perfectly enlightened as the root mandala of enlightened mind characterized as being the indivisibility of stainless space (*dbyings*) and wisdom (*ye shes*), in which the three kinds of mandalas are inseparable.

What are the three mandalas? The three mandalas are the ground of Anuyoga:
+ the primordial mandala of ultimate reality, which is related to the female consort Kuntu Zangmo
+ the naturally and spontaneously present mandala, which is related to the male consort Kuntu Zangpo
+ the root mandala of enlightened mind, which is related to the child of their supreme exaltation

PATH

The path of Anuyoga, and the ground mentioned above, are included within the three yogas:

+ yoga of the cause of activity (*bya ba rgyu'i rnal 'byor*)
+ yoga of the conditions that perform the activity (*byed pa rkyen gyi rnal 'byor*)
+ yoga of the result that is free from activity (*bya bral 'bras bu'i rnal 'byor*)

RESULT

The result of Anuyoga can be categorized in many ways. Regarding the final result of the path of Anuyoga, Dudjom Rinpoché quotes from the *Secret Discourse's Summation of Meaning* (*don bsdus*):

> The result is perfect Buddhahood,
> An infinity subsumed within twenty-five aspects
> Of wisdom body, speech, mind, noble qualities, and Buddha
>   activities;
> This is a spontaneously perfected omniscience.

COLLECTIONS OF ANUYOGA TEXTS

The collections in which Anuyoga are taught include: the *Four Root Discourses* (*rtsa ba'i mdo bzhi*), such as *All-Gathering Awareness* (*kun 'dus rig pa*); the *Six Tantras That Clarify the Six Parameters* (*mtha' drug gsal bar byed pa'i rgyud drug*); the *Twelve Rare Tantras* (*dkon rgyud bcu gnyis*); and the *Seventy Literary Transmissions* (*lung gi yi ge bdun bcu*).

UNLOCKING THE PROFOUND MEANING: THE INDISPENSABLE KEY OF THE SIX PARAMETERS AND FOUR METHODS OF INTERPRETATION

Dudjom Rinpoché next explains—before entering into an explanation of Great Perfection—that the extraordinary tantras, scriptures, pith instructions, and definitive secret tantras that contain the extremely profound vajra words have never been established through reasoning or scriptural authority of nominal sophistry. Instead, the indispensable key that unlocks the meaning of these extraordinary texts are the six parameters (*mtha' drug*) and four methods of interpretation (*tshul bzhi*).

SIX PARAMETERS

Why are these referred to as the "six parameters"? Because all secret words and meanings in tantra are appraised using these six ways of understanding. Nothing goes beyond these parameters. The six parameters that characterize the tantras are their:

+ provisional meaning
+ definitive meaning
+ implied meaning
+ unimplied meaning
+ literal meaning
+ non-literal meaning

Dudjom Rinpoché points out that a single phrase of vajra words may contain many different meanings directed toward those who realize or do not realize the ultimate meaning of things.

The first of the six parameters is the provisional meaning. This refers to skillful means needed in the context of introducing the inner structure of mandalas, symbols, hand gestures, burnt offerings, the creation stage, and tantric feasts.

The second parameter, the definitive meaning, is given in the context of texts that teach the channels, winds, and *bindus* of the perfection stage, and also the natural state of naturally luminous mind.

The third parameter is the use in texts of implied meaning, which is of three types:

+ time
+ meaning
+ intention

For instance, the first type of implied meaning, related to time, is exemplified by the statement from the *Reciting the Names of Manjushri*:

Completely enlightened in one instant.

The second type of implied meaning, related to meaning, is when what is said means something else. Dudjom Rinpoché gives the following example from the *Great Magical Display Tantra*:

Having stolen her from all the Buddhas,
The noble daughter of the sublime deity should be enjoyed.

Dudjom Rinpoché explains that this means one must enjoy the mother of all Buddhas, Prajnaparamita, sublime transcendent wisdom.

The third type of implied meaning is related to intention. Dudjom Rinpoché gives the following example from the Hévajra Tantra:

You should kill living beings.

In this case, "living beings" represents clinging to self, so the statement really means that you should eliminate self-clinging.

The fourth parameter, where the meaning is not implied but obvious, is given in the following example by Dudjom Rinpoché:

You should not kill living beings.
You should not tell lies.

The fifth parameter is the literal meaning and refers to those texts that should be taken literally, such as ritual texts that include mandalas, burnt offerings, tormas, and so forth.

The sixth parameter is the non-literal meaning and refers to texts written in the symbolic language of the Buddhas. Dudjom Rinpoché gives the example of the word *ali-kali*. This usually refers to the vowels (*ali*) and consonants (*kali*) of the Tibetan alphabet, but is also code for sexual union and liberation.

FOUR METHODS OF INTERPRETATION

Dudjom Rinpoché explains that the four methods of interpretation that characterize the tantras are:
1. literal method
2. general method
3. concealed method
4. ultimate method

First, the literal method is based on texts of grammar and logic.
Second, the general method is of three kinds:

1. the general method that counteracts regret regarding having entered and practiced lower vehicles
2. the general method that counteracts regret regarding involvement in the inner tantras due to thinking that the conduct involved with these tantras is debased because it lacks cleanliness and other aspects of purity and so forth, as found in the lower vehicles
3. the general method related to the creation stage, since creation stage meditation is common to both the creation and perfection stages and includes meditation on the celestial palaces, wisdom deities, and so forth

Third, is the concealed method. This refers to teachings and practices that are concealed from novices so they do not create wrong views for themselves.

Fourth is the ultimate method. This refers to the conclusion of the path, which is the perfection stage of luminosity, or ultimate reality.

Dudjom Rinpoché explains that these four methods of interpretation are utilized because a single phrase of vajra words can be understood according to the faculties of different practitioners, and without possessing the pith instructions, one cannot realize the real secret key point. If one possesses these four methods to aid in the interpretation of a text, then one can easily come to realize the wisdom mind of the secret Vajrayana.

GREAT PERFECTION ATIYOGA

The Great Perfection is the culmination of all paths to be traversed and the summit of all vehicles. Dudjom Rinpoché explains the Great Perfection in two sections:
superiority of the Great Perfection over the lower vehicles
its classifications

SUPERIORITY OF THE GREAT PERFECTION

Dudjom Rinpoché explains that the Great Perfection is superior to the lower vehicles because:

> This king among vehicles holds stainless space—the originally pure nature of mind whose nature is clear light, the naturally present changeless self-manifest wisdom that is naturally and

spontaneously present in oneself—to be the original ground of the Great Perfection.

In contrast, the eight lower vehicles are based upon intellectual contrivance and fabrication. Dudjom Rinpoché explains that from the perspective of the Great Perfection:

> The eight lower levels have intellectually fabricated and contrived that which is changeless solely due to fleeting thoughts that never experience what truly is. They apply antidotes to and reject that which is not to be rejected. They refer to as flawed that in which there is nothing to be purified, with a mind that desires purification. They have created division, with respect to that which cannot be obtained, by their hopes and fears that it can be obtained elsewhere. And they have obscured wisdom, which is naturally present, by their efforts in respect to that which is free from effort and free from needing to be accomplished. Therefore, they have had no chance to make contact with genuine ultimate reality as it is (*rnal ma'i de kho na nyid*).

Therefore, the natural Great Perfection, which refers to the nature of mind that transcends mind, is superior to the eight lower vehicles, which are created and fabricated by the mind. Dudjom Rinpoché further explains:

> In this way, the natural Great Perfection is present as the nature of mind that transcends ordinary mind, as the uncompounded clear light of wisdom that is awareness, such as that all noble qualities of the essential nature are spontaneously present.

It is this extremely rare and precious summit of all Buddhist teachings—the Great Perfection—that Dudjom Rinpoché is "placing in the palm of our hand" in the text *Essential Advice for Solitary Meditation Practice*.

EXPLANATION OF THE TERM "GREAT PERFECTION" (DZOGCHEN)

Nowadays, the term "Great Perfection" is quite common among Buddhist practitioners, but what does this term actually mean? Dudjom Rinpoché explains it as follows:

It is called the Great Perfection (*Dzogchen*) because it refers to self-manifest wisdom, unrestricted and without extremes, in which the meaning of all vehicles abides and is *perfected* (*dzog*) in a single essence; or it is called the Great Perfection because all enlightened phenomena are *perfected* (*dzog*) within the present natural state of awareness, the nature of phenomena, without deliberate analysis by means of mental fixation.

DEFINITION OF THE SANSKRIT TERM *ATIYOGA* (HIGHEST YOGA)

As for the definition of the word *atiyoga*, Dudjom Rinpoché writes:

[The Sanskrit] word *ati* means *shintu* in Tibetan ["very" or "extremely" in English]. It also carries the connotations of "supreme," "highest," "perfection," "pinnacle," and "innermost essence." The [Sanskrit] word *yoga* means [in Tibetan] *naljor* (*rnal 'byor*) ["union" in English]. Since it is the culmination of all yogas it is called *shintu naljor* [in Tibetan, *atiyoga* in Sanskrit], the "highest yoga." Since it is the essence of all aspects of the perfection stage (*dzog rim*), there is nothing else to be traversed higher than this. This is indicated by the word "great" [*chenpo* in Tibetan] since through it the unborn nature of phenomena—which is like the sky, extremely vast and difficult to examine—is directly pointed out.

CLASSIFICATIONS

DIVISIONS OF ATIYOGA

+ Atiyoga has three divisions:
+ Mind Class (*sems sde*)
+ Vast Expanse Class (*klong sde*)
+ Pith Instruction Class (*man ngag sde*)

Dudjom Rinpoché explains these as follows:

The Mind Class teaches that all phenomena are liberated from the extreme of being an object of renunciation because they are none other than the nature of mind. The Vast Expanse Class teaches that all conditioned phenomena are free of activity and are liberated from the extreme of needing antidotes because they are perfectly encompassed within the vast expanse of the female Buddha Kuntu Zangmo, the nature of phenomena. The Pith Instruction Class teaches that the defining characteristics of truth are liberated from both extremes—being an object of renunciation or in need of an antidote—because they are established according to ultimate reality as it is.

MIND CLASS (*SEMS SDE*)

Dudjom Rinpoché describes the Mind Class as follows:

> The philosophical approach of the Mind Class is that the compounded truth of the path—which is conditioned and fettered by firm perceptions that cling to the stages of vehicles, the two truths, the six *paramitas*, the two stages, and so forth—is resolved in vast stainless space, liberated from aspects of cause and result, virtuous and harmful actions, and acceptance or rejection, to be the wisdom of great purity and evenness—the original stainless space of phenomena that is the nature of enlightened mind, or the essential nature of ultimate truth free from conceptual elaboration. To put it concisely, all phenomena that dualistically appear within subject and object are transcended.

The distinctive attribute of the Mind Class is that mind is self-liberated at the very moment it arises. Dudjom Rinpoché quotes from *All-Creating King*:

> Phenomenal existence, the universe and beings contained within,
> All Buddhas and sentient beings
> Are created by mind...

Dudjom Rinpoché summarizes the philosophical approach of the Mind Class as follows:

> All conditioned phenomena that appear are perfected within the stainless space of enlightened mind—*dharmata*—without having

to apply the seal of *dharmata* to all phenomena that appear. The awareness of appearances as simply the display (*rtsal*) or play (*rol pa*) [of *dharmata*] accompanies them without identifying them as such.

Dudjom Rinpoché supports this by citing the glorious Naropa:

The nature of diverse phenomena
Is *dharmata*, thereby inseparable.
Therefore, in the luminous nature of mind—wisdom mind,
In which [appearances and *dharmata*] are indivisible—
Everything that appears is *dharmata*.
The essence of everything that appears
Is seen as the very heart of wisdom
And is inexpressible in its very essence.

CLASSIFICATION OF TEXTS

Dudjom Rinpoché explains that although the tantras of the Mind Class of Atiyoga consist of millions of verses, they can be subsumed within various classification systems. For instance, they can be subsumed within the *Three Vast Expanses* (*klong gsum po*):

1. *Vast Expanse of the Inexpressibility of the Nature of Phenomena* (*chos nyid brjod du med pa'i klong*)
2. *Vast Expanse in Which the View Is Not Non-existent* (*lta ba min pa med pa'i klong*)
3. *Vast Expanse in Which There Is No Conduct* (*spyod pa yin pa med pa'i klong*)

The Mind Class texts can also be classified as 1,003 supreme sections of tantras entitled: *Fifty Unerring Nails of Dharmata* (*chos nyid la 'chugs pa med pa'i gzer bu lnga bcu*); *Five Hundred and Eleven Situations in Which Objects Are Viewed as Mind* (*yul sems la lta ba'i gnas lnga brgya bcu gcig*); *Twenty Thousand Simultaneous Distinctions between Appearances and Mind* (*snang sems cig char du shan 'byed pa khri phrag gnyis*); *Fifty Thousand Resolutions Regarding the View of Direct Vision* (*lta ba thod rgal du la bzla ba lnga khri*); and *One Thousand Situations That Cut through Concepts of Being in Meditation* (*sgom yod rtog pa gcod pa'i gnas chig stong*).

VAST EXPANSE CLASS (*KLONG SDE*)

Dudjom Rinpoché explains the Vast Expanse Class as follows:

> In the vast expanse of female Buddha Always Noble (Kuntu
> Zangmo)—self-manifest wisdom, the nature of phenomena—all
> conditioned phenomena that appear are simply the ornaments of
> that array's manifestation in and of itself. Other than this, phe-
> nomena do not exist as bound or liberated nor as objects that arise
> or their arising. Phenomena are not considered to appear as the
> display or play of mind as in the Mind Class. The philosophical
> approach of the Vast Expanse Class is to establish with certainty
> the infinity of primordial liberation without any analysis of
> whether they have dependent existence, lack existence, are non-
> existent, or whether they are pure or impure.

To support this explanation, Dudjom Rinpoché cites the Lama Naropa's
Means for Attaining Ultimate Reality As It Is (*de kho na nyid sgrub pa'i
thabs*):

> Effortless, non-conceptual awareness—
> An uncontrived expanse of exaltation—manifests in and of itself.
> It manifests as the spontaneously present expanse of wisdom,
> Naturally occurring and pervasive as the sky.
>
> This enlightened mind's display that manifests in and of itself
> Is wisdom magic's expanse of exaltation.
> It actually radiates as wisdom awareness-holders,
> Who are a self-occurring magical manifestation.

CLASSIFICATION OF TEXTS

As for the texts of the Vast Expanse Class, according to Dudjom Rinpoché
there are considered to be eleven thousand chapters and six million four
hundred thousand verses, subsumed under the titles of three thousand
tantras that extensively teach the way of the Vast Expanse Class. These can
be included in the *Eighty Thousand Aspects of Reaching a Final Decision*
(*la bzla ba khri phrag brgyad*). They are also subsumed within *Twenty
Thousand Aspects of Distinction* (*shan 'byed khri phrag gnyis*). They can

also be condensed within *Nine Hundred Conclusions* (*'gag dgu brgya*). If the *Two Thousand Essentials* (*gnad nyis stong*) and the *Fifty Nails* (*gzre bu lnga bcu*) are included, they are subsumed within three categories: *Liberation from Activity* (*byas grol*), *Liberation in the Establishment [of Reality]* (*bzhag grol*), and *Naked Liberation* (*cer grol*).

PITH INSTRUCTION CLASS (*UPADESHA*)

SUPERIORITY OVER THE MIND CLASS AND THE VAST EXPANSE CLASS

Dudjom Rinpoché explains that the Pith Instruction Class is superior to the Mind Class and the Vast Expanse Class. The Mind Class emphasizes the profound aspect, emptiness rather than luminosity. There is not the realization of the display of luminosity as being the nature of phenomena. This can lead to a subtle clinging to deliberate examination.

In the Vast Expanse Class, although the profound and luminous aspects have both been accomplished, thereby avoiding the pitfall of deliberate examination that clings to the nature of phenomena, one can nearly become lost in a pitfall on the side of emptiness. On the other hand, according to Dudjom Rinpoché, the Pith Instruction Class is superior to both the Mind Class and Vast Expanse Class because from its point of view, all phenomena appear from the spontaneous natural display (*rtsal*)—the radiant manifestation in and of itself of the primordially pure inexpressible essence, the great transcendence of ordinary mind—and are gathered within the stainless space that is the nature of phenomena free from elaborations.

Dudjom Rinpoché cites the *Supreme Array of Ati* (*a ti bkod pa chen po*) to support this claim of the superiority of the Pith Instruction Class:

> O Vajrapani!
> If the Pith Instruction Class is not established,
> There will be those who cling to deliberate examination
> And, in particular, those who will believe in nothing at all.
> Therefore, this definitive secret essence—
> Like a butter lamp amid darkness,
> Like an elephant among oxen,
> Like a lion among wild animals,
> Or like a horseman among those on foot—
> Is superior to them all.

Dudjom Rinpoché further explains that the Pith Instruction Class is in no way a dualistic approach. It is inconceivable and inexpressible, and goes directly to the essential point. This is supported by citing Manjushri:

> Awareness is utterly luminous by nature,
> Originally pure as the sky.
> Primordially, the characteristics of phenomena have been abandoned.
> There is neither phenomena nor the nature of phenomena:
> It is similar to substanceless space,
> Free from all words and letters.

CLASSIFICATION OF THE PITH INSTRUCTION CLASS

The Pith Instruction Class can be classified into three categories:
1. random (*kha 'thor*)
2. oral tradition (*kha gtam*)
3. teaching that accords with its own textual tradition of the tantras (*rgyud rang gzhung du bstan pa*)

RANDOM

The first is the random category of Pith Instructions. Dudjom Rinpoché writes:

> Wisdom that transcends ordinary mind instantaneously manifests without regard for differentiation or exclusion. Its subdivisions are twofold: from the perspective of the establishment of ultimate reality there is the Pith Instruction That Concludes the Path (*bzhag pa lam gyi mtha' gcod pa'i man ngag*); and from the perspective of liberation there is the Pith Instruction That Actualizes the Pure Path (*grol ba tobs dag pa lam mngon gyur gyi man ngag*).

ORAL TRADITION

The second is the oral instruction category of Pith Instructions. Dudjom Rinpoché explains:

> Its essence is free from ordinary mind and is undeluded. Its nature undermines the source of thoughts. Its characteristics are

unidentifiable. Its subdivisions are twofold: the oral tradition that permeates all discourse (*gleng ba yongs la bor ba'i kha gtam*); and the oral tradition that unpredictably expresses in speech (*khar phog dus med pa'i kha gtam*).

TEACHING THAT ACCORDS WITH ITS OWN TEXTUAL TRADITION OF THE TANTRAS

The third category of Pith Instructions is the teaching that accords with its tantras' own textual tradition. Dudjom Rinpoché explains:

> Its essence is that it is the source of all Buddha's Words. Its nature is that since it is free of samsara and enlightenment, it is effortless, without an object to accept or reject. Since the nature of phenomena does not abide in words or language, it is untouched by debates about emptiness.

The subdivisions of this category of Pith Instructions are fourfold:
1. n a manner of full summation of the view (*lta ba sgang dril ba*)
2. in a manner of blood-letting that removes hindrances (*gtar ga gegs sel ba*)
3. in a manner of revealing the hidden (*gab pa ngon du phyung pa*)
4. in a manner of naturally clear explanations (*bshad pa rang gsal gyi tshul*).

TEXTS OF THE PITH INSTRUCTION CLASS

As for the texts of the Pith Instruction Class, Dudjom Rinpoché writes that in the Buddha's Words it is said that there are infinite categories of Pith Instruction texts. These categories include the four categories of the Pith Instruction Class that are subsumed into the Three Vast Expanses:
1. Vast Expanse of Ceaseless Display (*rol pa 'gag pa med pa'i klong*)
2. Vast Expanse in Which There Is Nothing Not Liberated in Ordinary Mind (*blo la ma grol ba med pa'i klong*)
3. Vast Expanse in Which the Essence Is Neither Good Nor Bad (*ngo bo la bzang ngan med pa'i klong*)

The essence of the Pith Instructions is also fourfold:
1. revealing the key point (*gnad bkrol ba*)

2. distilling the principles (*'gag bsdam pa*)
3. pointing out [awareness] (*ngo sprad pa*)
4. striking the manifest naturally vital point (*mngon sum rang gnad la dbab pa*)

THE VIEW AND PATH OF THE PITH INSTRUCTION CLASS

According to the tradition of the Pith Instruction Class of the Great Perfection, it is considered to be the essence, the heart of all teachings, because it directly uses one's own awareness as the object of practice. Dudjom Rinpoché explains this as follows:

> One's own awareness itself is the domain that is cultivated as wisdom. It transcends the mind that has the nature of the eight consciousnesses of conditioned grasping (*zag pa bcas pa'i nye bar len pa*).

Dudjom Rinpoché points out the necessity of directing one's intention toward awareness that transcends mind and also points to the importance of distinguishing between mind and wisdom. To emphasize this, Dudjom Rinpoché cites the scriptural authority of the Great Perfection tantra *The Lion's Perfect Display* (*seng ge rtsal rdzogs*):

> Habitual tendencies in relation to mind and wisdom are insubstantial.
> Although wisdom has been freed from all habitual tendencies,
> Mind amasses diverse habitual tendencies.
> If you do not distinguish between mind and wisdom,
> The root of objective phenomena is not cut through.
> Therefore, although the nature of phenomena is free of circumstances, it becomes difficult to realize.

A very special feature of the Pith Instruction Class is the four modes of liberation:
1. primordial liberation (*ye grol*)
2. self-liberation (*rang grol*)
3. naked liberation (*cer grol*)
4. liberation from extremes (*mtha' grol*)

Dudjom Rinpoché explains these four modes of liberation as follows:

> This very awareness, from time immemorial, is primordially liberated because its very essence is untainted by samsaric phenomena so that the perpetual cause (*nyer len gyi rgyu*) of existence has ceased.
>
> It is self-liberated because—uncontrived by any antidote—all that arises is liberated independent of any other liberating activities, like a snake's knot naturally uncoiling.
>
> It is directly liberated, because all consciousnesses of the eight aggregates are naturally liberated with great instantaneous lightening-like suddenness, without the duality of subject and object.
>
> It is liberated from extremes because it does not abide within the three times or as anything knowable.

CUTTING THROUGH SOLIDITY (TREKCHÖ) AND DIRECT VISION (TÖGAL)

Dudjom Rinpoché now explains that for this to be appropriately realized, one must proceed upon two paths: Cutting through Solidity, or *Trekchö* (*khregs chod*), and Direct Vision of Reality, or *Tögal* (*thod rgal*). Cutting through Solidity establishes the primordially pure abiding nature, while Direct Vision of Reality establishes the spontaneously present visionary experiences. A detailed discussion of Cutting through Solidity and Direct Vision of Reality is beyond the scope of this introduction and is best received directly from a qualified Great Perfection master.

REVIEW OF THE RESULTANT VEHICLES

Dudjom Rinpoché now reviews the outer and inner tantras in order "to facilitate understanding." Because much of this material is not actually covered in the general overview just completed, and because it adds greatly to an understanding of the nine vehicles, it is worthwhile exploring this section.

Distinction between the Outer and Inner Tantras

The first section of Dudjom Rinpoché's review succinctly describes the distinctions between the outer and inner tantras. There are five distinctions according to the Nyingma tradition as represented by Lord Dropukpa (*rje sgro phug pa*), who brought together the intention of the four pillars—the spiritual sons of Zurchungpa.[330] The five distinctions between the outer and inner tantras are by way of:

+ view
+ the way that spiritual attainment is received
+ empowerments
+ conduct
+ results

Distinction: View

Dudjom Rinpoché quotes Lord Dropukpa:

> As for the distinction of the view: In the inner tantric vehicles the nature of mind is realized to be the supreme nature (*bdag nyid chen po*); and in the outer tantric vehicles there is no such realization. As it is said in Indrabhuti's *Array of the Path* (*lam rnam bkod pa*):
>
>> Since those who hold to the three Buddha families and five Buddha families do not realize the supreme nature (*bdag nyid chen po*),
>> I have spoken of them as being the same as the common vehicles.[331]

Distinction: How Spiritual Attainment Is Received

As for the second distinction, how spiritual attainment is received: In the outer tantric vehicles spiritual attainment is requested by aspiring toward and attending upon the wisdom deity; in the inner tantric vehicles spiritual attainment is held to be naturally present because, through realization of the supreme nature, the nature of mind manifests in and of itself as the mandala of wisdom bodies and wisdom. As it is said in the *Questions and Answers of Vajrasattva* (*rdo rje sems dpa'i zhus lan*):

> In reply to the question, "What is the distinction between the yogins of the outer and inner Mantrayana in regard to receiving spiritual attainment?," [Vajrasattva said]:

For example, just as a king has commanded his minister,
Outer tantra's method is to bestow spiritual attainment from
above.
As a king holds dominion once the kingdom is offered by his
subjects,
Self-originating Great Perfection is the unsurpassable way.

And as it is said in the Secret Essence:

This wondrous, magical, amazing phenomena...

And so on.

Distinction: Empowerments

As for the third distinction, that of empowerments: The outer tantric vehicles are unable to obtain the three higher sublime empowerments, and the inner tantric vehicles are principally invested with these three.

Distinction: Conduct

As for the fourth distinction, that of conduct: The inner tantric vehicles can perform conduct in which the twenty samsaric phenomena are embraced through skillful means, and the outer tantric vehicles cannot.

Distinction: Result

As for the fifth distinction, their result: The outer tantric vehicles can unite a practitioner with the result (full enlightenment) in three, five, or seven lifetimes and so forth, and the inner tantric vehicles can unite a practitioner in this life.

A Concise Review of the Three Higher Vehicles

Next, Dudjom Rinpoché gives a concise review of each of the six tantric vehicles:
The three lower vehicles:
1. Kriya
2. Upa
3. Yoga

and the three higher vehicles:
1. Maha
2. Anu
3. Ati

As Dudjom Rinpoché's writings translated for this book deal primarily with the three higher vehicles—the vehicles of the inner tantras of skillful means—I will take this opportunity to explore them through Dudjom Rinpoché's concise review.

Dudjom Rinpoché lists the three inner tantras as:
1. Mahayoga tantras (*rgyud ma ha yo ga*)
2. Anuyoga transmissions (*lung a nu yo ga*)
3. Atiyoga pith instructions (*man ngag a ti yo ga*)

Distinction of the Three Inner Tantric Vehicles Based upon View

Concerning the distinctions between these three, Dudjom Rinpoché quotes Lord Zurchungpa's (*rje zur chung pa*) reply to a question raised by Lenchab Barwa (*glan chab bar ba*):

> Mahayoga manifests as the magical display (*cho 'phrul*) of awareness. Anuyoga manifests as one's own awareness's (*rang rig*) dynamic energy (*rtsal*). Atiyoga is the manifestation (*rang snang*) of awareness in and of itself. Garab Dorjé has said:
>
>> [The three inner tantric vehicles refer respectively to] magical display, dynamic energy, and manifestation in and of itself.

Dudjom Rinpoché explains these three inner vehicles' distinctive qualities in terms of view:

> Mahayoga realizes all phenomena to be the magical display of the nature of mind, the inseparability of appearance and emptiness. Anuyoga realizes all phenomena as the dynamic energy of the nature of mind, the non-duality of stainless space and wisdom. Atiyoga realizes all phenomena to be the manifestation in

and of itself of the nature of mind, self-manifest wisdom that is primordially without birth or cessation. This was held to be the most precious point by both Datik Chö Shakya[332] and Lenchab Barwa.

Kyo Gong Bupa said:

> The inner tantric vehicles place a greater or lesser emphasis on view, meditation, and conduct:
> Conduct is most important for Mahayoga.
> Samadhi [that is, meditation] is most important for Anuyoga.
> View is most important for Atiyoga.

Also, Lharjé Rok said:[333]

> It is called creation stage Mahayoga because the wisdom deity is generated by means of the three samadhis.
> It is called perfection stage Anuyoga because the deity is generated in a perfect way not depending upon the three samadhis.
> It is called Great Perfection Atiyoga without creation because it is free from both creation and perfection stages.
> Alternatively, Mahayoga is strongly focused upon the ten factors of tantra.[334] Anuyoga has less fixation on them, and Atiyoga is free of fixation on them.

And Menyak Jung-drak said:[335]

> Though the three aspects of creation and perfection are present in each vehicle, Mahayoga emphasizes the creation stage; Anuyoga emphasizes the perfection stage; and Great Perfection is free from both their efforts.

Chal-lo Kunga Dorjé also eloquently described this as the distinction between these terms' definitions.

In *The Great Chariot*, the supreme, omniscient Longchenpa has said:

> Mahayoga father tantras are the nature of skillful means of

appearances helpful to disciples who are predominantly angry and have many thoughts. Anuyoga mother tantras are the incisive knowledge of the perfection stage that is the ultimate reality of emptiness helpful to those who are predominantly desirous and delight in the stillness of mind. It is taught that Atiyoga is the nature of non-duality helpful to those who are predominantly ignorant and energetic. In the *Vast Array* it is said:

> The creation stage is for those who would transcend mind. The perfection stage is for those who would possess the very essence of mind. And the Great Perfection is for those who are supreme and most secret.

In *Resting in the Nature of Mind* (*sems nyid ngal so*), the omniscient Longchenpa also said:

> Mahayoga emphasizes vital energy (*rlung*) and the skillful means of the creation stage.
> Anuyoga emphasizes the elements and the incisive knowledge of the perfection stage.
> Atiyoga emphasizes the wisdom of the non-duality of everything.

A Concise Review of Mahayoga

Dudjom Rinpoché explains the Mahayoga vehicle within the context of:

- ✦ essence (*ngo bo*)
- ✦ definition of terms (*nges tshig*)
- ✦ classification (*dbye ba*)

Essence

Dudjom Rinpoché describes Mahayoga's essence:

> Its nature is that liberation is attained through the application of realization and familiarization in the inseparable meaning of superior truth by predominant reliance upon the creation stage of skillful means.

Definition of Terms

Dudjom Rinpoché defines the term Mahayoga (*rnal 'byor chen po*):

> The Tibetan term *naljor chenpo* (*rnal 'byor chen po*) comes from
> the [Sanskrit] *mahayoga* [in English, "superior union with gen-
> uineness"]. It is far superior to the outer yogas because it unites
> (*'byor*) the mind to non-dual truth.

Classification

The Mahayoga vehicle is classified according to six topics:
1. the twofold entrance: through empowerments and the actual entrance
   of the threefold meditative contemplation
2. view
3. discipline
4. meditation
5. conduct
6. result

TWOFOLD ENTRANCE

First, empowerment is the entrance into Mahayoga. In relation to Mahayoga there are four empowerments. In addition to the vase empowerment
that occurs in common with the three outer tantras, there are also the three
supreme uncommon empowerments: the secret empowerment, wisdom
empowerment, and the "fourth empowerment."

Second, the actual entrance is through the threefold meditative contemplation:
1. the yoga of great emptiness: incisive knowledge
2. the magical display of compassion: skillful means
3. the subtle and coarse symbols

Dudjom Rinpoché supports this by citing the *Tantra of Self-Manifest
Awareness* (*rig pa rang shar gyi rgyud*):

> The entrance is the threefold meditative contemplation.

VIEW

Second, the view of Mahayoga. Dudjom Rinpoché explains the view as follows:

> Ultimate truth is held to be awareness manifesting without elaboration, spontaneously accomplished as the essential cause. Relative truth is held to be that all thoughts that are the display (*rtsal*) of that awareness manifest in and of themselves as a mandala of wisdom bodies and wisdom. Neither ultimate nor relative truth is biased toward emptiness or phenomena because their essence manifests as an indivisible evenness. When we use the conventional expression "indivisible," this refers to an indivisibility that is free from being within the field of one's experience, since it transcends being an object of thought or expression that perceives it. Accordingly, it is said in the *Array of the Path* (*rnam bkod*):

> > The truth of the superior indivisibility of evenness,
> > While it is indeed shown everywhere by terms,
> > Actually transcends being an object of thought or speech.

> It is said in *Stages of the Path*:

> > To be freed from clinging to these terms,
> > Thought and expression are transcended within both conventional designations.

DISCIPLINE

Third, the discipline of Mahayoga. Dudjom Rinpoché states that according to the Nyingma tradition:

> It is said that there are twenty-eight tantric commitments (*samaya*) of Mahayoga. In the *Magical Key of Further Discernment* (*yang 'byed 'phrul mig gyi lde*) it says:

> > As for the limits guarded by Mahayoga:
> > There are the three sets of root tantric commitments and
> > the twenty-five branches to guard.

The root tantric commitments are those of wisdom body, speech, and mind. The branch tantric commitments are given in the *Magical Key of Further Discernment*:

> There are those to be practiced, those not to be given up, those to be accepted, those to be known, and those to be accomplished.

MEDITATION

Fourth, the meditation of Mahayoga. Dudjom Rinpoché explains that there are two traditions:

+ sadhana class (*sgrub sde*)
+ tantra class (*rgyud sde*)

SADHANA CLASS

There are five classes of sadhanas of the wisdom deities as described by Dudjom Rinpoché:

1 *Sadhana for Attaining the Wisdom Body of the Joyful Buddhas by Relying on the Four Centers of the Wisdom Body of Manjushri ('jam dpal gyi sku 'khor lo bzhi la brten nas bde gshegs sku'i sgrub pa)*

2 *Sadhana of Lotus Speech by Relying on the Three Neighs of Hayagriva (rta mgrin gyi rta skad thengs gsum la brten nas pad ma gsung gi sgrub pa)*

3 *Sadhana of Indestructible Mind by Relying on the Authentic and Sole Accomplishment, Awareness, Naturally Present Wisdom, Which Is the Mind of Yangdak (yang dag gi thugs rig pa rang byung gi ye shes yang dag grub pa gcig pu la brten nas thugs rdo rje'i sgrub pa)*

4 *Sadhana of the Nectar Attributes That Perfectly Reveal All Things of Samsara and Enlightenment as the Noble Qualities of Mahottara (che mchog gi 'khor 'das kyi chos thams cad yon tan du rdzogs par ston pa bdud rtsi yon tan gyi sgrub pa)*

5 *Sadhana of the Enlightened Activity of Vajrakilaya, Which Emphatically Teaches the Skillful Means for Subduing Malicious Beings by Rites of Sorcery (phur pa'i mngon spyod kyi las kyis gdug pa can 'dul ba'i thabs gtso bor ston pa phur ba phrin las kyi sgrub pa)*

TANTRA CLASS

As regards the tantra class, Dudjom Rinpoché explains that Mahayoga is generally classified according to father, mother, and non-dual tantras:

In the father tantras, such as that of Guhyasamaja (*gsang 'dus*), it is held that there is practice in the way of non-conceptual empty luminosity because the father tantras emphasize the aspect of the skillful means of the creation stage and also the vital energy (*rlung*) of its perfection stage.

In the mother tantras, such as those of Cakrasamvara (*bde mchog*), Hévajra (*dgyes rdo rje*), and Yangdak, the elaborations of the creation stage are fewer, and it is held that there is practice in a way that is non-conceptual regarding emptiness and exaltation and in which the perfection stage of wisdom emphasizes the bodhicitta essence.

In the non-dual tantras, such as the *Magical Net* (*sgyu 'phrul drwa ba*), the stages of creation and perfection are in integral union (*zung du 'jug*), and it is said that there is practice that emphasizes exaltation, luminosity, non-conceptual wisdom that arises from the channels, vital energy, and *tiklé* of the perfection stage, and especially the supreme wisdom of luminosity.

In this context, if we explain meditation from the point of view of the *Secret Essence Root Tantra*, then as it is said in the *Three Stages*:

> It is said that there are two specific kinds of meditation:
> The stages of meditation with characteristics and
> Ultimate reality as it is [that is, meditation without characteristics].

Therefore, there is meditation both with and without characteristics.

First, meditation with characteristics includes both the creation and perfection stages. As for the creation stage, it refers to the practice in which the wisdom deity and concepts are meditated upon as inseparable by emphasizing the successive creation of the mandala based upon the three meditative absorptions. There are two aspects to the creation stage: devotional meditation (*mos bsgom*) and certain perfection (*nges rdzogs*).

First, devotional meditation is practicing even though one has not attained stability in meditative absorption. One completes the branches of the creation stage ritual during one night's meditation session on the form of the wisdom deity. The second, certain perfection, refers to the five yogas of the conditioned paths of accumulation and application, and the four types of unconditioned awareness-holders.

As for the perfection stage, there are the pith instructions that hold and subdue through the upper gate and the pith instructions of the realms' display through the lower gate. Therefore, it is said in the *Three Stages*:

There are instructions for the upper and lower gates.

The second, meditation without characteristics, refers to meditation on the meditative absorption of the nature of phenomena as it is (*de bzhin nyid*).

CONDUCT

Fifth, the conduct of Mahayoga. Dudjom Rinpoché describes the conduct that a Mahayoga practitioner engages in as follows:

Any phenomena of samsara can be practiced without attachment since it is accepted with confidence in skillful means. It is said in the *Magical Key to the Storehouse* (*bang mdzod 'phrul lde*):

Creation stage Mahayoga
Engages in the practices of *tana, gana,*
And the five nectars that are tantric commitment substances
Through conduct that perceives great skillful means.

RESULT

Sixth, the result of Mahayoga. Dudjom Rinpoché describes the results of Mahayoga practice as follows:

In one life or in the intermediate state, one realizes the supreme nature that is the spontaneously accomplished five wisdom bodies. It is said in the *Guhyasamaja-tantra* (*gsang 'dus*):

> This, the supreme nature of the Transcendent Conqueror
> [Buddha]
> Arising from the undivided three kayas,
> Fully adorned with the ocean of wisdom,
> Will be attained in this very life.

And in the *Wisdom Essence* (*ye shes thig le*):

> Immediately after abandoning this body,
> The result will be effortlessly accomplished.

A Concise Review of Anuyoga

The transmission Anuyoga is also explained by Dudjom Rinpoché in terms of:

- essence
- definition of terms
- classification

Essence

First, as for the essence, Dudjom Rinpoché explains:

> Its nature is that liberation is attained through the union of realization and familiarization of the truth of the non-duality of stainless space and wisdom by means of relying mainly upon the perfection stage of incisive knowledge.

Definition of Terms

Second, Dudjom Rinpoché defines the term *anuyoga*:

> The [Sanskrit] *anuyoga* is called *jé su naljor* (*rjes su rnal 'byor*) [in Tibetan], "subsequent yoga" [in English], since it emphasizes the path of desire involved (*rjes*) with incisive knowledge.

Classification

Third is the classification of Anuyoga. Dudjom Rinpoché describes six categories:

1. twofold entrance
2. view
3. discipline
4. meditation
5. conduct
6. result

TWOFOLD ENTRANCE

The first category in the classification of Anuyoga, is the twofold entrance:

1. empowerment
2. actual entrance

As for empowerment, there are a variety of classification systems. Dudjom Rinpoché explains there are thirty-six empowerment rituals subsumed within the four categories of outer, inner, attainment, and secret empowerments. Dudjom Rinpoché cites a passage from the *Analysis of Empowerment's Meaning* (*dbang don rnam par 'byed pa*):

> Ten empowerments bring about possession of the enlightened family.
> Eleven empowerments bring about the inner secret.
> Thirteen empowerments are known as "the great Lama."
> Two empowerments perfect the empowerment of the nine vehicles.

The second aspect of the twofold entrance to Anuyoga is the actual entrance, through which one enters by means of the non-duality of stainless space and wisdom.

VIEW

The second category in the classification of Anuyoga is the view. Dudjom Rinpoché explains the view as follows:

> All phenomena are one's own mind, and that itself is the pure vast expanse of the space of the female consort Kuntu Zangmo, whose nature is unborn and free of elaborations. It is also called the "primordial mandala just as it is." In this respect, it is also

said in the *General Discourse That Gathers All Intentions*:

> Since that which has arisen from mind is emptiness,
> Everything that has arisen from it is empty.

Awareness, itself unborn though unceasing in every respect, radiates as a mandala of self-manifest light and is called "Wisdom Buddha Kuntu Zangpo" or the "Natural Spontaneously Accomplished Mandala." In the same text it is said:

> Unseen upon examination,
> It manifests everything.

The inseparable illumination of these two mandalas is the great exaltation child of the non-duality of stainless space and wisdom, the root mandala of enlightened mind. In accord with this, it is again said in the *Sutra That Gathers All Intentions*:

> That which is called "secret mantra" is ultimate reality as it is, in which appearance and non-appearance are non-dual. It is liberated from the essence of duality and does not have any fixation whatsoever on a middle between two things.

For this reason all phenomena are seen as primordially Buddha in the root mandala of enlightened mind, whose nature is inseparable from the three mandalas.[336]

DISCIPLINE

The third category in the classification of Anuyoga is discipline. There are root and branch tantric commitments that must be kept. From among the various classification systems Dudjom Rinpoché explains these tantric commitments based upon the sixty-sixth chapter of the *Sutra Synthesizing the Wisdom Mind of All Buddhas* (*sangs rgyas thams cad kyi dgongs pa 'dus pa'i mdo*). Based upon this text, there are nine enumerations, namely:

1. four tantric commitments definitive to the important scriptures
2. twenty-eight common tantric commitments
3. four superior tantric commitments

4. twenty-three relating to discipline
5. twenty relating to attainment
6. four relating to continuity of behavior
7. five negative forms of energy to be abandoned
8. four enemies to be destroyed
9. tantric commitment of the view

MEDITATION

The fourth category in the classification of Anuyoga is meditation. A detailed explanation of the meditation associated with Anuyoga falls outside the scope of this introduction, but generally, Dudjom Rinpoché explains that Anuyoga meditation comprises both the path of skillful means and the path of liberation. The path of skillful means involves the yoga of meditation that works with the four or six cakras. The path of liberation comprises non-conceptual meditation, meditation utilizing elaborations such as mantra recitation, and meditation in which the universe and all beings contained within distinctly radiate as the mandala of deities in an instantaneous manner, like a fish leaping from water.

CONDUCT

The fifth category in the classification of Anuyoga is conduct. Dudjom Rinpoché explains conduct as follows:

> Generally, conduct emphasizes evenness. As it is said in the *Magical Key to the Storehouse*:
>
>> The perfection stage Anuyoga
>> Is the perfect rapture of the inseparability of stainless space and wisdom.
>
> When classified in detail, there are three types of conduct: bestowal of blessings, overwhelming, and skillful means. The *Sutra Synthesizing the Wisdom Mind of All Buddhas* says:
>
>> Conduct that bestows blessings,
>> Conduct that is skillful, and conduct that overwhelms
>> Are like space, a king, and water that extinguishes a mass of fire.

RESULT

The sixth category in the classification of Anuyoga is the result. The result is the actualization of the essence in one lifetime. This is the wisdom body of great exaltation that is the unity of the four wisdom bodies. Dudjom Rinpoché quotes from the *Magical Key to the Storehouse*:

> The vehicle of Anuyoga,
> In one lifetime, without hindrance,
> Definitely proceeds to the level of Buddha.

Concise Review of Atiyoga

The pith instruction Atiyoga is explained in terms of:

+ essence
+ definition of terms
+ classification

Essence

First, as for the essence, Dudjom Rinpoché writes:

> It is the skillful means that directly liberates the ultimate truth that we are primordially Buddha and whose nature is free from conduct to be accepted or rejected, free from hope or fear.

Definition of Terms

Second, Dudjom Rinpoché defines the term *atiyoga*:

> [The Sanskrit] word *atiyoga* is translated as *shintu naljor* (*shin tu rnal 'byor*) [in Tibetan], "highest yoga" [in English], since it is the culmination of the perfection stage of both the creation and perfection stages, and since it is the summit of all vehicles.

Classification

Third is the classification system of Atiyoga. There are six categories:

1. twofold entrance
2. view
3. discipline
4. meditation

5. conduct

6. result

TWOFOLD ENTRANCE

Dudjom Rinpoché explains that the first category in the classification of Atiyoga is the twofold entrance: empowerment and the actual entrance. The first entrance, empowerment, refers to the ripening caused through the empowerment of awareness's display (*rig pa'i rtsal dbang*). The second entrance, the actual entrance, is entering by means of not entering anything at all. Dudjom Rinpoché supports this by citing *All-Creating King*:

> Regarding the Buddha's teachings there is nothing to be done,
> Thus it is entered effortlessly.

VIEW

The second category in the classification of Atiyoga is the view. As Dudjom Rinpoché explains:

> All phenomena, everything that seemingly exists (*snang srid*) subsumed within samsara and enlightenment, are held to be effortlessly and primordially enlightened in the essence of self-manifest wisdom, dharmakaya, the supreme *tiklé*. As it is said in the *Vast Space of Vajrasattva* (*rdo rje sems dpa'i nam mkha' che*):
>
> > Having been effortlessly liberated through self-originating
> > wisdom,
> > The path of liberation is shown.
>
> And it is said in *The Great Garuda* (*khyung chen*):
>
> > Self-manifest wisdom always abides as it is, without concepts.

DISCIPLINE

The third category in the classification of Atiyoga is discipline. This is explained by Dudjom Rinpoché as follows:

The tantric commitments of non-existence (*med pa*), non-substantial evenness (*phyal ba*), oneness (*gcig pu*), and spontaneous presence (*lhun grub*) should not be transgressed. As it is said in the *Magical Key of Further Discernment* (*yang 'byed 'phrul mig gyi lde*):

> The tantric commitments of Atiyoga
> Are non-existence, non-substantial evenness, oneness,
> And spontaneous presence.
> Do not transgress their significance.

MEDITATION

The fourth category in the classification of Atiyoga is meditation. Dudjom Rinpoché begins by citing the *Supreme Array of Ati* (*a ti bkod pa chen po*):

> For those who hold to mind, there is the Mind Class;
> For those who hold to space, there is the Vast Expanse Class;
> And for those who are free of gradual effort, there is the Pith
>   Instruction Class.

Dudjom Rinpoché comments on the above quotation:

> In accord with this quotation, the Mind Class refers to resting within the nature of empty awareness, dharmakaya. The Vast Expanse Class refers to resting within the nature of phenomena, without activity or effort. And the Pith Instruction Class refers to resting within the nature of phenomena, primordially liberated, free from conduct that accepts or rejects.
>
> Generally, meditation in the tradition of the Great Perfection is subsumed within Cutting through Solidity (*khregs chod*) and Direct Vision (*thod rgal*). It is said in *The Pearl Necklace* (*mu tig phreng ba*):

> The practice is Cutting through Solidity and Direct Vision.

CUTTING THROUGH SOLIDITY

Based upon this, the first (Cutting through Solidity) is to rest without moving from the nature of the view of primordial purity. Dudjom Rinpoché explains:

> It is said in *The Great Garuda (khyung chen)*:
>
>> Naturally remaining is to abide.
>
> And Master Garab Dorjé has said:
>
>> The nature of mind is primordially Buddha.
>> In mind, like the sky, there is no origination and no cessation.
>> Having realized the real meaning of the evenness of all
>>   phenomena,
>> If without being sought it is settled within, that is meditation.

By meditating in this way, there are four creation stages of the paths and levels:

1. abiding
2. unmoving
3. evenness
4. spontaneous presence

DIRECT VISION

Next, Dudjom Rinpoché briefly describes the second practice, Direct Vision. This practice relies on the six essentials (*gnad drug*) that gradually give rise to the four visionary appearances, through which the ultimate goal is achieved.

CONDUCT

The fifth category in the classification of Atiyoga is conduct. Dudjom Rinpoché explains conduct as follows:

> Since all phenomena arise as the display of the nature of phenomena, conduct means there is nothing to accept or reject. It is said in the *Vast Space of Vajrasattva (nam mkha' che)*:
>
>> Everything is accomplished through doing nothing.

RESULT

The sixth category in the classification of Atiyoga is the result. Dudjom Rinpoché explains the result as follows:

> Abiding from this very moment on the level of the sponta-neously perfected Buddha Kuntu Zangpo, you reach your desti-nation. Since the four confidences have reached full measure, samsara is liberated in enlightenment. This is also stated in the *Magical Key of Further Discernment* (*yang 'byed 'phrul mig gyi lde*):

> As for the result of the Great Perfection, Atiyoga,
>   In the original seed—enlightenment—
>   The unobtainable fruit ripens by itself.

CONCLUSION TO THE EXPLANATION OF THE NINE VEHICLES SECTION

After reviewing the nine vehicles according to the Nyingma tradition based on the writings of His Holiness Dudjom Rinpoché, we can appreciate that the Buddhist teachings are extensive and profound.

Appendix 2
Transmission of the Literary Expression of Buddha's Teachings

W E HAVE SEEN in Appendix 1, an explanation of the nine vehicles, the special place these pith instruction teachings hold within the vast spectrum of Buddhist teachings. To further our appreciation of the rarity and great worth of this category of instruction—the Pith Instruction Class of the Great Perfection—it is useful to understand its place within the vast classification system of Buddha's teachings. To this purpose we will now review the copious enumerations and classification systems for the transmission of the literary expression of Buddha's teachings as contained within the Buddha's Word (*bka'*) and the treatises (*bstan bcos*). Unless otherwise noted, the following section is entirely based on His Holiness Dudjom Rinpoché's detailed classification on the subject as found in his text *The Festival of Delight in Which the Expression of Eloquent Teachings Manifest.*[337]

Transmission of the Literary Expression

Transmission of the literary expression (*rjod byed*) of the Buddha's teachings (*chos*) has two aspects:
1. the excellently spoken Buddha's Word (*bka'*)
2. the treatises (*bstan bcos*) composed by accomplished or learned masters that comment upon the intention of the Buddha's Word

THE BUDDHA'S WORD

Dudjom Rinpoché explains the Buddha's Word in three categories:
1. characteristics (*mtshan nyid*)
2. meaning of the words (*sgra don*)
3. classification (*dbye ba*)

Characteristics of the Buddha's Word

Buddha's Word consists of scriptures that originate from the extraordinary Teacher, Buddha, which are preserved in the Discourse Collection (Sutrapitaka) and Tantra Collection (Tantrapitaka). Dudjom Rinpoché writes that these scriptures have four special qualities according to the *Discourse That Inspires One's Higher Intentions*:

1. having meaningful subject matter
2. containing stainless words of description
3. functioning to abandon the passions of the three realms
4. the result indicating the benefits and advantages of peace

Dudjom Rinpoché also explains the four special qualities as follows:

1. They teach the three trainings as the subject matter.
2. They possess stainless words of explanation.
3. They possess the three kinds of valid cognition as evidence.[338]
4. The result is virtuous in the beginning, middle, and end.

Meaning of the Words

Dudjom Rinpoché explains that the Tibetan word *ka* (*bka'*, Buddha's Word) is derived from the Sanskrit word *subhashita*. *Su* in this context means "excellent" and *bhashita* means "that which has been taught." Therefore, because they are "excellently taught" they are *subhashita*. How are they excellently taught? Dudjom Rinpoché explains that these scriptures are excellently taught through ten aspects and cites the *Rational System of Detailed Explanation* (*rnam bshad rigs pa*):

How are they excellently taught? It is through ten aspects:

1. their genuine source
2. their scope
3. their approach
4. their excellent teaching
5. their detailed analysis
6. their support itself
7. causing comprehension
8. their designations
9. their time
10. their complete grasp of noble qualities

Classification of Buddha's Word

Dudjom Rinpoché explains that Buddha's Word is classified in five ways, in terms of:

1. controlling condition
2. time
3. categories
4. function as antidote
5. power

1. Controlling Condition

First, when classified according to the controlling condition, there are three categories of Buddha's Word:

1. given in oral teachings (*zhal nas gsungs pa*)
2. given through blessings (*byin gyis brlabs pa*)
3. given by permission blessing (*rjes su gnang ba'i bka'*)

Buddha's Word Given in Oral Teachings

First, Dudjom Rinpoché explains that when Buddha's Word is classified as given in oral teachings there are two aspects:

1. teachings delivered impromptu by the Buddha at gatherings (*ston pas mdun bsus nas gsungs pa ni sdud pa lta bu*), such as *The Concise Perfection of Wisdom* (*sdud pa*)[339]
2. teachings given at the request of an assembly, such as *Reciting the Names of Manjushri* (*'jam dpal mtshan brjod*)[340]

Buddha's Word Given through Blessings

Second, when Buddha's Word is classified as given through blessings (*byin gyis brlabs pa*), Dudjom Rinpoché explains it as threefold:

1. Buddha's Word given through the blessing of his wisdom body (*skus byin gyis brlabs pa'i bka'*)
2. Buddha's Word given through the blessing of his wisdom speech (*gsung gis byin gyis brlabs pa'i bka'*)
3. Buddha's Word given through the blessing of his wisdom mind (*thugs kyis byin gyis brlabs pa'i bka'*). Dudjom Rinpoché describes three aspects to this last category. First, this includes Buddha's Word given through the blessing of the samadhi of his wisdom mind (*thugs ting nge 'dzin gyis byin gyis brlab pa'i bka'*). For example, the *Heart*

Sutra, in which Buddha went into "the samadhi on the profundity of phenomena" (*zab mo snang ba'i ting nge 'dzin*) and taught through a dialogue between Chenrezi and Shariputra. Next, there is the Buddha's Word given by the blessing of the power of the truth of Buddha's mind (*thugs bden pa'i stobs kyis byin gyis brlabs pa'i bka'*), such as sounds emanating from the environment—from the sky, animals, and trees—due to the accomplished power of Buddha. Third, there is Buddha's Word given through the blessing of the power of Buddha's compassion.

Buddha's Word Given by Permission Blessing

Third, when Buddha's Word is classified as those given by permission blessing (*rjes su gnang ba'i bka'*) it refers to those teachings that were compiled by councils after Buddha's parinirvana that begin "Thus have I heard" and end "Manifest praise to the teaching given by the Lord Buddha."

2. Time

Dudjom Rinpoché explains that when Buddha's Word is classified according to time, it is classified as three successive turnings of the wheel of the Dharma (*chos 'khor rim pa*). The first turning was concerned with the four truths (*bden bzhi*); the second turning was concerned with characteristiclessness (*mtshan nyid med pa*); and the third turning was concerned with the ultimate definitive meaning (*don dam rnam par nges pa*).

3. Categories

Dudjom Rinpoché explains that when the Buddha's Word is classified according categories, there are twelve or nine branches of the scriptures (*gsung rab*). Dudjom Rinpoché lists the twelve branches as cited in the commentary to the *Perfection of Wisdom in Eight Thousand Lines* (*brgyad stong 'grel chen*):[341]

These twelve classes are the twelve branches of Buddhist scriptures (*gsung rab*):
1. discourses (*mdo sde*)
2. aphorisms in prose and verse (*dbyangs bsnyad*)
3. prophetic declarations (*lung bstan*)
4. verse (*tshigs bcad*)

5. meaningful expressions (*ched brjod*)
6. narratives (*rtogs pa brjod*)
7. parables (*de lta byung*)
8. legends (*gleng gzhi*)
9. extensive teachings (*shin tu rgyas*)
10. tales of past lives (*skye rabs*)
11. established instructions (*gtan phab*)
12. marvelous events (*rmad du byung ba*)

Dudjom Rinpoché explains that the classification into nine branches excludes the sections on narratives, parables, and established instructions as cited in the *Clearly Worded Commentary* (*tshig gsal*)[342] by Candrakirti.

Dudjom Rinpoché explains that the twelve branches of Buddhist scriptures can be condensed into the Three Collections (*pitaka; sde snod*) as cited in the *Minor Precepts of the Vinaya* (*lung phran tshegs*):

✦ The *Collection of Discourses* (*Sutrapitaka; mdo sde*) subsumes: the discourses; aphorisms in prose and verse; prophetic declarations; verses; and meaningful expressions.

✦ The *Collection of Discipline* (*Vinayapitaka; 'dul bar bsdus*) subsumes: the legends (*gleng gzhi*); narratives (*rtogs pa brjod*); parables (*de lta byung*); and tales of past lives (*skyes rabs*).

✦ The *Collection of Abhidharma* (*Abhidharmapitaka; mngon chos*) subsumes: the extensive teachings; marvelous events; and established instructions.

NOTE ON THE SECRET MANTRA TEXTS

Dudjom Rinpoché writes that in this context, the secret mantra texts are considered by most followers of the Nyingma tradition to belong to the Bodhisattva Collection of extensive teachings as cited in the *Magical Net of Manjushri* (*'jam dpal sgyu drwa*), though the learned scholar Narton Sengé-Ö (*snar ston seng ge 'od*) said they belong either to the section of established instructions or that of marvelous events.

4. Function as antidote

Dudjom Rinpoché explains:

When classifying Buddha's Word according to its function as an antidote, it consists of eighty-four thousand collections of Buddhist teachings (*chos kyi phung*). It says in the *Questions by the Four Goddesses* (*lha mo bzhis zhus pa*):[343]

> The Great Sage classified the doctrine into eighty-four thousand collections of teachings.

Dudjom Rinpoché then explains that these collections can be subsumed within four categories related to their function as antidotes to the three poisons. There are twenty-one thousand collections of spiritual teachings that correspond in equal proportions to desire, anger, ignorance, and the three, yielding a total of eighty-four thousand. There are twenty-one thousand spiritual teachings contained within the *Collection of Discipline* as antidotes to the twenty-one thousand kinds of desire (*'dod chags*). There are twenty-one thousand spiritual teachings contained within the *Collection of Discourses* as antidotes to the twenty-one thousand kinds of anger (*zhe sdang*). There are twenty-one thousand spiritual teachings contained within the *Collection of Abhidharma* as antidotes to the twenty-one thousand kinds of ignorance (*gti mug*). And there are twenty-one thousand spiritual teachings in equal proportion contained within the *Mantric Collection of the Awareness-holders* (*rig pa 'pa sngags kyi sde snod*) as antidotes to the twenty-one thousand kinds of conduct resulting from these three poisons.

Regarding the *Mantric Collection of the Awareness-holders* mentioned above, Dudjom Rinpoché states that some masters say that mantra should belong within the *Collection of Abhidharma* as the inner Abhidharma, and some scholars include it within the *Collection of Discourses*. According to Dudjom Rinpoché, his tradition is not in contradiction with the earlier Lamas who made these assertions and states it is best to classify the mantra texts as a separate collection called either the *Awareness-holders' Collection* or the *Fourth Collection*. Dudjom Rinpoché mentions that the Great Perfection tantra called *All-Creating King* (*kun byed rgyal po*) classifies the tantric texts as the *Fourth Collection*.

5. Power

There are several ways of classifying the Buddha's Word according to vehicles based on their power. The word "vehicle" in English, *theg pa* in Tibetan, and *yana* in Sanskrit is used quite often in Buddhist texts, such as in Sutrayana, Mahayana, Vajrayana, and so forth, so it might be worth quoting Dudjom Rinpoché's explanation of why this term is used:

> Generally, the [Tibetan word] *theg pa* [vehicle] was derived from the [Sanskrit] word *yana* since one travels to higher and higher paths, just as one gets into a means of transport; thus, it is called a "vehicle" (*theg pa*).

The vehicles are classified in many ways. Sometimes the Buddha's Word is classified as two vehicles: the Lesser Vehicle (*theg pa chung ngu*) and the Greater Vehicle (*theg pa chen po*). Sometimes it is classified as three causal vehicles: the vehicles of the hearers (*thos*), solitary sages (*rang*), and bodhisattvas (*byang sems*). There is also a fourfold classification that includes the three causal vehicles and the resultant vehicle (Vajrayana). Dudjom Rinpoché quotes from the *Magical Net of Manjushri*:

> One renounces through the three vehicles
> And abides in the result through the single vehicle
> [the Vajrayana].

The vehicles can also be classified as fivefold by adding the vehicle of the higher realms of samsara (the god and human realms), which leads one to the other four vehicles mentioned above. Dudjom Rinpoché supports this by citing the *Secret Essence Tantra* (*gsang ba'i snying po*):[344]

> The vehicle of gods and humans, of hearers, of solitary sages, of bodhisattvas, and the Unsurpassable Vehicle [make five].

The vehicles can also be classified as nine. Dudjom Rinpoché quotes from *All-Creating King* (*kun byed rgyal po*):

> While there exists but one,
> It appears as nine vehicles.

Dudjom Rinpoché emphasizes that the different vehicles are not separate paths, but instead, they are similar to rungs of a ladder that leads to enlightenment. To support this point he explains:

What system is followed in this context? The classification into numerous vehicles has been made provisionally; their circumstances and the greater and lesser degree of their importance were taught as skillful means for the training of disciples. It is intended that when these vehicles have each arrived at the result of their respective paths, they are continued still higher in the supreme teaching of the Vajrayana, the sole path on which all Buddhas have progressed. Those others [hearers, solitary sages, and bodhisattvas] are taught merely as paths leading to this vehicle. They are paths that are to be traversed until perfect enlightenment and are positioned like rungs of a ladder. Therefore Nagarjuna has said:

> This method, which is like rungs of a ladder, has been taught
> by the perfect Buddha.

Dudjom Rinpoché then explains that according to "our" tradition the vehicles are classified as four:
1. Hearer Vehicle
2. Solitary Sage Vehicle
3. Bodhisattva Vehicle
4. Mantra Vehicle

The Mantra category can be classified into six. The three lower classes of tantras:
+ Kriyatantra
+ Caryatantra (also referred to as Upatantra)
+ Yogatantra

and the three higher classes of tantras, the creation and perfection stages belonging to Highest Yogatantra:
+ Mahayoga
+ Anuyoga
+ Atiyoga

Dudjom Rinpoché then explains:

In general, it is appropriate either to apply the name "single vehicle" to all the Buddhist teachings subsumed under the level of enlightenment, or apply the names of the individual vehicles to each in particular, because they are the path to be journeyed toward omniscience.

These nine vehicles are: the hearers, solitary Buddhas, bodhisattvas, Kriyatantra, Caryatantra, Yogatantra, Mahayoga, Anuyoga, and Atiyoga.

Dudjom Rinpoché also mentions that from the ultimate perspective—an individual abiding in the natural state—it is said there is no vehicle whatsoever, and he substantiates this with a quotation from the *Sutra of the Descent to Lanka (lang gshegs)*:

> When the mind becomes transformed,
> There is neither vehicle nor passenger.

Conclusion

In conclusion, Dudjom Rinpoché reaffirms that within the Nyingma tradition all Buddha's teachings are explained in terms of nine vehicles, or alternatively as nine stages of a single vehicle:

> As it is said in the *Tantra of the Great Self-Manifestation of Awareness (rig pa rang shar)*:

> The sublime Buddhist teachings are:
> The discourses, extensive teachings,
> and very extensive teachings.
> The very extensive teachings are
> the inconceivable eighty-four thousand categories of teachings,
> an extremely vast number,
> inconceivable, immeasurable,
> ineffable, and far beyond all thought.
> Extensive teachings such as these
> are considered to have nine classifications:
> Those of hearers, solitary sages, and likewise the bodhisattvas;
> The vehicles of Kriya, Upa, and likewise Yoga are explained.

There are also the Maha, Anuyoga, and likewise Great Perfection
Ati.
In this way, it is explained in nine aspects.

These nine vehicles will not be discussed as this point. I refer the reader
to Appendix 1 for a detailed explanation of the nine vehicles.

TREATISES (*bstan bcos*)

The treatises comment upon the intention of Buddha's Word and are
explained through three categories:
1. characteristics of the treatises
2. meaning of the words
3. classification of the treatises

Characteristics of the Treatises
Dudjom Rinpoché explains the characteristics of the treatises:

> A simple treatise (*bstan bcos tsam*) is characterized as a scrip-
> tural teaching (*lung gi chos*) that is arranged in such a way as to
> present one's own philosophical approach (*grub mtha'*) to others.
> Any treatise that possesses four unique qualities is characterized
> as a pure treatise, while those lacking any of the four unique
> qualities are categorized as nominal treatises (*bstan bcos ltar
> snang*).

Dudjom Rinpoché explains these four unique qualities as follows:
1. First is the unique quality of motivation. This pertains to a
   writer whose mind is undistracted, whose words and meaning
   are based in incisive knowledge, and who writes out of compassion to help others.
2. Second is the unique quality of expressive words that can be
   properly written in metrical verses (*sdeb sbyor*).
3. Third is the unique quality of the subject matter (*brjod bya
   don*), which indicates the methods for those disciples who
   require training and aspire to liberation.
4. Fourth is the unique quality of purposeful composition, which

has the power to lead one to the attainment of liberation through study and the consideration of these words.

Meaning of the Words

Dudjom Rinpoché explains that the Tibetan word *tan chö* (*bstan bcos*, "treatise" in English) is derived from the Sanskrit word *shastra*, which is made up of *shabana*, "to change," and *traya*, "to protect." He then elaborates:

> It is called *shabana* [in Sanskrit], "to change," since in its causal aspect it changes the three poisons of the passions into the three higher trainings;[345] and it is called *traya* [in Sanskrit], "to protect", since in its resultant aspect it protects from the sufferings of samsara and from rebirth in the lower realms. Therefore, since it has the qualities of change (*'chos*) and protection (*skyob*), it is a treatise (*bstan bcos*). As it is said in the *Rational System of Detailed Explanation* (*rnam bshad rigs pa*):
>
>> It changes (*'chos*) all enemies that are the passions
>> And protects (*skyob*) from rebirth in the lower realms.
>> Since it has the qualities of change and protection, it is called a
>>   treatise (*bstan bcos*).
>> Treatises having both these qualities do not exist in other
>>   traditions.

Classification of the Treatises

Treatises are classified in six ways:

1. level of composition
2. purpose of their composition
3. individual authors
4. manner of composition
5. explaining according to the Buddha's Word
6. the meaning they express

1. Treatises Classified According to the Level of Composition

Treatises classified according to the level of their composition are of four kinds: meaningless, ordinary meaning, reverse meaning, and meaningful. Dudjom Rinpoché mentions a Sanskrit text describing dentistry for crows, the *Kakadantaparik-shastra,* as an example of a meaningless text. Texts in the category of having mere ordinary meaning are treatises on the four common sciences (*rig gnas bzhi*). Those of reverse meaning are the treatises of non-Buddhists who hold extreme views of nihilism or eternalism. The treatises that fall into the category of meaningful treatises are those on the inner science of Buddhism (*sangs rgyas pa'i nang rig*).

Dudjom Rinpoché explains that according to the *Yogacara Bhumi* there are nine types of treatises taught in three sets. The first set includes treatises that are: meaningless, of reverse meaning, and meaningful. The second set includes those that are: deceptive, lacking compassion, and that abandon suffering. The third set includes treatises devoted to debate, polemics, and attainment.

Dudjom Rinpoché points out that the first two types of treatises of each set are nominal treatises of a lower level, while the last one of each set is a genuine treatise of a sublime level.

2. Treatises Classified
According to the Purpose of Composition

There are three types of treatises when classified according to the purpose of their composition. First, there are those that summarize the vast meaning of the Buddha's Word, such as the *Abhidharma-samuccaya* (*mngon pa kun las btus pa*). Second, there are those that are compilations (*'khrugs pa go rim*), such as the *Root Discourse of the Vinaya* (*'dul ba mdo rtsa ba*). And third, there are those treatises that reveal the profound meaning, such as the *Mahayanottara-tantra Shastra* (*theg chen rgyud bla ma'i bstan bcos*).

3. Treatises Classified
According to Individual Authors

Dudjom Rinpoché explains that there are five types of treatises when classified according to their individual authors (*rtsom byed gang zag*):

First, treatises composed based upon the teachings given by perfect Buddhas, such as the *Five Transmissions of the Assembly of Joyous Buddhas* (*bde 'dus kyi lung lnga*), composed by Vajradharma; and the *Five Doctrines of Maitreya* (*byams chos sde lnga*).

Second, treatises written based upon the teachings given by arhats, such as the *Seven Sections on the Abhidharma* (*mngon pa sde bdun*).

Third, treatises written based upon the teachings given by sublime bodhisattvas, such as the extensive treatises of the *Five Sections on the Levels* (*sa sde lnga*); concise treatises known as the *Compendium of Abhidharma* (*mngon pa kun las btus pa*); and the *Collection of the Greater Vehicle* (*theg pa chen po bsdus pa*). These were all composed by Arya Asanga, a bodhisattva abiding on the third level (*bhumi*).

Fourth, treatises written after prophecies (*lung bstan*) had been obtained from wisdom deities, such as the *Compendium of Valid Cognition* (*Pramanasamuccaya; tshad ma kun las btus pa*) by Dignaga; and the *Seven Treasuries of Scriptures* (*gsung rab mdzod bdun*) by Kunkhyen Longchen Rabjampa.

Fifth, treatises written by ordinary learned panditas to present their own philosophical approach and to refute the reverse views of others. One such text mentioned by Dudjom Rinpoché is the *Eight Dissertations* (*Ashtaprakarana; sde brgyad*) composed by the pre-eminent scholar Vasubandhu.

4. Treatises Classified
According to the Manner of Their Composition

According to Dudjom Rinpoché, there are two categories of treatises when classified according to the manner of their composition:

+ treatises designated as commentaries on the Buddha's Word
+ treatises that are written independently based upon the meaning of the Buddha's Word

First, Treatises Designated as Commentaries on the Buddha's Word

These are of four types:

First, extensive commentaries that establish in detail both the word and meaning of the Buddha's Word, such as the *Commentary on the Praktimoksha Sutra in Fifty Sections* (*Pratimoksha-sutratika; so thar gyi mdo'i 'grel pa bam po lnga bcu pa*), and the *Great Commentary on the Kalacakra Tantra Entitled Stainless Light* (*Vimalaprabha; dus 'khor 'grel chen dri ma med pa'i 'od*).

Second, word-for-word commentaries (*tshig 'grel*) that elaborately explain the words in conjunction with annotations, such as the *Commentary on the Collection of Meaningful Expressions* (*Udana-vargavrtti; ched du brjod pa'i tshom kyi 'grel pa*), and *Dispelling Darkness in the Ten Direc-*

tions: A Commentary on the Secret Essence (*snying 'grel phyogs bcu mun sel*) by Kunkhyen Longchenpa.

Third, commentaries that discern points that are difficult to understand, such as the *Commentary on the Concise Perfection of Wisdom* (*Sancaya-gathapanjika; sdud pa'i 'grel pa*).

Fourth, commentaries that subsume and establish the main point (*don gyi gtso bo*) are commentaries that summarize the main points of a text (*bsdus don*), such as the *Condensed Commentary on the Secret Essence* (*Guhyagarbhapindartha; snying 'grel pindartha*) by Vimalamitra, and the *Chapterless Commentary on the Supplementary Magical Net* (*le lag gi sa ma 'grel*) by the great Mahapandita Rongzompa.

SECOND, TREATISES WRITTEN INDEPENDENTLY ON THE MEANING OF THE BUDDHA'S WORD

These are of three types:

First, those that completely teach the meaning of one text of Buddha's Word, such as the *Root Discourse of the Vinaya* (*Vinayamulasutra; 'dul ba mdo rtsa ba*) composed by Gunaprabha, the *Ornament of Emergent Realization* (*Abhisamayalamkara; mngon rtogs rgyan*) by Maitreyanatha, and the *Sequence of the Path of the Magical Net* (*Mayajala-vajrakarmakrama; sgyu 'phrul lam rim*) written by Buddhaguhya.

Second, those that teach the meaning of a fragmentary text of Buddha's Word, such as the *Stanzas on the Novitiate* (*Shramanera-karika; dge tshul gyi ka ri ki*).

Third, those that teach the meaning of many texts of Buddha's Word. These include treatises such as the *Compendium of Lessons* (*Shiksha-samuccaya; bslab btus*) composed by Shantideva, and the *Precious Treasury of Noble Qualities* (*yon tan rin po che'i mdzod*) composed by the omniscient Jigmé Lingpa.

5. Treatises Classified
According to the Buddha's Word That They Explain

Treatises classified according to the Buddha's Word they explain are those treatises that comment on the general teachings of Buddha's Word, including commentaries on their verbal structure, such as the grammatical treatises of the *Kalapasutra* and the *Grammar of Candragomin* (*Candra-vyakarana*), and commentaries on their meaning such as the *Seven Sections of Valid Cognition* by Dharmakirti.

Treatises on the Intention of the
Three Turnings of the Wheel of the Dharma
and the Collection of the Awareness-holders

Dudjom Rinpoché explains that there are also treatises that comment on the intention of the three turnings of the wheel of the Dharma of Buddha's Word, as well as the *Collection of the Awareness-holders*.

First turning of the wheel of the Dharma

The first category—which is threefold—are commentaries on the intention of the first turning of the wheel of the Dharma:

1. First, commentaries that establish the view, such as the *Treasure of Abhidharma (Abhidharmakosha; chos mngon pa mdzod)* by Vasubandhu.
2. Second, commentaries that establish conduct, such as the *Root Discourse of the Vinaya*.
3. And third, commentaries that establish the indivisibility of view and conduct, such as the *Great Treasure of Detailed Exposition (Vibhashakosha; bye brag bshad mdzod chen mo)*.

Intermediate turning of the wheel of the Dharma

The second category—which is threefold—are commentaries on the intention of the intermediate turning of the wheel of the Dharma:

1. First, commentaries that establish the view, such as the *Collection of Madhyamaka Reasoning (Yuktikaya; dbu ma rigs tshogs)* written by Nagarjuna.
2. Second, commentaries that establish conduct, such as *Entering the Conduct of Bodhisattvas (Bodhisattvacaryavatara; byang chub sems dpa'i spyod pa la 'jug pa)* by Shantideva.
3. And third, commentaries that establish the inseparability of view and conduct, such as the *Ornament of Emergent Realization (Abhisamayalamkara; mngon rtogs rgyan)*.

Third turning of the wheel of the Dharma

The third category—which is threefold—are commentaries on the intention of the final word of Buddha, the third turning of the wheel of the Dharma:

1. First, commentaries that establish the view, such as the *Unexcelled Continuum of the Greater Vehicle (Mahayanottara-tantra Shastra;*

theg chen rgyud bla ma'i bstan bcos) and *Discerning the Middle and the Extremes* (*Madhyantavibhaga; dbus mtha' rnam 'byed*).

2. Second, commentaries that establish conduct, such as the *Twenty Verses on the Bodhisattva Vow* (*Bodhisattva-samvaravimshaka; sdom pa nyi shu pa*) by Shantarakshita.

3. And third, commentaries that establish the indivisibility of view and conduct, such as the *Ornament of the Sutras of the Greater Vehicle* (*Mahayana-sutralamkarakarika; theg pa chen po mdo sde rgyan*) by Maitreya.

COLLECTION OF THE AWARENESS-HOLDERS

The fourth category—which is threefold—is that of the *Collection of the Awareness-holders*, also referred to as the *Fourth Collection*. Dudjom Rinpoché explains that treatises in this collection comment on the intention of the four or six classes of tantra.

1. First, commentaries that establish the view, such as *Garland of Views: A Collection of Upadesha* (*Upadesha-darshanamala; man ngag lta ba'i phreng ba*) by the great master Padmasambhava.

2. Second, commentaries which establish conduct, such as *Clarification of Samaya* (*Samayavivyakti; dam tshig gsal bkra*) by Lilavajra.

3. Third, commentaries which establish the indivisibility of view and conduct, such as the *Sequence of the Path of the Magical Net* (*Maya-jala-pathakrama; sgyu 'phrul lam rim*) by Buddhaguhya.

6. Treatises Classified According to the Meaning They Express

Treatises classified according to the meaning they express are twofold:

1. treatises that teach quantitatively
2. treatises that teach qualitatively

TREATISES THAT TEACH QUANTITATIVELY

First, those that teach quantitatively are classified in two ways: common quantitative treatises and uncommon quantitative treatises.

COMMON QUANTITATIVE TREATISES

Dudjom Rinpoché explains the common quantitative treatises as being treatises explicating worldly traditions such as guides for distinguishing precious gems, horses, clothes, land, and so forth, such as the ancient Indian text called the *Point of Human Sustenance* (*Nitishastrajantu-poshan-abindu*). Dudjom Rinpoché explains that these treatises can lead to the higher realms of humans and gods which can then be a stepping stone to liberation; he then supports this by citing the *Hundred Verses on Incisive Knowledge* (*shes rab brgya pa*):[346]

> If positive human traditions are practiced well,
> The journey to the god realms is not far off.
> Climbing the stairway of men and gods,
> One is close to liberation.

UNCOMMON QUANTITATIVE TREATISES

Dudjom Rinpoché next explains the uncommon quantitative treatises as being treatises that establish the first four of the five sciences (*rig gnas lnga*):

1. arts
2. medicine
3. grammar
4. logic

The fifth is the inner science of the teachings of Buddha.

The Science of the Arts. There are three categories regarding the science of the arts. Supreme among the arts of form are methods for constructing receptacles of Buddha's body, speech, and mind such as statues, books, and stupas. Supreme among the arts of speech are the songs of praise in the form of offerings to the Buddhas. And supreme among the arts of mind are the extraordinary aspects of the wisdom produced through study, reflection, and meditation.

The Science of Medicine. Medical science is usually explained under four headings: the illness and the person to be healed; the remedy that heals, including life-style, medicine, and diagnosis; the types of healing, which include prolonging life free of disease and healing disease when it occurs; and the healer: the doctors, nurses, and other health practitioners and care-givers. This is explained in treatises such as the *Commentary on the Intention of the Four Glorious Tantras of Medical Science* (*dpal ldan rgyud bzhi'i dgongs pa*) by Yutokpa.

The Science of Grammar. According to Dudjom Rinpoché, an important grammatical treatise known in India was the *Commentary of Panini* (*Panini vyakaranasutra*); and the two famous texts known in Tibet as the sun and moon are the treatises and instructions of the *Kalapasutra* (*sgra ka la pa*) and the *Grammar of Candragomin* (*Candravyakaranasutra; sgra tsandra*).

The Science of Logic. Logic is used as a means for comprehending that which is to be appraised by oneself, and as a means of communicating that understanding to others. Examples of treatises of logic given by Dudjom Rinpoché are the *Sutra of Valid Cognition* (*tshad ma mdo*) composed by the master Dignaga, and commentaries on its intention such as the *Seven Sections of Valid Cognition* (*tshad ma sde bdun*) composed by the glorious Dharmakirti.

FIVE MINOR SCIENCES
In addition, Dudjom Rinpoché mentions there are also five minor sciences—astrology, poetics, prosody, synonymies, and drama—which are usually categorized as branches of the artistic or grammatical sciences.

Astrology. First are the treatises on the science of astrology, which also includes the science of elemental divination and geomancy (*'byung rtsi*). Important astrological treatises are the *Commentary on the Kalacakra Tantra* (*dus 'khor rgyud 'grel*), the *Commentary on the Four Seats* (*gdan bzhi 'grel pa*), and a treatise held in common with non-Buddhists called the *Astrological Treatise Entitled Martial Conquest* (*Yuddha-jayanama-tantra-rajasvarodaya; gyul las rnam rgyal*). Explanations on geomancy can be found in such treatises as the *Mother and Son of the Clarifying Lamp* (*gsal sgron ma bu*).

Poetics. Second are the treatises on poetics, such as the *Mirror of Poetics* (*Kavyadarsha; snyan ngag me long dbyug pa can gyi gzhungs*) by Dandin.

Prosody. Third are the treatises on prosody such as the *Precious Source ofProsody* (*Chando-ratnakara; sdeb sbyor rin chen 'byung gnas*) by the master Shantipa.

Synonymies. Fourth are treatises on synonyms, homonyms, epithets, and so on, such as the *Treasury of Amarasimha* (*Amarokosha; 'chi med mdzod*).

Drama. Fifth are treatises on drama, such as the *Dramatical Treatise* (*Natyashastra; bha ra ta*).

TREATISES THAT TEACH QUALITATIVELY

Qualitative treatises teach methods for attaining liberation and omniscience and are exemplified in the Great Vehicle (Mahayana) by those of the Madhyamaka school that establish the selflessness of the individual and phenomena. Qualitative treatises include those such as the *Bodhisattva Levels* (*byang sa*) by Asanga, and *Entering the Conduct of Bodhisattvas* (*byang chub sems dpa'i spyod pa la 'jug pa*) by Shantideva. Masters at different levels compose these treatises. For instance, the superior type of master includes those who perceive the nature of phenomena, such as the glorious lord Nagarjuna and the sublime Asanga. The middling type of master includes those to whom permission to write was given by their wisdom deities, such masters as Dignaga and Candragomin. The lesser type of master includes those who are learned in the five sciences and possess the esoteric instructions of the lineage of Lamas, such masters as Shrigupta and Shakyamati.

The instructions of the lineages that these masters possess have five aspects regarding the explanation of the discourses:

1. relating purpose
2. condensed meaning
3. words along with meaning
4. response to objections
5. an outline that connects the text

Alternatively, the explanation of the tantras can be explained through five calculated approaches that conform to five headings given by Buddha as found in the *Clarifying Lamp* (*sgron gsal*)[347] by Candrakirti:

1. What is the tantra's title?
2. For whose benefit is it composed?
3. Who is the composer?
4. What is the scope?
5. What is its purpose?

The classification of the various texts related to the six categories of tantra—Kriya, Upa, Yoga, Mahayoga, Anuyoga, and Ati—will not be given at this point, as they were given within the context of the explanation of the nine vehicles as found in Appendix 1.

Word List

Abhidharma	*mngon chos kyi sde snod*	མངོན་ཆོས་ཀྱི་སྡེ་སྣོད་
abiding nature, natural state	*gnas lugs*	གནས་ལུགས་
accomplishment	*grub pa*	གྲུབ་པ་
attainment, spiritual attainment, siddhi	*dngos grub*	དངོས་གྲུབ་
actual entrance	*bya ba'i 'jug sgo*	བྱ་བའི་འཇུག་སྒོ་
advice	*bslab bya*	བསླབ་བྱ་
advice from my heart	*snying gtam du gdams pa*	སྙིང་གཏམ་དུ་གདམས་པ་
age of conflict	*rtsod ldan*	རྩོད་ལྡན་
All-Creating King	*kun byed rgyal po*	ཀུན་བྱེད་རྒྱལ་པོ་
all-encompassing evenness	*phyam brdal*	ཕྱམ་བརྡལ་
all-inclusive, encompassing	*'ub chub*	འུབ་ཆུབ་
all-pervasive	*brdal khyab*	བརྡལ་ཁྱབ་
all-pervasive evenness	*mnyam brdal*	མཉམ་བརྡལ་
altruistic mind, altruistic attitude	*sems bzang po*	སེམས་བཟང་པོ་
Always Noble, Buddha Always Noble, Kuntu Zangpo	*kun tu bzang po*	ཀུན་ཏུ་བཟང་པོ་
Ancient Translation school	*snga 'gyur*	སྔ་འགྱུར་
antidote, remedy	*gnyen po*	གཉེན་པོ་
Anuyoga of the perfection stage	*lung rdzogs a nu yo ga*	ལུང་རྫོགས་ཨ་ནུ་ཡོ་ག
Anuyoga transmissions	*lung a nu yo ga*	ལུང་ཨ་ནུ་ཡོ་ག
aphorisms in prose and verse	*dbyangs bsnyad*	དབྱངས་བསྙད་

ENGLISH	TRANSLITERATION	TIBETAN
appearances and awareness	snang rig	སྣང་རིག།
appears and exists, seemingly exists, phenomenal existence	snang srid	སྣང་སྲིད།
approach and accomplishment	bsnyen sgrub	བསྙེན་སྒྲུབ།
ascertain the view's basis	gzhi rtsa chod pa	གཞི་རྩ་ཆོད་པ།
aspiration and application mind of awakening	smon 'jug sems	སྨོན་འཇུག་སེམས།
aspiration prayer	smon lam	སྨོན་ལམ།
aspiration, will	'dun	འདུན།
aspirational empowerment	smon lam dbang bskur	སྨོན་ལམ་དབང་བསྐུར།
assemblage, mass, mandala	tshom bu	ཚོམ་བུ།
assurance	dbugs 'byin	དབུགས་འབྱིན།
at ease	rgya yan	རྒྱ་ཡན།
Atiyoga pith instructions	man ngag a ti yo ga	མན་ངག་ཨ་ཏི་ཡོ་ག།
attachment	chags zhen	ཆགས་ཞེན།
auspicious connections	rten 'brel	རྟེན་འབྲེལ།
awakening's ten stages	sa bcu	ས་བཅུ།
awareness' display, awareness' dynamic energy	rig pa'i rtsal	རིག་པའི་རྩལ།
awareness-holder of complete maturity	rnam smin rig 'dzin	རྣམ་སྨིན་རིག་འཛིན།
awareness-holder of indestructibility	rdo rje rig 'dzin	རྡོ་རྗེ་རིག་འཛིན།
awareness-holder of Mahamudra	phyag chen pa rig 'dzin	ཕྱག་ཆེན་པ་རིག་འཛིན།
awareness-holder with the power over longevity	tshe dbang ba'i rig 'dzin	ཚེ་དབང་བའི་རིག་འཛིན།

ENGLISH	TRANSLITERATION	TIBETAN
awareness-holders, *vidyadhara*	*rig 'dzin*	རིག་འཛིན་
awareness itself, one's own awareness	*rang rig*	རང་རིག་
awareness-holder of spontaneous presence	*lhun grub rig 'dzin*	ལྷུན་གྲུབ་རིག་འཛིན་
behavior	*spyod lam*	སྤྱོད་ལམ་
beyond mind's scope, transcends mind	*blo 'das*	བློ་འདས་
Blazing Fire Mountain pure realm	*me ri 'bar ba'i zhing khams*	མེ་རི་འབར་བའི་ཞིང་ཁམས་
blazing of blissful warmth in the body	*lus la bde drod 'bar ba*	ལུས་ལ་བདེ་དྲོད་འབར་བ་
Blood Drinker, *Héruka*	*khrag 'thung*	ཁྲག་འཐུང་
bodhisattva	*byang chub sems dpa'*	བྱང་ཆུབ་སེམས་དཔའ་
body of perfect rapture, *sambhogakaya*	*longs sku*	ལོངས་སྐུ་
Buddha, Transcendent Conqueror	*bcom ldan 'das*	བཅོམ་ལྡན་འདས་
Buddha's word	*bka'*	བཀའ་
Buddhist doctrine	*chos bstan*	ཆོས་བསྟན་
Buddhist practitioner	*chos pa*	ཆོས་པ་
Buddhist scriptures	*gsung rab*	གསུང་རབ་
Buddhist teaching, Buddhist practice, *dharma*, teachings, phenomena	*chos*	ཆོས་
burnt offerings	*sbyin sreg*	སྦྱིན་སྲེག་
carefree	*bag yangs*	བག་ཡངས་
carefree	*gu yang*	གུ་ཡང་
Caryatantra	*spyod pa'i rgyud*	སྤྱོད་པའི་རྒྱུད་

ENGLISH	TRANSLITERATION	TIBETAN
cascading mountain streams	*ri bo'i 'bab chu*	རི་བོའི་འབབ་ཆུ་
catalyst, circumstances, contributing conditions, adverse conditions	*rkyen*	རྐྱེན་
causal vehicle	*rgyu'i theg pa*	རྒྱུའི་ཐེག་པ་
celestial pure land	*mkha' spyod kyi zhing khams*	མཁའ་སྤྱོད་ཀྱི་ཞིང་ཁམས་
celestial realms	*mkha' spyod zhing*	མཁའ་སྤྱོད་ཞིང་
chain of delusion	*'khrul pa lu gu*	འཁྲུལ་པ་ལུ་གུ་
chandali, inner heat	*gtu mo*	གཏུ་མོ་
channels	*rtsa*	རྩ་
characteristics	*mtshan nyid*	མཚན་ཉིད་
clairvoyant	*mngon par shes pa*	མངོན་པར་ཤེས་པ་
clear faith	*dang ba'i dad pa*	དང་བའི་དད་པ་
clear light, luminosity	*'od gsal*	འོད་གསལ་
clearly and nakedly	*rjen lhang nge*	རྗེན་ལྷང་ངེ་
clinging	*zhen*	ཞེན་
co-emergent, innate	*lhan cig skyes*	ལྷན་ཅིག་སྐྱེས་
Collection of Discipline, *vinayapitaka*	*'dul ba'i sde snod*	འདུལ་བའི་སྡེ་སྣོད་
Collection of Discourses *sutrapitaka*	*mdo sde'i sde snod*	མདོ་སྡེའི་སྡེ་སྣོད་
collection, *pitaka*	*sde snod*	སྡེ་སྣོད་
commentaries	*khrid yig*	ཁྲིད་ཡིག་
commitment being	*dam tshig pa*	དམ་ཚིག་པ་
compassion (H)	*thugs kyis dgongs*	ཐུགས་ཀྱིས་དགོངས་

ENGLISH	TRANSLITERATION	TIBETAN
Compassionate One, Chenrezi	*lha rdzogs thugs*	ལྷ་རྫོགས་ཐུགས་
complete	*mthar phyin*	མཐར་ཕྱིན་
complete protector, lord of the mandala	*'khor lo'i mgon*	འཁོར་ལོའི་མགོན་
completely empty void	*chad du stong*	ཆད་དུ་སྟོང་
conceited attachment	*rlom zhen*	རློམ་ཞེན་
conceptual meditation	*rtog sgom*	རྟོག་སྒོམ་
conceptual mind, dualistic mind	*yid dran*	ཡིད་དྲན་
conditioned phenomena	*chos can*	ཆོས་ཅན་
conduct	*spyod pa*	སྤྱོད་པ་
confident faith	*yid ches dad pa*	ཡིད་ཆེས་དད་པ་
confirmation, reassurance	*dbugs dbyung*	དབུགས་དབྱུང་
consciousness	*rnam shes*	རྣམ་ཤེས་
consciousness	*shes pa*	ཤེས་པ་
consciousness' six collections	*tshogs drug*	ཚོགས་དྲུག་
consecration	*rab gnas*	རབ་གནས་
contemplative practice, tantric practice, yogic practice, practice	*rnal 'byor*	རྣལ་འབྱོར་
continuity, *tantra*, mindstream, stream of being	*rgyud*	རྒྱུད་
controlling condition	*bdag rkyen*	བདག་རྐྱེན་
correct physical posture	*lus gnad*	ལུས་གནད་
correct teachings	*yang dag chos*	ཡང་དག་ཆོས་
cultivate the experience, cultivate spiritual practice	*sgrub pa nyams len*	སྒྲུབ་པ་ཉམས་ལེན་

ENGLISH	TRANSLITERATION	TIBETAN
cultivate, meditate	*sgom pa*	སྒོམ་པ་
cultivation	*sgrub*	སྒྲུབ་
cut to the root	*rtsa ba ma gcod*	རྩ་བ་མ་གཅོད་
cutting through solidity	*khregs chod*	ཁྲེགས་ཆོད་
cycle of profound treasures	*zab gter skor*	ཟབ་གཏེར་སྐོར་
deceptive illusions	*slu byed sgyu ma*	སླུ་བྱེད་སྒྱུ་མ་
deep concentration, *samadhi*	*ting nge 'dzin*	ཏིང་ངེ་འཛིན་
decide upon	*thag chod*	ཐག་ཆོད་
describe	*brjod pa*	བརྗོད་པ་
defilement	*grib pa*	གྲིབ་པ་
definition of terms	*nges tshig*	ངེས་ཚིག་
definitive truth	*nges don*	ངེས་དོན་
deliberate examination	*yid dpyod*	ཡིད་དཔྱོད་
delusion	*'khrul pa*	འཁྲུལ་པ་
demons	*'dre*	འདྲེ་
demons	*gdon*	གདོན་
desirable things, sense pleasures	*'dod yon*	འདོད་ཡོན་
desire	*'dod chags*	འདོད་ཆགས་
devotion	*mos gos*	མོས་གོས་
devotion is the sole sufficient cure	*mos gus dkar po chig thub*	མོས་གུས་དཀར་པོ་ཅིག་ཐུབ་
devotional meditation	*mos bsgom*	མོས་བསྒོམ་

ENGLISH	TRANSLITERATION	TIBETAN
dharmakaya	*chos sku*	ཆོས་སྐུ་
diligence	*brtson 'grus*	བརྩོན་འགྲུས་
direct instructions	*dmar khrid*	དམར་ཁྲིད་
direct path	*nye lam*	ཉེ་ལམ་
direct vision, Tögal	*thod rgal*	ཐོད་རྒལ་
directly liberates	*rang thog tu grol bar byed pa*	རང་ཐོག་ཏུ་གྲོལ་བར་བྱེད་པ་
disciple	*gdul bya*	གདུལ་བྱ་
disciple	*rjes su bzung*	རྗེས་སུ་བཟུང་
discipline	*tshul khrims*	ཚུལ་ཁྲིམས་
disciplined mindfulness	*'jur dran*	འཇུར་དྲན་
discourse, *sutra*	*mdo*	མདོ་
display, enjoy	*rol pa*	རོལ་པ་
display, power, dynamic energy, creative energy, expressive power, force	*rtsal*	རྩལ་
displays itself	*snang tshul*	སྣང་ཚུལ་
dissolve	*yal shor*	ཡལ་ཤོར་
distilling the principles	*'gag bsdam pa*	འགག་བསྡམ་པ་
distraction	*rnam g.yengs*	རྣམ་གཡེངས་
domain, object	*yul*	ཡུལ་
doubt	*the tshom*	ཐེ་ཚོམ་
dualistic grasping, clinging, the subject	*'dzin pa*	འཛིན་པ་

ENGLISH	TRANSLITERATION	TIBETAN
dualistic perception	*gnyis snang*	གཉིས་སྣང་
dualistic thought	*gnyis rtog*	གཉིས་རྟོག
ease, relax, rest	*lhug*	ལྷུག
effort	*'bad rtsol*	འབད་རྩོལ
ego-clinging	*bdag 'dzin*	བདག་འཛིན
eight aggregates	*tshogs brgyad*	ཚོགས་བརྒྱད་
eight worldly concerns	*'jig rten chos brgyad*	འཇིག་རྟེན་ཆོས་བརྒྱད་
eight-fold path	*'phags lam yan lag brgyad*	འཕགས་ལམ་ཡན་ལག་བརྒྱད་
elaborations, formulations	*spros pa*	སྤྲོས་པ་
embodiment of all buddhas	*spyi gzugs*	སྤྱི་གཟུགས་
empowerment	*dbang bskur*	དབང་བསྐུར་
emptiness	*stong pa nyid*	སྟོང་པ་ཉིད་
empty resonance	*drags stong*	དྲགས་སྟོང་
enactment	*las sbyor*	ལས་སྦྱོར་
enemies	*dgra*	དགྲ་
energetically creating	*rtsol sgrub*	རྩོལ་སྒྲུབ་
energy center, *cakra*, wheel, mandala	*'khor lo*	འཁོར་ལོ་
enlightened activity	*phrin las*	ཕྲིན་ལས་
enlightened family, family, buddha family, class	*rigs*	རིགས་
enlightened mind, mind of awakening, *bodhicitta*	*byang chub sems*	བྱང་ཆུབ་སེམས་དཔའ་
enlightenment, Buddha	*sangs rgyas*	སངས་རྒྱས་

ENGLISH	TRANSLITERATION	TIBETAN
enlightenment's form body, *rupakaya*, body in form	*gzugs sku*	གཟུགས་སྐུ
enlightenment's forms, *kaya*, wisdom bodies	*sku*	སྐུ
enthusiastic faith	*'dod pa'i dad pa*	འདོད་པའི་དད་པ
erudition, great knowledge, wisdom, scholar	*mkhas pa*	མཁས་པ
essence	*dwangs ma*	དྭངས་མ
essence	*ngo bo*	ངོ་བོ
essential advice	*gnad kyi slab bya*	གནད་ཀྱི་སླབ་བྱ
essential keys, essential vital point	*gnad kyi snying po*	གནད་ཀྱི་སྙིང་པོ
essential nature, basic nature, fundamental nature, nature of reality	*gshis lugs*	གཤིས་ལུགས
establish	*gtan la phab pa*	གཏན་ལ་ཕབ་པ
establish confidence	*gding 'cha'*	གདིང་འཆའ
eternal goal, lasting goals	*gtan gyi 'dun ma*	གཏན་གྱི་འདུན་མ
eternalism	*rtag pa*	རྟག་པ
evenness	*mnyam nyid*	མཉམ་ཉིད
ever present	*lhan skyes*	ལྷན་སྐྱེས
everlasting refuge, eternal refuge	*gtan gyi skyabs*	གཏན་གྱི་སྐྱབས
exaltation, bliss, happiness	*bde ba*	བདེ་བ
exalted succession	*rgyal rabs*	རྒྱལ་རབས
exhilarating	*a la la*	ཨ་ལ་ལ
existence	*srid pa*	སྲིད་པ

ENGLISH	TRANSLITERATION	TIBETAN
existence as it is	snang srid	སྣང་སྲིད་
experiential cultivation, practice	nyams len	ཉམས་ལེན་
explanation	bshad pa	བཤད་པ་
extremely agitated	rab 'tshugs	རབ་འཚུགས་
exult	ya la la	ཡ་ལ་ལ་
fabrication, contrived	bcos	བཅོས་
faculties, sense faculties	dbang po	དབང་པོ་
faith	dad pa	དད་པ་
fall away	zhig shor	ཞིག་ཤོར་
familiarization, to familiarize	goms	གོམས་
fearful	ya ngad	ཡ་ངད་
fearless activity, fearless conduct, tantric discipline, discipline	brtul zhugs	བརྟུལ་ཞུགས་
female Buddha, female consort	yum	ཡུམ་
female demons	sen mo	སེན་མོ་
final conclusion	mtha' sdud	མཐའ་སྡུད་
five aspects of excellence	phun sum tshogs pa lnga	ཕུན་སུམ་ཚོགས་པ་ལྔ་
five degenerations	snyigs ma lnga bdo	སྙིགས་མ་ལྔ་བདོ་
five sciences	rig gnas lnga	རིག་གནས་ལྔ་
flaws, faults	skyon	སྐྱོན་
fortunate aeon	skal pa bzang po	སྐལ་པ་བཟང་པོ་
four aspects to turn the mind [away from *samsara*]	blo ldog rnam pa bzhi	བློ་ལྡོག་རྣམ་པ་བཞི་

ENGLISH	TRANSLITERATION	TIBETAN
four essential recollections	*dran pa nyer gzhag*	དྲན་པ་ཉེར་གཞག
four modes of interpretation	*tshul bzhi*	ཚུལ་བཞི
four naturally manifest lights	*rang byung sgron ma bzhi*	རང་བྱུང་སྒྲོན་མ་བཞི
four obscurations	*sgrib bzhi*	སྒྲིབ་བཞི
four paths of learning	*slob pa'i lam bzhi*	སློབ་པའི་ལམ་བཞི
four visions	*snang ba bzhi*	སྣང་བ་བཞི
four wisdom bodies	*sku bzhi*	སྐུ་བཞི
fresh, fresh state	*so ma*	སོ་མ
gathering, collection, accumulation, group, Tantric feast	*tshogs*	ཚོགས
general topics	*spyi don*	སྤྱི་དོན
generating the mind of awakening	*byang sems bskyed pa*	བྱང་སེམས་བསྐྱེད་པ
generation stage	*bskyed rim*	བསྐྱེད་རིམ
generosity	*sbyin pa*	སྦྱིན་པ
genuine reality, ultimate reality	*rnal ma'i de kho na nyid*	རྣལ་མའི་དེ་ཁོ་ན་ཉིད
genuine, genuine nature, original	*gnyug ma*	གཉུག་མ
Glorious Copper-Colored Mountain	*dpal ri*	དཔལ་རི
glorious lama, glorious spiritual master	*dpal ldan bla ma*	དཔལ་ལྡན་བླ་མ
glorious sublime lama, glorious sublime spiritual master	*dpal ldan bla ma dam pa*	དཔལ་ལྡན་བླ་མ་དམ་པ
great dynamic energy	*rtsal chen*	རྩལ་ཆེན
great exaltation	*bde ba chen*	བདེ་བ་ཆེན
great meditator	*sgom chen*	སྒོམ་ཆེན

ENGLISH	TRANSLITERATION	TIBETAN
great transference rainbow body	'pho chen 'ja' lus	འཕོ་ཆེན་འཇའ་ལུས་
Greater Vehicle, *Mahayana*	theg pa chen po	ཐེག་པ་ཆེན་པོ་
ground *tantra*	gzhi rgyud	གཞི་རྒྱུད་
ground's luminosity	gzhi'i 'od gsal	གཞི་འི་འོད་གསལ་
guidance, instruction	khrid	ཁྲིད་
guru *yoga*	bla ma'i rnal 'byor	བླ་མའི་རྣལ་འབྱོར་
habitual tendencies, habits	bag chags	བག་ཆགས་
harmful thoughts	gnod sems	གནོད་སེ་མས་
hearers, study, hearing	thos pa	ཐོས་པ་
heart (H)	thugs	ཐུགས་
heart advice	zhal gdams	ཞལ་གད་མས་
heart-disciple	thugs kyi sras	ཐུགས་ཀྱི་སྲས་
heart's essence	thugs kyi bcud	ཐུགས་ཀྱི་བཅུད་
hero, spiritual warrior, *daka*, brave warrior	dpa' bo	དཔའ་བོ་
Highest Yogatantra	rnal 'byor bla med	རྣལ་འབྱོར་བླ་མེད་
hindrances	'gal byed	འགལ་བྱེད་
how joyful, satisfied	blo re bde	བློ་རེ་བདེ་
ignorance, stupidity	gti mug	གཏི་མུག་
immediacy of awareness	rig pa spyi blugs	རིག་པ་སྤྱི་བླུགས་
immortal vase body	gzhon nu bum sku	གཞོན་ནུ་བུམ་སྐུ་
impermanence	mi rtag	མི་རྟག་

ENGLISH	TRANSLITERATION	TIBETAN
incisive knowledge, supreme wisdom	*shes rab*	ཤེས་རབ་
indestructible stainless space	*rdo rje dbyings*	རྡོ་རྗེ་དབྱིངས་
indivisible, inseparable	*dbye ba med*	དབྱེ་བ་མེད་
inner clarity	*gting gsal*	གཏིང་གསལ་
inner clarity, inner luminosity	*snang gsal*	སྣང་གསལ་
inner radiance, display	*mdangs*	མདངས་
inner science of Buddhism	*sangs rgyas pa'i nang rig*	སངས་རྒྱས་པའི་ནང་རིག
inspiration	*bskul ba*	བསྐུལ་བ་
instruction manuals	*khrid yig gi gzhung*	ཁྲིད་ཡིག་གི་གཞུང་
instruction, reading transmission, scripture	*lung*	ལུང་
instructions, oral instructions	*gdams ngag*	གདམས་ངག
intermediate state, *bardo*	*bar do*	བར་དོ་
intricate array, display	*yo lang*	ཡོ་ལང་
introduce, pointing out (awareness)	*ngo sprad pa*	ངོ་སྤྲད་པ་
introduction, to introduce	*ngo 'phrod*	ངོ་འཕྲོད་
irrelevant teachings	*bshad yam chos*	བཤད་ཡམ་ཆོས་
Joyous Buddha	*bde bzhin shegs pa*	བདེ་བཞིན་གཤེགས་པ་
karma, action	*las*	ལས་
karmic circulating energies	*las rlung*	ལས་རླུང་
karmic obscurations	*las kyi sgrib pa*	ལས་ཀྱི་སྒྲིབ་པ་
karmic wheel of existence	*srid pa las kyi 'khor lo*	སྲིད་པ་ལས་ཀྱི་འཁོར་ལོ་

ENGLISH	TRANSLITERATION	TIBETAN
key essential point, vital point, key point,	*gnad*	གནད་
kingdom	*rgyal thabs*	རྒྱལ་ཐབས་
knowable	*shes bya*	ཤེས་བྱ་
Kriyatantra	*bya ba'i rgyud*	བྱ་བའི་རྒྱུད་
Lake Born Vajra	*mtsho skyes kyi rdo rje*	མཚོ་སྐྱེས་ཀྱི་རྡོ་རྗེ་
Land of the Exalted, India	*'phags yul*	འཕགས་ཡུལ་
lasting victory	*gtan du rgyal ba*	གཏན་དུ་རྒྱལ་བ་
layman's vows of individual liberation	*so thar dge bsnyen sdom*	སོ་ཐར་དགེ་བསྙེན་སྡོམ་
legends	*gleng gzhi*	གླེང་གཞི་
leisures and attainments	*dal 'byor*	དལ་འབྱོར་
Lesser Vehicle	*theg pa chung ngu*	ཐེག་པ་ཆུང་དུ་
liberate, deliver, save	*sgrol ba*	སྒྲོལ་བ་
liberated from extremes	*mtha' grol*	མཐའ་གྲོལ་
Life and Liberation Supplications, prayer based on life story	*rnam thar gsol 'debs*	རྣམ་ཐར་གསོལ་འདེབས་
life-sustaining channel	*srog rtsa*	སྲོག་རྩ་
literal meaning	*tshig gi don*	ཚིག་གི་དོན་
Lord of Secrets, *Vajrapani*	*gsang bdag*	གསང་བདག་
lord of yogins	*rnal 'byor dbang phyug*	རྣལ་འབྱོར་དབང་ཕྱུག་
lord-protector	*mgon po*	མགོན་པོ་
lose warmth	*drod 'chor*	དྲོད་འཆོར་

ENGLISH	TRANSLITERATION	TIBETAN
luminosity, illumination	*gsal ba*	གསལ་བ་
magical apparitions	*cho 'phrul*	ཆོ་འཕྲུལ་
magical display	*sgyu 'phrul*	སྒྱུ་འཕྲུལ་
magical, magical display	*sgyu ma*	སྒྱུ་མ་
Mahayoga	*rnal 'byor chen po*	རྣལ་འབྱོར་ཆེན་པོ་
Mahayoga tantras	*rgyud ma ha yo ga*	རྒྱུད་མ་ཧ་ཡོ་ག་
male demons	*rgyal po*	རྒྱལ་པོ་
malevolent beings	*gdug pa*	གདུག་པ་
mandala	*dkyil 'khor*	དཀྱིལ་འཁོར་
manifestation body, *nirmanakaya*	*sprul sku*	སྤྲུལ་སྐུ་
manifold illumination	*snang stong 'bar*	སྣང་སྟོང་འབར་
Mantric Collection of the Awareness-holders	*rig pa 'dzin pa sngags kyi sde snod*	རིག་པ་འཛིན་པ་སྔགས་ཀྱི་སྡེ་སྣོད་
material body	*gdos bcas phung po*	གདོས་བཅས་ཕུང་པོ་
May this prove virtuous and excellent	*dge legs*	དགེ་ལེགས་
meditation	*bsam gtan*	བསམ་མ་གཏན་
mental body	*yid lus*	ཡིད་ལུས་
mental constructs	*blo byas*	བློ་བྱས་
mental images	*don spyi*	དོན་སྤྱི་
mentally stable	*blo brtan*	བློ་བརྟན་
metrical verses	*sdeb sbyor*	སྡེབ་སྦྱོར་
mind	*sems*	སེམས་

ENGLISH	TRANSLITERATION	TIBETAN
mind	yid	ཡིད་
mind class	sems sde	སེ་མས་སྟེ་
mind stream (H)	dgongs rgyud	དགོངས་རྒྱུད་
mind training	blo sbyong	བློ་སྦྱོང་
mind treasures	thugs gter	ཐུགས་གཏེར་
mind, intellect, intellectual activity, intent	blo	བློ་
mindfulness	dran shes	དྲན་ཤེས་
mindfulness, remember	dran pa	དྲན་པ་
mind's comprehension	blo yul	བློ་ཡུལ་
mind's nature, your	rang gi sems nyid	རང་གི་སེ་མས་ཉིད་
miraculous powers	rdzu 'phrul	རྫུ་འཕྲུལ་
mirage	mig 'phrul	མིག་འཕྲུལ་
mirage	smig sgyu	སྨིག་སྒྱུ་
misconceptions	sgro 'dog	སྒྲོ་འདོག་
motivation	kun slong	ཀུན་སློང་
my own perceptions	rang snang	རང་སྣང་
naked liberation, direct liberation	cer grol	ཅེར་གྲོལ་
narratives	rtogs pa brjod	རྟོགས་པ་བརྗོད་
Natural Great Perfection	rang bzhin rdzogs pa chen po	རང་བཞིན་རྫོགས་པ་ཆེན་པོ་
natural manifest display	rang rtsal rol pa	རང་རྩལ་རོལ་པ་
natural manifestation, manifests in and of itself, one's own phenomena	rang snang	རང་སྣང་

ENGLISH	TRANSLITERATION	TIBETAN
natural meditation	*rang bzhin bsam gtan*	རང་བཞིན་བསམ་ག་གཏན་
natural mind, innate mind	*gnyug ma'i sems*	གཉུག་མའི་སེ་སེམས་
natural state, naturally settled state, natural repose,	*rang babs*	རང་བབས་
naturally liberated, self-liberated	*rang grol*	རང་གྲོལ་
naturally abides	*rang gnas*	རང་གནས་
naturally relax	*rang du klod*	རང་དུ་ཀློད་
naturally settle, naturally remain, settle naturally	*rang bzhag*	རང་བཞག་
nature	*rang bzhin*	རང་བཞིན་
nature of mind	*sems ngo*	སེ་མས་ངོ་
nature of phenomena, nature or reality, *dharmata*	*chos nyid*	ཆོས་ཉིད་
negative actions	*sdig*	སྡིག་
negative acts	*las ngan*	ལས་ངན་
negative circumstances	*'gal mkhyen*	འགལ་མཁྱེན་
negative forces, *mara*, demons	*bdud*	བདུད་
nevertheless	*gal te na*	གལ་ཏེ་ན་
nihilism	*chad*	ཆད་
non-action	*byar med*	བྱར་མེད་
non-dual truth	*gnyis med kyi don*	གཉིས་མེད་ཀྱི་དོན་
non-duality	*gnyis su med*	གཉིས་སུ་མེད་
non-existence	*med pa*	མེད་པ་

ENGLISH	TRANSLITERATION	TIBETAN
non-fixation, without reference, non-conceptual	dmigs med	དམིགས་མེད་
non-substantial evenness	phyal ba	ཕྱལ་བ་
not be turned back	las phyir mi ldog	ལས་ཕྱིར་མི་ལྡོག་
not foraging	mi slong ba	མི་སློང་བ་
oath-bound guardians	dam can	དམ་ཅན་
object of worship	mchod gnas	མཆོད་གནས་
obscuration of habitual tendencies	bag chags kyi sgrib pa	བག་ཆགས་ཀྱི་སྒྲིབ་པ་
obscuration of passions	nyon mongs kyi sgrib pa	ཉོན་མོངས་ཀྱི་སྒྲིབ་པ་
obscurations	sgrib pa	སྒྲིབ་པ་
observer of monastic precepts	sdom brtson	སྡོམ་བརྩོན་
obstacles	bar chad	བར་ཆད་
offering-practice rituals	sgrub mchod	སྒྲུབ་མཆོད་
omniscience	rnam pa thams cad mkhyen pa	རྣམ་པ་ཐམས་ཅད་མཁྱེན་པ་
oneness, only	gcig pu	གཅིག་པུ་
open and relaxed	gu yangs blo bde	གུ་ཡངས་བློ་བདེ་
openness	kha yan	ཁ་ཡན་
oral instructions	gdams ngag	གདམས་ངག་
oral instructions	zhal gdams	ཞལ་གདམས་
oral tradition	kha gtam	ཁ་གཏམ་
oral transmission lineage (of supreme beings)	snyan brgyud	སྙན་བརྒྱུད་

ENGLISH	TRANSLITERATION	TIBETAN
ordinary knowing, ordinary awareness, ordinary mind	*tha mal gyi shes pa*	ཐ་མལ་གྱི་ཤེས་པ་
ordinary meaning	*don dman*	དོན་དམན་
original abiding nature	*gdod ma'i gnas lugs*	གདོད་མའི་གནས་ལུགས་
original basic nature, original essential nature	*gnyug ma'i gshis lugs*	གཉུག་མའི་གཤིས་ལུགས་
original ground	*gdod ma'i gzhi*	གདོད་མའི་གཞི་
original ground	*gzhi*	གཞི་
original lord-protector	*gdod ma'i mgon po*	གདོད་མའི་མགོན་པོ་
original mindfulness	*gnyug ma'i dran pa*	གཉུག་མའི་དྲན་པ་
original natural mind, my innate knowing, original awareness	*gnyug ma'i shes pa*	གཉུག་མའི་ཤེས་པ་
original, primordial	*gdod ma*	གདོད་མ་
own nature, natural face, true nature	*rang ngo*	རང་ངོ་
palace	*pho brang*	ཕོ་བྲང་
parables	*de lta byung*	དེ་ལྟ་བྱུང་
path of accumulation	*tshogs lam*	ཚོགས་ལམ་
path of application	*sbyor lam*	སྦྱོར་ལམ་
path of meditation	*sgom lam*	སྒོམ་ལམ་
path of seeing	*mthong lam*	མཐོང་ལམ་
paths and levels	*sa lam*	ས་ལམ་
patience	*bzod pa*	བཟོད་པ་
perfect conduct	*yang dag spyod*	ཡང་དག་སྤྱོད་
personal deity	*phug gi lha*	ཕུག་གི་ལྷ་

ENGLISH	TRANSLITERATION	TIBETAN
philosophical approach, philosophical system, tenet	*grub mtha'*	གྲུབ་མཐའ་
pith instructions, *upadesha*	*man ngag*	མན་ངག་
point of resolution	*tshar tshad*	ཚར་ཚད་
post-meditation, after sitting meditation	*rjes thob*	རྗེས་ཐོབ་
post-meditation's conduct	*rjes thob spyod lam*	རྗེས་ཐོབ་སྤྱོད་ལམ་
power and strength	*dbang shed*	དབང་ཤེད་
power of recollection	*dran pa'i stob*	དྲན་པའི་སྟོབ་
practical instructions, practice procedures	*lag len*	ལག་ལེན་
practice, spiritual practice	*sgrub pa*	སྒྲུབ་པ་
practitioner, yogin, adept	*rnal 'byor pa*	རྣལ་འབྱོར་པ་
precious master	*rin po che*	རིན་པོ་ཆེ་
preparation	*sbyor*	སྦྱོར་
present awareness, present knowing	*da lta'i shes pa*	ད་ལྟའི་ཤེས་པ་
primordial liberation	*ye grol*	ཡེ་གྲོལ་
primordial presence	*ye yin*	ཡེ་ཡིན་
primordial purity	*ka dag*	ཀ་དག་
primordially existent	*ye grub*	ཡེ་གྲུབ་
profound instructions	*gdams ngag*	གདམས་ངག་
profound meaning	*zab don*	ཟབ་དོན་
profound treasures	*zab gter*	ཟབ་གཏེར་
prophecy, prophetic declarations	*lung bstan*	ལུང་བསྟན་

ENGLISH	TRANSLITERATION	TIBETAN
protectors and guardians	*skyong srung ma*	སྐྱོང་སྲུང་མ་
protectors of the Teachings, dharma protectors	*chos skyongs*	ཆོས་སྐྱོངས་
provisional	*gnas skabs*	གནས་སྐབས་
pure appearances, pure view, pure vision	*dag snang*	དག་སྣང་
pure conduct	*tshangs spyod*	ཚངས་སྤྱོད་
pure drop	*dwangs ma'i thig le*	དྭངས་མའི་ཐིག་ལེ་
pure realms	*zhing khams*	ཞིང་ཁམས་
purity and impurity	*gtsang dme*	གཙང་དྨེ་
qualities, noble qualities	*yon tan*	ཡོན་ཏན་
rainbow body	*'ja' lus*	འཇའ་ལུས་
reach consummation, destination is reached	*mtha' ru phyin*	མཐའ་རུ་ཕྱིན་
reach full measure	*tshad du phyin pa*	ཚད་དུ་ཕྱིན་པ་
realization	*rtogs pa*	རྟོགས་པ་
realm of an aeon of illumination	*sgron me'i zhing khams*	སྒྲོན་མེའི་ཞིང་ཁམས་
realms of phenomena	*chos khams*	ཆོས་ཁམས་
recognition, awareness, natural mind, knowing, wisdom	*shes pa*	ཤེས་པ་
recognize	*ngo shes pa*	ངོ་ཤེས་པ་
recognize, recognize one's natural face	*rang ngo shes*	རང་ངོ་ཤེས་
recollection of mind	*sems dran pa nyer gzhag*	སེ་མས་དྲན་པ་ཉེར་གཞག་
regent, representative	*rgyal tshab*	རྒྱལ་ཚབ་

ENGLISH	TRANSLITERATION	TIBETAN
relax	*lhug pa*	ལྷུག་པ་
relax at ease	*klod kyis klod*	གློད་ཀྱིས་གློད་
relax, let go,	*kha yan du klod*	ཁ་ཡན་དུ་གློད་
relaxed, settling	*lhug 'jog*	ལྷུག་པར་འཇོག་
remote retreat	*dben sa*	དབེན་ས་
renunciate, abandon	*spangs pa*	སྤངས་པ་
renunciation	*nges 'byung*	ངེས་འབྱུང་
resolve	*gdar sha chod*	གདར་ཤ་ཆོད་
resolve, decisive, conclude	*thag gcod*	ཐག་གཅོད་
resonance, compassion, compassionate qualities	*thugs rje*	ཐུགས་རྗེ་
respect	*mos pa*	མོས་པ་
resplendent enjoyment	*longs spyod*	ལོངས་སྤྱོད་
rest at ease	*lhug par bzhag*	ལྷུག་པར་བཞག་
rest in evenness	*mnyam par bzhag*	མཉམ་པར་བཞག་
resting	*bzhag*	བཞག་
resultant vehicle	*'bras bu'i theg pa*	འབྲས་བུའི་ཐེག་པ་
revealing the key point	*gnad bkrol ba*	གནད་བཀྲོལ་བ་
reverse meaning, wrong meaning	*don log*	དོན་ལོག་
reverse point of view, wrong view	*log lta*	ལོག་ལྟ་
root spiritual master, root lama	*rtsa ba'I bla ma*	རྩ་བའི་བླ་མ་
sacred inherent potential	*dam pa'i rigs*	དམ་པའི་རིགས་

ENGLISH	TRANSLITERATION	TIBETAN
sacred places and regions	*gnas yul*	གནས་ཡུལ་
sacred substances	*dam rdzas*	དམ་རྫས་
sacred Teachings, sacred dharma	*dam chos*	དམ་ཆོས་
sadhana class	*sgrub sde*	སྒྲུབ་སྡེ་
samaya, tantric commitment	*dam tshig*	དམ་ཚིག་
samsara and *nirvana*	*'khor 'das*	འཁོར་འདས་
samsaric phenomena	*'khor ba'i chos*	འཁོར་བའི་ཆོས་
scholarship, nobility, and excellence,	*mkhas tsun grub*	མཁས་ཙུན་གྲུབ་
second Teacher (Guru Rinpoché)	*ston pa gnyis pa*	སྟོན་པ་གཉིས་པ་
secret empowerment	*gsang dbang*	གསང་དབང་
secret heart essence	*snying thig yang gsang*	སྙིང་ཐིག་ཡང་གསང་
secret practices	*gsang ba'i spyod*	གསང་བའི་སྤྱོད་
secular and religious laws	*lugs gnyis*	ལུགས་གཉིས་
self-manifest emanation body	*rang byung sprul sku*	རང་བྱུང་སྤྲུལ་སྐུ་
self-manifest magical display	*rang byung sgyu ma*	རང་བྱུང་སྒྱུ་མ་
self-manifest primordial wisdom	*rang byung ye shes*	རང་བྱུང་ཡེ་ཤེས་
series of successive lives	*tshe rabs*	ཚེ་རབས་
settle	*zhog*	ཞོག་
settle, rest	*'jog pa*	འཇོག་པ་
seven branches of enlightenment	*byang chub yan lag bdun*	བྱང་ཆུབ་ཡན་ལག་བདུན་
significance, meaning, truth	*don*	དོན་
six essentials	*gnad drug*	གནད་དྲུག་

ENGLISH	TRANSLITERATION	TIBETAN
six parameters	*mtha' drug*	མཐའ་དྲུག
skillful means, methods	*thabs la mkhas pa*	ཐབས་ལ་མཁས་པ་
Snowy Land (Tibet)	*kha ba can*	ཁ་བ་ཅན་
solitary meditation practice	*ri chos*	རི་ཆོས་
solitary sages	*rang sangs rgyas*	རང་སངས་རྒྱས་
song of yearning	*gdung glu*	གདུང་གླུ
songs of realization, *doha*	*gur*	གུར་
songs of tantric gatherings	*tshogs glu*	ཚོགས་གླུ
source of refuge	*skyabs gnas*	སྐྱབས་གནས་
sovereign of the teachings, Dharma King	*chos kyi rgyal po*	ཆོས་ཀྱི་རྒྱལ་པོ་
special deity	*lhag pa'i lha*	ལྷག་པའི་ལྷ་
sphere, *bindu, tik lé*, essence	*thig le*	ཐིག་ལེ་
spirits, negative spirits	*'byung po*	འབྱུང་པོ་
spiritual accomplishment, *siddhi*	*dngos grub*	དངོས་གྲུབ་
spiritual community, *sangha*	*dge 'dun*	དགེ་འདུན་
spiritual companions	*mched grog*	མཆེད་གྲོག
spiritual experiences	*nyams myong*	ཉམས་མྱོང་
spiritual master, wisdom master, master, lama, guru	*bla ma*	བླ་མ་
spiritual maturity and liberation	*smin grol*	སྨིན་གྲོལ་
spiritual vehicle, *yana*	*theg pa*	ཐེག་པ་
spiritual verse, songs of realization, *doha*	*mgur*	མགུར་

ENGLISH	TRANSLITERATION	TIBETAN
spontaneous presence, spontaneously accomplished	*lhun grub*	ལྷུན་གྲུབ་
stainless space	*dbyings*	དབྱིངས་
starving spirits, demons	*'gong po*	འགོང་པོ་
state of happiness, carefree, happy	*blo bde*	བློ་བདེ་
stillness, abide, dwell, sacred place	*gnas pa*	གནས་པ་
strive for	*don du gnyer*	དོན་དུ་གཉེར་
subject and object	*yul dang yul can*	ཡུལ་དང་ཡུལ་ཅན་
sublime guide	*ded dpon*	དེད་དཔོན་
substanceless space	*dngos po med pa'i mkha'*	དངོས་པོ་མེད་པའི་མཁའ་
supplication prayer	*gsol ba 'debs pa*	གསོལ་བ་འདེབས་པ་
suppression	*dgag*	དགག་
supreme guide	*dran mchog*	དྲན་མཆོག་
supreme knowledge	*mkhyen pa*	མཁྱེན་པ་
supreme knowledge, wisdom, love, and power	*mkhyen brtse nus*	མཁྱེན་བརྩེ་ནུས་
supreme nature, epitome	*bdag nyid chen po*	བདག་ཉིད་ཆེན་པོ་
supreme treasure revealer	*gter chen*	གཏེར་ཆེན་
supreme wisdom consort, supreme wisdom	*shes rab ma*	ཤེས་རབ་མ་
swift path	*myur lam*	མྱུར་ལམ་
taintless, untainted	*zag med*	ཟག་མེད་
tales of past lives, series of lives,	*skye rabs*	སྐྱེ་རབས་
tantra of skillful means	*thabs kyi rgyud*	ཐབས་ཀྱི་རྒྱུད་

English	Transliteration	Tibetan
tantra, mantra	*sngags*	སྔགས་
tantric collection, tantra class, *tantrapitaka*	*rgyud sde*	རྒྱུད་སྡེ་
tantric feast celebration	*tshogs kyi dga' ston*	ཚོགས་ཀྱི་དགའ་སྟོན་
tantric master	*sngags kyi slob dpon*	སྔགས་ཀྱི་སློབ་དཔོན་
tantric monk	*ngags ban*	ངགས་བན་
ten unvirtuous actions	*mi dge ba bcu*	མི་དགེ་བ་བཅུ་
terms	*ming*	མིང་
terrestrial pure land	*sa spyod zhing khams*	ས་སྤྱོད་ཞིང་ཁམས་
thinking, movement of thoughts	*'gyu*	འགྱུ་
thoughts and memories	*dran rtog*	དྲན་རྟོག་
thoughts of wrong views	*log pa'i rnam rtog*	ལོག་པའི་རྣམ་རྟོག་
thoughts, concepts	*rnam rtog*	རྣམ་རྟོག་
three phases of birth	*skye gsum*	སྐྱེ་གསུམ་
Tibet	*bsil ldan*	བསིལ་ལྡན་
totally open	*ha chad de*	ཧ་ཆད་དེ་
tradition	*bka' srol*	བཀའ་སྲོལ་
tradition	*ring lugs*	རིང་ལུགས་
train, cultivate, practice	*bsgrub pa*	བསྒྲུབ་པ་
transference (of consciousness)	*'pho ba*	འཕོ་བ་
treasure trove	*gter mdzod*	གཏེར་མཛོད་
treasures, hidden teachings	*gter ma*	གཏེར་མ་

ENGLISH	TRANSLITERATION	TIBETAN
treatise	*bstan bcos*	བསྟན་བཅོས་
Triple Gems	*dkon mchog gsum*	དཀོན་མཆོག་གསུམ་
true virtuous friend	*yang dag dge ba'i bshes gnyen*	ཡང་དག་དགེ་བའི་བཤེས་བ
trust	*yid ches*	ཡིད་ཆེས་
truth of origination	*kun 'byung*	ཀུན་འབྱུང་
turn the Teachings' wheel, turn the *dharma* wheel	*chos kyi 'khor bsgyur*	ཆོས་ཀྱི་འཁོར་བསྒྱུར་
two goals, two benefits	*don gnyis*	དོན་གཉིས་
ultimate nature of reality	*don dam gshis gyi gnas lugs*	དོན་དམ་གཤིས་ཀྱི་གནས་
ultimate nature, ultimate truth	*don dam*	དོན་དམ་
ultimate reality as it is	*yin lugs*	ཡིན་ལུགས་
ultimate reality, as it is	*de bzhin nyid*	དེ་བཞིན་ཉིད་
ultimate reality, nature of reality	*de kho na nyid*	དེ་ཁོ་ན་ཉིད་
unassailable state	*btsan sa*	བཙན་ས་
unconditioned	*'dus ma byas*	འདུས་མ་བྱས་
uncontrived	*ma bcos*	མ་བཅོས་
uncontrived all-pervasive equality	*mnyam brdal ma bcos*	མཉམ་བརྡལ་མ་བཅོས་
undistracted	*yengs med*	ཡེངས་མེད་
unimpeded	*zang thal*	ཟང་ཐལ་
union, integral union, inseparable	*zung 'jug*	ཟུང་འཇུག་
unobstructed	*sha ra ra*	ཤ་ར་ར་
unrelenting	*thang lhod*	ཐང་ལྷོད་

ENGLISH	TRANSLITERATION	TIBETAN
unrestricted, free, unconfined	*rgya yan*	རྒྱ་ཡན་
untainted	*ma 'dres pa*	མ་འདྲེས་པ་
upheaval, challenge	*lhongs*	ལྷོངས་
upheavals of negative karma	*las ngan lhongs*	ལས་ངན་ལྷོངས་
upward moving circulating energy	*gyen rgyu'i rlung*	གྱེན་རྒྱུའི་རླུང་
utterly free and spacious	*gu yangs phya ler 'gro*	གུ་ཡངས་ཕྱ་ལེར་འགྲོ་
Vajrayana	*rdo rje theg pa*	རྡོ་རྗེ་ཐེག་པ་
valid cognition	*tshad ma*	ཚད་མ་
vast expanse	*klong*	ཀློང་
vast expanse class	*klong sde*	ཀློང་སྡེ་
vehicle of characteristics, *sutrayana*	*mtshan nyid theg pa*	མཚན་ཉིད་ཐེག་པ་
vehicle of tantra	*sngags kyi theg pa*	སྔགས་ཀྱི་ཐེག་པ་
Venerable Saraha	*mda' bsnun zhabs*	མདའ་བསྣུན་ཞབས་
verse	*tshigs bcad*	ཚིགས་བཅད་
Victorious One's heirs, *bodhisattvas*	*rgyal sras*	རྒྱལ་སྲས་
Victorious One's teachings' wheel, wheel of the Victorious One's doctrine	*rgyal bstan chos 'khor*	རྒྱལ་བསྟན་ཆོས་འཁོར་
view of primordial purity	*ka dag gi lta ba*	ཀ་དག་གི་ལྟ་བ་
view, point of view	*lta ba*	ལྟ་བ་
visionary experiences	*nyams snang*	ཉམས་སྣང་
vital energy, subtle energy, wind, *prana*	*rlung*	རླུང་

ENGLISH	TRANSLITERATION	TIBETAN
vow-breaker	*dam nyams*	དམ་ཉམས་
vows	*sdom pa*	སྡོམ་པ་
wheel of life, *samsara*	*'khor ba*	འཁོར་བ་
wheel of tantric feast gathering, tantric feast-wheel	*tshogs kyi 'khor lo*	ཚོགས་ཀྱི་འཁོར་ལོ་
wisdom, primordial wisdom	*ye shes*	ཡེ་ཤེས་
wisdom being	*ye shes pa*	ཡེ་ཤེས་པ་
wisdom deity	*yi dam*	ཡི་དམ་
wisdom deity body	*lha sku*	ལྷ་སྐུ་
wisdom mind (H), mind (H)	*thugs rgyud*	ཐུགས་རྒྱུད་
wisdom mind transmission	*dgongs brgyud*	དགོངས་བརྒྱུད་
wisdom mind, realization, think (H), consider (H)	*dgongs*	དགོངས་
without any fixed point of reference, without fixation, beyond understanding	*gtad med*	གཏད་མེད་
word, phrase	*tshig*	ཚིག་
words from my heart	*snying gtam*	སྙིང་གཏམ་
worthy recipient	*snod rung*	སྣོད་རུང་
wrong paths	*log lam*	ལོག་ལམ་
Yogatantra	*rnal 'byor rgyud*	རྣལ་འབྱོར་རྒྱུད་
yogi	*rtogs ldan*	རྟོགས་ལྡན་

Abbreviations

CWDR   *Collected Works of His Holiness Dudjom Rinpoche* (*bdud 'joms 'jigs bral ye shes rdo rje yi gsung 'bum dam chos rin chen nor bu'i mdzod*) published by Dupjung Lama, Madhav Nikunj, Kalimpong, W.B., 1978.

Das   *Tibetan-English Dictionary* of Chandra Das.

T   *A Complete Catalogue of the Tibetan Buddhist Canons.* Tohoku University Catalogue of the Dergé (*sde dge*) Edition of the Canon. Sendai, 1934.

NSTB   *The Nyingma School of Tibetan Buddhism,* volume 1, Gyurme Dorje and Matthew Kapstein. Boston: Wisdom Publications, 1991.

NGB   *Collected Tantras of the Nyingmapa. rnying ma'i rgyud 'bum.* Thimpu: Jamyang Khyentse Rinpoche, 1973, 36 vols. Catalogue by E. Kaneko, Tokyo, 1982.

P   *The Tibetan Tripitaka, Peking Edition.* 168 vols. Tokyo-Kyoto: Suzuki Research Foundation, 1955–61.

LC   Library of Congress

TsDzCm   *An Encyclopaedic Tibetan-English Dictionary,* letters *ka-nya.*

Bibliography

PUBLICATIONS IN TIBETAN

All-Creating King (kun byed rgyal po). T828. NGB, vol. 1.

Analysis of Empowerment's Meaning (dbang don rnam par 'byed pa). Unidentified.

Array of the Path of the Magical Net (sgyu 'phrul lam rnam bkod pa; Skt. *Maya-patha-vyavastha-pana)*. Indrabhuti. P4737.

The Collected Gter-ma Rediscoveries of Gter-chen Bdud-'joms-gling-pa. Volume 19. Edited by H. H. bdud-joms 'jigs bral ye shes-rdo-rje. Kalimpong, West Bengal, India: Dupjung Lama, Madhav Nikunj. Dudjom Lingpa.

Collected Works of Dudjom Rinpoché (bdud 'joms 'jigs bral ye shes rdo rje yi/ gsung 'bum dam chos rin chen nor bu'i mdzod). Vols. 1, 2, 4, and 13. His Holiness Dudjom Rinpoché, Jigdral Yeshé Dorjé.

Commentary on Difficult Points Entitled, Endowed with Wisdom (dka' 'grel ye shes ldan; Skt. *Shribuddha-kapala-tantrapanjika-jnanavati)*. Saraha. T1652.

Commentary on Meditation in Mudra (phyag rgya bsam gtan; Skt. *Maya-jala-mudra-dhyana)*. P4732. Vimalamitra.

Commentary on the Perfection of Incisive Knowledge in Eight Thousand Lines (brgyad stong 'grel chen; Skt. *Ashtasahasrika-prajnaparamita-vyakhyab-hisamaya-lamkaraloka)*. Haribhadra. T3791.

The Festival of Delight in Which the Expression of Eloquent Teachings Manifests: A Concise Detailed Presentation of the Nyingmapa Teachings, The Ancient Translation School of Secret Mantra (gsang sngags snga 'gyur rnying ma ba'i bstan pa'i rnam gzhag mdo tsam brjod pa legs bshad snang ba'i dga' ston). In the *Collected Works of Dudjom Rinpoché*, vol. 2, pp. 277–423. His Holiness Dudjom Rinpoché, Jigdral Yeshé Dorjé.

Freedom Path's Illuminating Light: Preliminary Practice's Developmental Instructions for the Profound, Secret Dakini's Heart Essence (zab gsang

mkha' 'gro'i snying thig gi sngon 'gro'i khrid rim thar lam snang sgron).
In the *Collected Works of Dudjom Rinpoché*, vol. 13, pp. 25–421. His Holiness Dudjom Rinpoché, Jigdral Yeshé Dorjé.

General Sutra Which Gathers All Realization (*spyi mdo dgongs pa 'dus pa*).
LCSB, vols. 10–12.

The Glorious Secret Essence Tantra of the Glorious Magical Net of Vajrasattva
(*rdo rje sems dpa'i sgyu 'phrul drwa ba'i rgyud dpal gsang ba'i snying po*;
Skt. *Guhyagarbha-tattvavinishcayamahatantra*). T832.

The Great Chariot (*shing rta chen mo*). Autocommentary to *Resting in the
Nature of Mind* (*sems nyid ngal so*), part of the *Trilogy of Rest* (*ngal gso
skor gsum*). 4 vols. Gangtok, Sikkim: Dodrupchen Rinpoché, 1973.
Longchen Rabjampa

The Great Garuda (*khyung chen*). NGB, vol. 1.

Great Magical Display Tantra (*sgyu 'phrul chen po*; Skt. *Mahamaya Tantra*).
T425.

*Heart Advice of My Always Noble Spiritual Master: Instructions on the Pre-
liminary Practice of the Heart Essence* (*snying thig sngon 'gro'i khrid yig
kun bzang bla ma'i zhal lung*). Sichuan, China: Sichuan Ethnic National-
ity Publications, 1989. Patrul Rinpoché.

Hévajra Tantra (*kye yi rdo rje*; Skt. *Hevajra-tantraraja*). T417–8.

Hundred Verses on Incisive Knowledge (*shes rab brgya pa*; Skt. *Prajnashatakanamaprakarana*). Nagarjuna. T4328.

The Lion's Perfect Display (*seng ge rtsal rdzogs*). NGB, vol. 9.

Matrix of Mystery (*gsang ba 'dus pa*; Skt. *Guhyasamaja Tantra*). T442–3.

Magical Key of Further Discernment (*yang 'byed 'phrul mig gyi lde*). NGB,
vol. 2.

Magical Key to the Storehouse (*bang mdzod 'phrul gyi lde mig*). NGB, vol. 2.

Magical Net of Manjushri (*'jam dpal sgyu 'phrul drva ba*). T360.

Means for Attaining Ultimate Reality As It Is (*de kho na nyid sgrub pa'i
thabs*). Naropa. Unidentified.

Minor Precepts of the Vinaya (*'dul ba lung phran tshegs*; Skt. *Vinayaksu-
dragama*). T6.

Pearl Necklace (mu tig phreng ba). NGB, vol. 9.

Questions and Answers of Vajrasattva (rdo rje sems dpa'i zhus lan; Skt. *Vajrasattva-prasnottara)*. P5082.

Questions by the Four Goddesses (lha mo bzhis zhus pa; Skt. *Caturdevipariprc-cha)*. T446.

Rational System of Detailed Explanation (rnam par bshad pa'i rigs pa; Skt. *Vyakhyayukti)*. Vasubandhu. T4061.

Reciting the Names of Manjushri ('phags pa 'jam dpal gyi mtshan yang dag par brjod pa; Skt. *Manjushrinamasamgiti)*. T360.

Secret Discourse's Summation of the Meaning (don bsdus; Skt. *Guhyasu-trapindartha)*. P4751.

Song of Encouragement to Read the Seven Treasuries, The Excellent Words of Omniscient Longchen Rabjampa (klong chen mdzod bdun la blta bar bskul ba). In the *Collected Works of Dpal-sprul O-rgyan-'jigs-med-chos-kyi-dbang-po* (Gangtok: Sonam T. Kazi, 1970-1971), vol. 1, pp. 149–58. Patrul Rinpoché.

The Special Teachings of the Glorious Wise King (mkhas pa shri rgyal po'i khyad chos). In the *Collected Works of Dpal-sprul O-rgyan-'jigs-med-chos-kyi-dbang-po* (Gangtok: Sonam T. Kazi, 1970-1971), vol. 4. Patrul Rinpoché.

Stages of the Path of the Magical Net (sgyu 'phrul lam rim; Skt. *Mayajala-pathakrama)*. Buddhaguhya. P4720.

Supreme Array of Ati (a ti bkod pa chen po). NGB, vol. 2.

Sutra of the Descent to Lanka (mdo lang kar gshegs pa; Skt. *Lankavatarasu-tra)*. T103.

Synopsis of the Illumination of Suchness (de kho na nyid snang ba'i don bsdus; Skt. *Tattvalokavyakhya)*. T2510.

Tantra of the Extensive Version of the Magical Net (sgyu 'phrul drwa ba rgyas pa). NGB, vol. 14.

Tantra of the Great Self-Manifestation of Awareness (rig pa rang shar chen po'i rgyud). NGB, vol. 10.

Tantra of Self-Manifest Awareness (rig pa rang shar gyi rgyud). NGB, vol. 10.

Three Stages (rim pa gsum; Skt. *Mayajalopadesha-kramatraya).* Vimalamitra. P4742.

Vajra Tent (rdo rje gur; Skt. *Vajra-panjaratantra).* T419.

Vast Space of Vajrasattva (rdo rje sems dpa'i nam mkha' che). NGB, vol. 2.

Wisdom Essence (ye shes thig le; Skt. *Jnanatilakatantra).* T422.

Publications in English

Barron, Richard, translator. *The Autobiography of Jamgön Kongtrul.* Ithaca, NY: Snow Lion Publications, 2003.

Chöying Tobden Dorjé. *The Treasury of Discourses and Tantras (mdo rgyud rin po che'i mdzod).* Translated by Ngawang Zangpo. Unpublished, in the private collection of Lama Tharchin Rinpoché.

Dargyay, Eva M. *The Rise of Esoteric Buddhism in Tibet.* Delhi: Motilal Banarsidass, 1979.

Dowman, Keith, translator. *The Divine Madman: The Sublime Life and Songs of Drukpa Kunley.* Clearlake, CA: Dawn Horse Press, 1983.

Dudjom Jigdral Yeshé Dorjé. *The Nyingma School of Tibetan Buddhism: Its Fundamentals and History.* Volume 1, *The Translations.* Translated by Gyurme Dorje. Boston: Wisdom Publications, 1991.

———. *Perfect Conduct: Ascertaining the Three Vows.* Translated by Khenpo Gyurme Samdrub and Sangye Khandro. Boston: Wisdom Publications, 1996.

Dudjom Lingpa. *Buddhahood Without Meditation: A Visionary Account Known as* Refining One's Perception (Nang-jang). Translated by Richard Barron. Junction City, CA: Padma Publishing, 1994.

Guenther, Herbert. *Ecstatic Spontaneity: Saraha's* Three Cycles of Doha. Berkeley: Asian Humanities Press, 1993.

Gyalwa Changchub and Namkhai Nyingpo. *The Lady of the Lotus-Born: The Life and Enlightenment of Yeshé Tsogyal.* Translated by the Padmakara Translation Group. Boston: Shambhala Publications, 1999.

Gyurme Dorje and Tudeng Nima, translators. *An Encyclopaedic Tibetan-English Dictionary: A Revised Version of Bod rGya Tshig mDzod Chen Mo.*

Volume 1: *Ka-Nya*. Beijing: The Nationalities Publishing House; London: The School of Oriental and African Studies, 2001.

Harding, Sarah, translator. *Machik's Complete Explanation*. Ithaca, NY: Snow Lion Publications, 2003.

Jamgön Kongtrul. *The Treasury of Knowledge. Book Five: Buddhist Ethics*. Translated by the Kalu Rinpoché Translation Group. Ithaca, NY: Snow Lion Publications, 2003.

———. *The Treasury of Knowledge. Book One: Myriad Worlds*. Translated by the Kalu Rinpoché Translation Group Ithaca, NY: Snow Lion Publications, 2003.

———. *The Teacher-Student Relationship*. Translated by Ron Garry. Ithaca, NY: Snow Lion Publications, 1999.

Lama Chonam and Sangye Khandro, translators. *The Lives and Liberation of Princess Mandarava: The Indian Consort of Padmasambhava*. Boston: Wisdom Publications, 1998.

Lama Tharchin. *A Commentary on the Dudjom Tersar Ngöndro: The Preliminary Practice of the New Treasures of Dudjom*. Watsonville, CA: Vajrayana Foundation, n.d.

Lhalungpa, Lobsang P., translator. *The Life of Milarepa*. Boston: Shambhala Publications, 1985.

Longchen Rabjam. *The Practice of Dzogchen*. Introduced, translated, and annotated by Tulku Thondup. Ithaca, NY: Snow Lion Publications, 1996.

———. *The Precious Treasury of the Way of Abiding*. Translated by Richard Barron. Junction City, CA: Padma Publishing, 1998.

———. *The Precious Treasury of the Basic Space of Phenomena*. Translated by Richard Barron. Junction City, CA: Padma Publishing, 2001.

———. *A Treasure Trove of Scriptural Transmission: A Commentary on* The Precious Treasury of the Basic Space of Phenomena. Translated by Richard Barron. Junction City, CA: Padma Publishing, 2001.

Ngawang Zangpo, translator. *Guru Rinpoché: His Life and Times*. Ithaca, NY: Snow Lion Publications, 2002.

———. *Sacred Ground: Jamgon Kongtrul on "Pilgrimage and Sacred Geography."* Ithaca, NY: Snow Lion Publications, 2001.

Padmasambhava (root text); Jamgon Kongtrul the Great (commentary). *The Light of Wisdom*. Translated by Erik Pema Kunzang. Boston: Shambhala Publications, 1995.

Patrul Rinpoche. *The Words of My Perfect Teacher: Kunzang lama'i shelung*. Translated by the Padmakara Translation Group. San Francisco: Harper-Collins Publishers, 1994.

Rigdzin Kunzang Tobden Angpo. *Removing the Darkness of Doubt: The Suddenly Arising Song Which Deciphers the Symbols of the Yogi's Three Secrets*. Translated by Tulku Thubten and Ron Garry. Unpublished, in the private collection of Lama Tharchin Rinpoché.

Shabkar. *The Life of Shabkar: The Autobiography of a Tibetan Yogin*. Translated by Matthieu Ricard. Albany, NY: State University of New York Press, 1994.

Thinley Norbu. *The Small Golden Key: to the Treasure of the Various Essential Necessities of General and Extraordinary Buddhist Dharma*. Translated by Lisa Anderson. Boston: Shambhala Publications, 1993.

———. *Welcoming Flowers: From Across the Cleansed Threshold of Hope. An Answer to the Pope's Criticism of Buddhism*. New York: Jewel Publishing House, 1997.

———. *White Sail: Crossing the Waves of Ocean Mind to the Serene Continent of the Triple Gems*. Boston: Shambhala Publications, 1992.

Tulku Thondup. *Buddhist Civilization in Tibet*. London and New York: Routledge and Kegan Paul, Inc., 1987.

———. *Hidden Teachings of Tibet: An Explanation of the Terma Tradition of the Nyingma School of Buddhism*. London: Wisdom Publications, 1986.

———. *Masters of Meditation and Miracles: The Longchen Nyingthig Lineage of Tibetan Buddhism*. Boston: Shambhala Publications, 1996.

Notes

1. From the *Collected Works of Dudjom Rinpoché* (CWDR), vol. 13, p. 341.

2. From *Heart Gem for Fortunate Disciples*.

3. *The Autobiography of Jamgön Kongtrul: A Gem of Many Colors*, translated and edited by Richard Barron (Chökyi Nyima), p. xv.

4. There is actually precedent for doing this in the Tibetan Buddhist tradition, where many texts, even with titles are often referred to by an abbreviated name such as *Entering Conduct* (*spyod 'jug*) as opposed to its actual complete title *Entering the Conduct of Bodhisattvas* (*byang chub sems dpa'i spyod pa la 'jug pa*); or sometimes a text is referred to by its first few words such as the song of tantric gatherings known as "The Assembly Palace of Great Exaltation" (*tshogs khang bde chen*), instead of its proper title, "The Melodious Tamboura of the Lotus: The Concise Fulfillment of the Dakinis."

5. From "Lama, incomparable lord." See p. 64.

6. See p. 296. *The Festival of Delight in Which the Expression of Eloquent Teachings Manifest: A Concise Detailed Classification of the Nyingmapa Teachings, the Ancient Translation School of Secret Mantra* (*gsang sngags snga 'gyur rnying ma ba'i bstan pa'i rnam gzhag mdo tsam brjod pa legs bshad snang ba'i dga 'ston*), from CWDR, vol. 2.

7. See Appendix 1 of this book, p. 321.

8. See p. 163 of this work for a suggested reading list of life stories of realized masters.

9. *kun mkhyen klong chen rab 'byams pa'i gsung rab mdzod bdun la blta bar bskul ba bzhugs*, from Patrul Rinpoché's *Collected Works*, published in Gangtok, Sikkim in 1970–71 by Sonam Kazi from Dudjom Rinpoché's xylograph collection, p. 79.

10. The *Seven Treasuries* are: *The Treasury of the Basic Space of Phenomena* (*chos dbyings rin po che'i mdzod*); *The Treasury of the Way of Abiding* (*gnas lugs rin po che'i mdzod*); *The Treasury of Pith Instructions* (*man ngag rin po che'i mdzod*); *The Treasury of Philosophical Approach* (*grub mtha' rin po che'i mdzod*); *The Treasury of the Supreme Vehicle* (*theg mchog rin po che'i mdzod*); *The Treasury of Words and Meanings* (*tshig don rin po che'i mdzod*); *The Wish-fulfilling Treasury* (*yid bzhin rin po che'i mdzod*).

11. See Dza Paltrul, *Heart Advice of My Always Noble Spiritual Master: Instructions on the Preliminary Practice of the Heart Essence* (*snying thig sngon 'gro'i khrid yig kun bzang bla ma'i zhal lung*), p. 273.

12. CWDR, vol. 13, p. 340.2.

13. Dza Paltrul, *Heart Advice of My Always Noble Spiritual Master*, pp. 501–2.

14. CWDR, vol. 13, p. 341.

15. CWDR, vol. 13, p. 224.

16. Dza Paltrul, *Heart Advice of My Always Noble Spiritual Master*, p. 246.

17. From *The Treasury of Discourses and Tantras* translated by Lama Ngawang, soon to be published by Snow Lion Publications.

18. Always Noble, Kuntu Zangpo, is the original primordial Buddha, who has never been deluded, since the very beginning, having recognized all phenomena as being the display of his own wisdom mind.

19. In this context I have translated the Tibetan word *dü* (*bdud*), which is a translation of the Sanskrit *mara*, as "negative forces". In general, mara represents clinging to a self and one's attachment and involvement with the eight worldly concerns. Often mara is discussed in the context of the four maras (*bdud bzhi*), negative forces or demons. According to the Sutrayana tradition, the four demons are: the demon of the aggregates; of the passions; of death; and of the child of the gods. According to the Vajrayana tradition, the four demons are: the material demon; the immaterial demon; the demon of exaltation; and the demon of pride. The material demon refers to external phenomena, whether things or other beings who do us harm. The immaterial demon refers to the three poisons—anger, desire, and ignorance. The demon of exaltation refers to attachment to such things as inner spiritual experiences. The demon of pride—the root of all demons—is clinging to a self. For an excellent and detailed account of mara, see Sarah Harding's introduction to and translation of *Machik's Complete Explanation*, pp. 33–8, and pp. 117–22. Also see Patrul Rinpoché's *The Words of My Perfect Teacher*, pp. 297–307.

20. The eight worldly dharmas are gain and loss; praise and blame; pleasure and pain; fame and infamy.

21. According to Lopön Jigmé, this passage refers to inner retreat. This is very important and contributes to the inner and direct nature of these teachings. Outer retreat means to retreat in a solitary, isolated location, such as forests or mountains. The practitioner leaves behind his home, family, friends, and the things that he or she enjoys, whether classical concerts, poetry readings, the theater, or a good baseball game. He sets physical boundaries that he is not allowed to transgress, and no one is permitted to enter. This is outer retreat. But what is most important is inner retreat. It is not enough to merely go to an isolated place, because you can still be very much engaged in the world by thinking about the outside world. The truly isolated place is to hold the thought of death in one's own heart, which is a support for diligence and perseverance in practice. It is important for the practitioner to be sick and tired of grasping on to one thing after another, which only perpetuates endless circling of samsara, the wheel of life. It is crucial that the practitioner set the inner retreat boundary, which is to give up thoughts of this life that are only involved with propping up the ego. To stay within physical retreat boundaries with your mind totally involved with the world you thought you left behind is to transgress the inner retreat boundary. Usually when you are in strict retreat, you do not see anyone except your spiritual master who is guiding your retreat. From the perspective of inner retreat, it is not enough not to see anyone; you must not become internally involved with the eight worldly concerns as they arise in your mind. Lopön Jigmé explains that someone who can make this type of inner retreat does not have to go to an isolated retreat to be in retreat but is in retreat even within the context of daily life. This is why the current text *Essential Advice for Solitary Meditation Practice* is not limited only to those who have gone to an isolated place to practice. This text is very profound since His Holiness is pointing out to us how to do inner retreat and inner practice, which can be applied in all contexts, whether in an isolated three-year retreat or in your daily life as a householder.

22. For a traditional explanation of these demons, see *Machik's Complete Explanation*, pp. 231–34. Actually, the entire book is the best resource to learn about the various demons and spirits that appear throughout Tibetan Buddhist practice and literature.

23. His Holiness writes this in the context of a culture in which spiritual practice was rewarded to the point of being a lucrative career.

24. In Buddhist countries this implies that the recipient would beg or receive support to stay in retreat.

25. This is a Tibetan expression that literally means "do not burn the nose of others." This means that a practitioner should not irritate, agitate, or be harsh to others.

26. "To abide in non-action" does not mean to be lazy, not to practice at all, or to become unemployed. It means not to engage in dualistic mind that clings to whatever phenomena appear in relation to your body, speech, and mind regardless of the physical activity in which you are engaged.

27. The common preliminary practices—the four aspects to turn the mind away from samsara—are to contemplate: the preciousness of human birth; impermanence and death; the inevitability of the cause and effect of karma; and the suffering within cyclic existence (samsara). By considering these four thoughts, one's mind is subdued, one turns away from preoccupation with cyclic existence, and one is inspired to practice the pure spiritual path, with determination and diligence, until enlightenment is attained. For in-depth teachings on this important subject, and for explanations on the uncommon preliminary practices, I highly recommend the following texts: the soon-to-be-released commentary on the concise version of the preliminary practices of the New Treasures of His Holiness Dudjom Rinpoché, written by Kyabjé Dungsé Thinley Norbu Rinpoché, as yet untitled; *The Words of My Perfect Teacher* by Patrul Rinpoché; *Resting in the Nature of Mind* (*sems nyid ngal gso*) by Kunkhyen Longchenpa, translated under the title *Kindly Bent to Ease Us*; and Dudjom Rinpoché's commentary on the long version of the preliminary practices of the New Treasures of His Holiness Dudjom Rinpoché, currently untranslated, located in CWDR, vol. *pa*, pp. 25–421.

28. These uncommon preliminary practices are an essential foundation for all Buddhist practice, including that of the Great Perfection.

29. This means that all phenomena without exception, existence as well as anything associated with the state of enlightenment, are the display of emptiness, just as the sun's rays are the display of the sun. Therefore, since the essence is primordially pure, sublime, unobstructed emptiness, its display is also primordially pure, without any exceptions at all.

30. According to Lopön Jigmé, "You should resolve all phenomena in this awareness" means that all phenomena—the outwardly perceived, substantial, inanimate phenomena, and the inner perceiving, insubstantial, animate subject—are resolved within awareness, the view of the Great Perfection as previously stated above.

31. A small child has no grasping to concepts regarding what is seen.

32. *bzhugs tshul*, translated here as "abiding state," is the honorific for the more commonly used *gnas tshul*.

33. There are many ways mindfulness is discussed and categorized, but in brief, my teacher explains mindfulness as being of two kinds: intentional mindfulness (*'du byed gyi dran pa*), and mindfulness of the nature of phenomena (*chos nyid kyi dran pa*). Intentional mindfulness is mindfulness based upon any effort whatsoever. Mindfulness of the nature of phenomena is effortless and uncontrived and is synonymous with abiding in the view, in awareness itself. Here, Garab Dorjé is referring to the mindfulness of the nature of phenomena, because he says "This is dharmakaya, not fabricated nor created by anyone."

34. In Sanskrit, *klesha*. The passions are ignorance (*ma rig pa*), desire (*'dod chags*), anger (*khong khro ba*), pride (*nga rgyal*), and jealousy (*phra dog*).

35. In Tibetan, the words for subject and object are *zung-wa dzin-pa* (*gzung ba 'dzin pa*). *Zung-wa* refers to that which is grasped, the object, and *dzin-pa* refers to that which grasps, the subject. They also have the connotations of that which is perceived and that which perceives, respectively.

36. At subject and object.

37. Literally, "Practice; do not let your heart rot!"

38. When meditating, the experiences of bliss, clarity, and emptiness automatically arise. If you cling to them, then you will become sidetracked from your goal of complete liberation. Clinging to bliss in meditation leads to rebirth in the desire realms; clinging to clarity leads to rebirth in the form god realms; and clinging to emptiness leads to rebirth in the formless god realms. All these realms are still within the endless wheel of life and, therefore, only lead to suffering.

39. There is a distinction made between the great meditator (*sgom chen*) and the practitioner of the Great Perfection. The great meditator, through practice, develops powerful concentration that leads to temporary states of peace in the highest god realms, where they may abide for many eons. Unfortunately, this is still within the context of the six realms of cyclic existence. As a result, when the karma that allows them to remain in this state of bliss, clarity, or non-conceptuality is exhausted, their circumstances change, and they will once again fall into lower states of existence, including that of the hell realms. This is because they know how to meditate, but not how to liberate. As Patrul Rinpoché writes in *The Special Commentary of the Wise Glorious King* (*mkhas pa shri rgyal po'i khyad chos*), a commentary to Garab Dorjé's *Three Lines That Strike the Vital Point* (*tshig gsum gnad 'degs*), "Therefore, it is said, 'Being able to meditate but not liberate—isn't that just like the meditation gods?' Those who place their trust in a meditation that is the mere meditation of mental resting that does not possess the key point of how to liberate will go astray into the meditative states of the upper realms." The authentic Great Perfection practitioner is not involved with this type of meditation based on a reference point, but with liberation. In the same text, Patrul Rinpoché teaches "For a practitioner (*rnal 'byor pa*), thoughts are liberated the moment they arise." pp. 29–30.

40. The Tibetan saying literally means "as one whose head is wreathed with salt." This means to be completely defeated, or completely lost.

41. Why is meeting someone you are familiar with like recognition's liberation of thoughts? Because you do not mistake your friend for someone else. You are not mistaken in recognizing your friend; you know immediately who this person is without thinking, guessing, or trying to figure it out. In the same way, thoughts are recognized as the display of awareness and so are simultaneously liberated.

42. The Tibetan word *naljorpa* (*rnal 'byor pa*) is the Tibetan translation of the Sanskrit *yogi*. *Naljorpa* is made up of two words *nal* and *jor*, and the particle *pa*. *Nal* refers to what is genuine and authentic. *Jor* refers to union. So *naljor* means in union with that which is genuine, and *pa* is a particle in Tibetan that means "the one who." So all together *naljorpa* means "one who is in union with that which is genuine."

43. The word *kyil* (*'khyil*) literally means to fill a container or space evenly. According to Lopön Jigmé, mind and body dissolve into basic space. They dissolve and fill space evenly, just as water, when poured into a vase, fills it equally, from top to bottom, side to side. This is the sense in which *kyil* means "attaining" the youthful vase body.

44. It is extremely important to pay attention to your post-meditation conduct. The best way to accomplish this is to keep your vows and tantric commitments responsibly. The vows and tantric commitments we take protect us from accumulating negative karma and help us to accumulate positive karma, which refines all karma making us sensitive enough to catch the disease of full realization from our Lama.

There are numerous categories of tantric commitments for Secret Mantrayana. As Dudjom Rinpoché explains in *Ascertaining the Three Vows* (*sdom gsum rnam nges*), his commentary to Ngari Panchen's renowned text on the three vows:

According to the *Mayajala* (*sgyu 'phrul*), there are fifteen root and branch samayas, from which three hundred and sixty are derived. According to the *Akhyata-tantra* there are ninety-seven samayas. In the *Samanaya-sutra* there are four basic tantric commitments, twenty-eight common tantric commitments, four additional tantric commitments, twenty-three of fearless conduct, twenty to accomplish, four corresponding to behavior, the abandonment of the five maras, the destruction of the four enemies, and further elaborations of the samaya that correspond to the view. In addition, each tantra elaborates on individual root and branch tantric commitments to be guarded.

Further, there are tantric commitments corresponding to samadhi, behavior, the partaking of food, objects from which never to be separated, and many other countless enumerations. (CWDR, vol. *nga*, p. 355.2)

In *Essential Advice*, Dudjom Rinpoché states, "Secret mantra's tantric commitments have many categories, but in a concise form they can be subsumed into one—tantric commitments of the wisdom body, speech, and mind of your root spiritual master." Dudjom Rinpoché explains this in the commentary quoted from just above:

The root tantric commitments correspond to the root Lama's wisdom body, speech, and mind. For wisdom body, speech, and mind there are outer, inner, and secret tantric commitments respectively, bringing the total to twenty-seven.

In actuality, the essence of these root tantric commitments is to realize the indivisibility of one's three doors with the condensed essence of all the buddhas. This is likened to realizing the root Lama's wisdom body, speech, and mind to be non-dual as the three vajras. The very word "guru" implies weight, which can be interpreted here as the weight of the tantric commitments corresponding to the guru and how, if they are allowed to deteriorate, they will be difficult to restore. The Tibetan equivalent of the word "Guru" is *Lama*, which means "unsurpassed."

Of the nine tantric commitments that correspond to the body, the first three are outer: to abandon stealing, sexual misconduct, and killing. The three inner tantric commitments are to abandon abusing one's family, as explained earlier, including one's own body; abusing the teachings and people related to the teachings; and forcing oneself to undergo unnecessary hardship, such as extreme ascetic discipline. The three secret tantric commitments are: to abandon striking, or even attempting to strike, the body of vajra brothers or sisters (this includes verbal abuse or criticism of ornaments or adornments they may be wearing); making sexual advances toward the Lama's consort; and walking on or over the Lama's shadow or acting unconscientiously with body and speech in the presence of the Lama.

The nine tantric commitments that correspond to speech begin with the three outer: to abandon lying, slander, and using harsh words. The three inner tantric commitments are: to abandon verbally disrespecting a Buddhist teacher, disrespecting anyone who contemplates the meaning, or disrespecting anyone who meditates upon the abiding nature (*gnas lugs*). The three secret tantric commitments are: to abandon disrespecting the speech of vajra brothers and sisters; speaking negative words about the conduct of the spiritual teacher; and disregarding any of the spiritual master's teachings or advice as well as the words of those in his immediate retinue.

There are nine tantric commitments that correspond to mind. The three outer are to abandon (1) harmful thoughts, (2) coveting, and (3) the reverse point of view. The three inner are: to abandon (1) wrong conduct, (2) carelessness (*bag med*), and (3) senseless chatter (*tho co*). The three secret are: (1) to abandon incorrect meditation practice—i.e., practice distorted by dullness (*bying*), agitation (*rgod*), mental wandering (*gol*), and obscurations (*sgrib*) as well as to abandon the reverse points of view (*log lta*); (2) grasping the extreme of eternalism (*rtag*); and (3) grasping the extreme of nihilism (*chad*). In addition, the secret tantric commitments include the abandonment of not paying attention (*yid la ma byed pa*) to view, meditation, and conduct throughout the three times of the day and night, as well as not paying attention to one's yidam deity, not paying attention to guru yoga, and not paying attention to being loving and affectionate toward one's vajra brothers and sisters.

These are the twenty-seven root samayas corresponding to the wisdom body, speech, and mind on the outer, inner, and secret levels. (CWDR, vol. *nga*, p. 346.)

This explanation by Dudjom Rinpoché clearly shows us the vital importance of our relationship to our Lama.

45. According to Buddhist cosmology, there are six realms of beings that constitute samsara: the hell realm, the starving spirit realm, the animal realm, the human realm, the realm of the jealous gods, and the god realm. A human being falls into the category of the human realm, one of six categories of sentient beings trapped in samsara, the wheel of life. From the Vajrayana point of view, in order to receive blessings that lead to full liberation, you must see your Lama as a fully enlightened buddha, who is entirely free from cyclic existence. Otherwise, it is said that if you see your Lama as a bodhisattva, you will receive the blessings of a bodhisattva, and if you see your Lama as an ordinary human being, you will merely receive the blessings of an ordinary person.

46. In other words, take everything I offer, body, speech, and mind. This means I am offering to help implement my spiritual master's activities for the benefit of others.

47. That is, carefully. In Tibet, medicine was prepared by grinding various natural ingredients.

48. Literally, "it doesn't make sense to throw ashes on your own head."

49. This refers to the practice of having others, such as Lamas, practitioners, or monastics, pray and perform special practices for you, such as *phowa*. Also, friends and relatives usually make offerings on the deceased's behalf, such as lighting butter lamps in temples and so forth.

50. This refers to the three types of vows related to the Vajrayana, Mahayana, and Hinayana respectively. See *Perfect Conduct*.

51. The promise a retreatant makes to stay in retreat until its conclusion. According to the instruction manual for the Mahayoga practice of the Vajrakilaya cycle called *The Razor That Destroys at a Touch*, the three ways of doing retreat are for a specific time period, for example, six months; until a pre-determined number of mantra recitations are completed, such as six million; or until realization is attained. See *The Fulfiller of Spiritual Attainments: An Instruction Manual for the Razor That Destroys at a Touch*. CWDR, vol. *ba*, pp. 533–63.

52. As just mentioned above, the refusal to practice and so forth.

53. One of four maras: the mara of the aggregates; the mara of the passions; the mara of the child of god; and the mara of the lord of death. For a description of these four maras, see Sarah Harding's *Machik's Complete Explanation*, pp. 36–7.

54. That is, that one has a realization of the consciousness transference practice (*phowa*).

55. This refers to the preliminary practices: taking refuge and generating bodhicitta; Vajrasattva; and mandala offerings. See *The Words of My Perfect Teacher*, pp. 171–295, for an in-depth discussion.

56. "The purification of ordinary phenomena into the wheel of purity" means to see all forms as the form of the wisdom deity, all sounds as the speech of the wisdom deity, and whatever arises within one's mind as the pure mind of the wisdom deity.

57. *tshogs kyi bdag po*.

58. "Tröma" refers to Tröma Nakmo, the Black Wrathful Goddess who is a fully enlightened buddha. The practices of the Mahayoga level are grouped under three categories: Lama, Wisdom Deity, and Dakini. The dakini category consists of outer, inner, secret, and innermost secret practices. Tröma Nakmo is the innermost secret dakini practice. These practices were revealed by Dudjom Lingpa and are an integral part of the Dudjom lineage.

59. This is His Holiness Dudjom Rinpoché's mind treasure from the Dorjé Drolö cycle. Tulku Orgyen Chemchok Düpa Tsal, who requested this prayer, is the lineage holder of the Drolö cycle and lives in eastern Tibet. He is one of the main teachers of Dudjom Rinpoché's current incarnation.

60. This indicates that Tulku Orgyen—who requested this instruction from His Holiness— is the designated heir to this specific teaching, the *Innermost Secret Gathering*.

61. This is the famous nuns' institution headed by the series of incarnations of Shukseb Dakini, the last of which was also a teacher of Chadral Rinpoché.

62. For a discussion of remaining in non-action regarding the nine types of activities, see *Buddhahood Without Meditation*, commonly known as the *Nang jang*, pp. 157–63.

63. For example, in a Mahayoga sadhana practice, the preliminary practice can consist of lineage prayers, taking refuge, bodhicitta, and the seven-branch prayer. The main practice can consist of visualization of the deity, invocation, request to remain, offerings, praise, and mantra recitation. The conclusion includes dissolution of the mandala and closing prayers, such as aspiration prayers to be reborn in the Copper-Colored Mountain, and long life prayers for your spiritual masters.

64. In this case, "present ordinary mind" (*tha mal gyi shes pa*) refers to pure awareness.

65. Although it is important to understand the view of the Great Perfection, it is also important to practice only under the supervision of a qualified master. It is of utmost importance not to use these teachings as a basis for practicing the Great Perfection on one's own as it can lead to detrimental results, such as creating internal obstacles that will naturally prevent one from practicing the correct Great Perfection path in the present and will slowly create obstacles preventing a connection with an authentic master and unbroken lineage in the future. So please be careful. These profound teachings by Dudjom Rinpoché on the view can be used as support for whatever practice one is doing because it is very helpful to bring the profound view into your preliminary practices of taking refuge, generating bodhicitta, purification through the practice of Vajrasattva, offering the mandala of the entire universe to all wisdom beings, and guru yoga. It is also extremely important to bring this profound view into your creation stage Mahayoga practice on wisdom deities. It is not appropriate to skip these practices and create one's own "Great Perfection" practice based upon the profound instruction of wisdom masters such as Dudjom Rinpoché. Please avoid this dangerous obstacle and practice according to your teacher's instructions, develop faith in the Great Perfection through reading these teachings, and if you do not have a teacher, my sincere advice is to search impeccably for a qualified master and an unbroken lineage. When these are found, develop faith and devotion toward this wisdom teacher, and then put effort into your practice.

66. The Lotus-Born (*pad ma 'byung*) refers to Padmasambhava, also known as Guru Rinpoché ("precious guru").

67. The three excellences are preparation, main practice, and conclusion. The preparation is to generate bodhicitta (*sbyor ba sems bskyed*); the main practice is to practice without reference points (*dngos gzhi dmigs med*); and the conclusion is to dedicate the merit (*rjes bsngo ba*).

68. The six-syllable mantra, Om mani pémé hung, is the mantra of the Lord of Compassion, Chenrezi.

69. The six collections (*tshogs drug*) refer to the six gatherings, or aggregates, of consciousness (*rnam shes tshogs drug*): eye consciousness (*mig gi rnam shes*); ear consciousness (*rna ba'i rnam shes*); nose consciousness (*sna'i rnam shes*); tongue consciousness (*lce'i rnam shes*); body consciousness (*lus kyi rnam shes*); and mind consciousness (*yid kyi rnam shes*).

70. The cave of Yangléshö is located in the southern end of the Katmandu Valley, near the village of Parping. The upper cave of Yangléshö is known as Asura Cave.

71. This text contains the very essence of all Buddhist practice; under the supervision of a qualified Lama, through this text alone, a qualified disciple can attain enlightenment in this very life. His Holiness's Great Perfection teachings as found in this book are inspiring. For one seriously interested in practicing these teachings it is essential to seek out a qualified spiritual master and diligently practice under his or her supervision. The Great Perfection is the essence of the profound eighty-four thousand teachings of Buddha. Under the guidance of a qualified spiritual master these teachings can lead to enlightenment in one lifetime. Without this guidance, this is not so easy to accomplish.

72. This section refers to the three lines of Garab Dorje: First, to directly recognize your true nature (*ngo rang thog tu sprad pa*); second, to decide upon one thing (*thag gcig thog tu bcad pa*); and third, to gain confidence in liberation (*gdeng grol thog tu bca' ba*). For a translation of Patrul Rinpoché's commentary to the three words of Garab Dorjé, see *The Special Teaching of Khepa Shri Gyalpo: Three Words Striking the Vital Point*, translated by Erik Pema Kunzang, in the compilation of various prayers and teachings called *Crystal Cave*.

73. Original mindfulness (*gnyug ma'i dran pa*) refers to the mindfulness of nature of phenomena (*dharmata*) that occurs without effort when abiding in pure awareness.

74. See note 41.

75. This refers to the lord Gyurmé Nédon Wangpo, the root Lama of Dudjom Rinpoché.

76. The italicized words were highlighted in the original text and mean "These words of instructions were given to Samten (*bsam gtan la/ gdams ngag 'di/ sprad*)." The rest of the words of the colophon elaborate upon this. It is a beautiful stylistic use of the Tibetan language that is frequently utilized.

77. From "From the beginning, the essential original nature of luminosity," p. 142.

78. See *The Life of Shabkar: The Autobiography of a Tibetan Yogin*, translated by Matthieu Ricard.

79. In Tibetan, the full name of "Glorious Mountain's Palace on Tail-Fan Island" is: *Rnga yab gling zang mdog dpal ri bo*.

80. Tsaritra is an extremely important pilgrimage place in central Tibet, not far from Kongpo. For Shabkar's pilgrimage to Tsari, see *The Life of Shabkar: The Autobiography of a Tibetan Yogin*, pp. 243–67.

81. This is the sacred place most often mentioned among the twenty-four or thirty-two sacred places.

82. That is, death and rebirth.

83. Lake Born Vajra is the name given to Guru Rinpoché by King Indrabhuti of Oddiyana. The king was childless and without an heir to his throne. One day Krishnadhara, the king's minister, was returning from the land of jewels when he saw a child, Guru Rinpoché, upon a lotus in the middle of Lake Danakosha in this land of Oddiyana. The king adopted this child and gave him the name Lake Born Vajra (Tsokyé Dorjé) and also Lotus-Born (Péma Jungné). CWDR, vol. *ka*, p. 93.

84. This temple was built under the direction of Dudjom Rinpoché.

85. "...bring my lord guru's intentions to completion" (*dgongs rdzogs*) relates to completing the Lama's projects after his passing.

86. Kongpo is a province in southeast Tibet.

87. This song of realization is written in seven sections: the three *kayas*—dharmakaya (Amitabha), sambhogakaya (Chenrezi), and nirmanakaya (Lotus-Born); the three roots— Lama, Yidam, and Dakini; and the dharmapalas.

88. *Sha ra ra* is synonymous with the Tibetan *thogs pa med pa*, "unobstructed."

89. The following tantric gathering song was written by His Holiness Dudjom Rinpoché in his previous incarnation as Dudjom Lingpa. This song is located in Dudjom Lingpa's Tröma volume, pp. 919–20. This song is structured around the five certainties (*nges pa lnga*), or perfections, of the sambhogakaya, body of perfect rapture. In general, the perfect place is the Supreme Highest Pure Land (*Akanishta*; '*og min chen po*). The perfect teachers are the five buddhas with their consorts. The perfect retinue are the fulfilled bodhisattvas. The perfect teachings are the highest Vajrayana teachings. The perfect time is the timelessness of primordial purity.

90. Mount Malaya has great significance for the transmission of the Buddha's teachings. It is one of the locations where the Buddha gave the third promulgation of his teachings. It is also a sacred location for the Great Perfection. Garab Dorjé's memory contained the six million four hundred thousand verses of the Natural Great Perfection. Vajrasattva, after conferring vase empowerment of awareness on him, commanded Garab Dorjé to write down these verbal tantras. On the summit of Mount Malaya, Garab Dorjé—along with the Indestructible Stainless Space Dakini, Yellow Exaltation Bestowing Dakini, and the Dakini of Limitless Noble Qualities—spent three years recording and correctly arranging these Great Perfection tantras.

91. From "Blessings Swiftly Received," p. 199.

92. See *The Words of My Perfect Teacher*, p. 311.

93. *The Life of Shabkar*, p. xviii.

94. Currently I am working on a translation of the life stories of the hundred great treasure-revealers, including concise life stories of Guru Rinpoché, Yeshé Tsogyal, King Trisong Déutsen, and the twenty-five disciples.

95. This is a play on words as Yeshé Dorjé is both the name of the relative Lama Dudjom Rinpoché, as well as a designation of the ultimate Lama, "indestructible wisdom."

96. The four training methods (*'dul ba rnam par bzhi*) are the four kinds of training of the supreme emanation body: training by the great merit of wisdom body (*sku bsod nams chen pos 'dul ba*); training by the direct perception of wisdom mind (*thugs mngon sum pas 'dul ba*); training by inconceivable miraculous abilities (*rdzu 'phrul bsam gyis mi khyab pas 'dul ba*); and training by knowledge conveyed in wisdom speech (*gsung rig pas 'dul ba*). See NSTB, pp. 131–2; and *Myriad Worlds*, p. 96 and p. 264, n. 4.

97. The fourth guide (*rnam 'dren bzhi*) refers to Shakyamuni Buddha, who is the fourth buddha out of one thousand that will manifest in this fortunate eon.

98. Dudjom Lingpa, His Holiness Dudjom Rinpoché's previous life, has incarnated for the benefit of beings as numerous great noble beings, taking various sublime forms such as an enemy-destroyer (*arhat*), awareness-holder (*vidyadhara*), wisdom scholar (*pandita*), and accomplished master (*siddha*), in both India and Tibet. His series of lives include some of the most sublime beings throughout Buddhist history, as seen in the previous prayer, *The Pearl Necklace: A Supplication to the Series of Lives of His Holiness Dudjom Rinpoché*. The Sanskrit word *arhat* was translated into Tibetan as *drachompa*, which means "enemy-destroyer," one who has destroyed the enemy of the passions. This is a title given to those initial disciples of Buddha who showed externally the path of the Hearer Vehicle (Shravakayana). The Sanskrit word *vidyadhara* was translated into Tibetan as *rikdzin (rig 'dzin)* and is the title given to those who have become fully enlight-

ened buddhas through the Secret Mantra Vehicle (Mantrayana). The Sanskrit word *pandita* was translated into Tibetan as *khépa* (*mkhas pa*), which means "wisdom scholar." This refers to someone who has reached the highest levels of Buddist scholarship, based not only upon intellectual knowledge, but also upon wisdom through practice—thus "wisdom" scholar. The Sanskrit word *siddha* was translated into Tibetan as *druptob* (*grub thob*), which means "accomplished master." Siddha comes from the same Sanskrit root as *siddhi*, which was translated into Tibetan as *ngödrup* (*dngos grub*), which means "spiritual attainment." The ultimate siddhi is that of becoming a fully enlightened buddha.

99. A reference to Sertak in the Golok region of eastern Tibet where Dudjom Lingpa was born.

100. As Dudjom Rinpoché mentions here, the Nub clan was a source of myriad scholars and accomplished masters, beginning with the great Nupchen Sangyé Yeshé (*gnubs chen sangs rgyas ye shes*). According to Dudjom Rinpoché (NSTB, pp. 607–16) Nupchen Sangyé Yeshé was born in 832 c.e. In his youth he received from Padmasambhava the empowerment of the Eight Transmitted Precepts and later received many tantras and pith instructions. He also relied upon many great masters in India and Nepal such as Shri Singha and Vimalamitra. In his autobiography (*Collected Works of Dudjom Lingpa*, vol. *dza*, pp. 105–397), Dudjom Lingpa mentions that there are five family lineages according to Chinese astrology (*ma ha tsi ni*) with correspondences of five families, five colors, and five elements: the Dong (*sdong*) family corresponds to the color brown and the earth element; the Ra (*dbra*) family to white and iron; the Dru (*'gru*) family to blue and water; and the Ga (*sga*) family to green and wood. Dudjom Lingpa writes that his father was of the Achak Dru clan (*a lchags 'gru*) and his mother was of the Mu Tshaga family (*dmu tsha sga*). In earlier times the Dru clan came to the province of Nub (*gnubs*), which gave rise to many sublime beings such as the aforementioned Sangyé Yeshé (*sangs rgyas ye shes*) and Gelong Namkhai Nyingpo (*dge slong nam mkha'i snying po*). This is called the family lineage of Nub. One group of this lineage, slowly over time, migrated eastward to the provence of Kham. Thus, this family lineage dispersed through out Kham and Do-mé. Dudjom Lingpa's father is connected to this lineage, that of the Nub family's lesser lineage of Rung, which was a very noble family that also gave rise to many realized beings. His name was Aten (*a bstan*), and his mother's name was Bo Dzok (*bo rdzogs*).

101. When Dudjom Lingpa entered his mother's womb, he was accompanied by countless dakinis with a shower of auspicious flowers raining down. His mother had many dreams in which dakas and dakinis provided protection and bathed him.

102. This probably refers to an instance related in Dudjom Lingpa's autobiography that occurred at the age of nine. On the night of the seventh day of the first month of winter, a dakini clad in a blue woolen cloak came to Dudjom Lingpa and told him that in the coming year he should travel to the northwest in order to meet a spiritual master named Jamyang who was an incarnation of the master Namkhai Nyingpo. With him Dudjom Lingpa would study and learn how to read and write. Dudjom Lingpa recounts that the dakini then gave him a skullcup filled with nectar that he drank in one gulp and his entired body became filled with great exaltation.

103. Manjushri is the lord of the Tathagata family; Chenrezi is the lord of the Padma family; and Vajrapani is the lord of the Vajra family.

104. The Glorious Copper-Colored Mountain is the pure land where Guru Rinpoché abides.

105. Here, "inferior tainted bliss" refers to the falling essence, and "sublime unconditioned pure conduct" refers to the sustaining bliss. These are terms used in the channels-energy practice (*rtsa-rlung*) of Anuyoga.

106. This verse relates to the level of Hinayana vows kept by Dudjom Lingpa.

107. This verse refers to the level of Dudjom Lingpa's Mahayana practice.

108. This verse refers to the tantric practice of creation stage Mahayoga practice.

109. The three forms of blazing primordial wisdom are: the blazing great exaltation of the body; the blazing power of speech; and the blazing realization of mind.

110. This refers to the enactment aspect of the creation stage of tantric practice.

111. The *roma* (ro ma) is one of the three chief channels (*nadi*) in the body. In males it is the right channel; in females, the left.

112. The *kyangma* (rkyang ma) is one of the three chief channels (*nadi*) in the body. In males it is the left channel; in females, the right.

113. The central energy channel, or *avadhuti*, is one of the three chief channels (*nadi*) in the body.

114. This refers to the perfection stage Anuyoga of tantric practice with characteristics.

115. *Chandali*, or inner heat, is a practice related to Anuyoga.

116. This refers to Great Perfection practice.

117. This refers to Great Perfection Direct Vision or *Tögal* (thod rgal) practice.

118. *lha rdzogs thugs.* If a treasure-revealer is a great treasure-revealer (*gter chen*), as Dudjom Lingpa was, he or she must reveal these three—a practice of Guru Rinpoché, a practice of the Great Perfection, and a practice of Chenrézi. Other treasure-revealers, regardless of how numerous their treasures, are called minor revealers of treasures (*gter phran*).

119. That is, a *ngagpa*, or *yogi*, that is, a tantric lay practitioner. For a description of the meaning of the ornaments of a yogi see *Removing the Darkness of Doubt: The Suddenly Arising Song Which Deciphers the Symbols of the Yogi's Three Secrets*, by Rigdzin Kunzang Tobden Angpo, from the private collection of Lama Tharchin Rinpoché. Translated by Tulku Thubten and Ron Garry.

120. Offering practice rituals (*sgrub mchod*) are elaborate rituals for deities, usually including self-empowerment.

121. His own family lineage, although there is a play on words here that alludes to the Buddha's eight bodhisattva disciples.

122. Thirteen of Dudjom Lingpa's disciples attained rainbow body.

123. Ngari is in western Tibet; Ü, central Tibet; Tsang, southern Tibet; Puwo is in southeastern Tibet; Bo Tsuk is located in Domé, in eastern Tibet; Kongpo is near Puwo; and Amdo and Kham are provinces of eastern Tibet.

124. From the perspective of the Nyingma tradition, Bérotsana (Bérotsana Lotsawa, whose name also appears as Vairocana or Vairotsana) is considered the most supreme of all translators. According to Dudjom Rinpoché, Bérotsana traveled from his native Nyemo Cakar in Tibet to the Great Nine-Storey Temple created by the miraculous power of the master Shri Singha. Bérotsana requested and received teaching on the effortless vehicle of Atiyoga. Shri Singha wrote down for Bérotsana the eighteen esoteric instructions of the Mind Class. In addition, Shri Singha bestowed upon him all the empowerments and esoteric instructions of the sixty tantras, along with the three branches of the Vast Expanse Class, the white, black, and variegated, which reveal that the goal is already naturally present. Shri Singha also taught Bérotsana the three ways to bring forth the fruit of instructions, the four cases when the teaching should be granted, and the four cases when they should not. Bérotsana also met Garab Dorjé in the great charnel ground of

Dhumasthira. He attained the true lineage of the six million four hundred thousand verses on the Great Perfection and attained the great accomplishment of simultaneous realization and liberation. Upon returning to Tibet, Bérotsana began giving teachings to the king on the causal vehicle by day and on the secret doctrine of the Great Perfection by night. At this time Bérotsana translated five texts of the Mind Class of the Great Perfection. Bérotsana attained the buddha body of integral union (*zung 'jug gi sku*) in Bhasing Forest, Nepal. CWDR, vol. *ka*, pp. 187–90.

125. Known as Nanam Dorjé Dudjom (*sna nam rdo rje bdud 'joms*), he was one of Guru Rinpoché's twenty-five disciples and had the ability to pass through a mountain of solid rock.

126. Terchen Zilnön Namkhé Dorjé (*zil gnon nam mkha'i rdo rje*) was a great treasure-revealer and mentioned by Dudjom Rinpoché as one of his two supreme teachers. Upon passing away he mostly vanished into rainbow light, which was accompanied by sound, light, earthquakes, and various other miracles. NSTB, p. 919.

127. Langdro Könchok Jungné (*lang gro dkon mchog 'byung gnas*) was one of Padmasambhava's twenty-five disciples, who later incarnated as the great treasure-revealer Ratna Lingpa.

128. *The Treasury of Precious Instructions* (*gdams ngag rin po che'i mdzod*) is one of the five treasuries of Jamgön Kongtrul Lodrö Taye. It contains a collection of thirteen volumes on the essential teachings of the eight practice lineages.

129. *lam rim ye shes snying po*. See *Light of Wisdom*, vol. 1 (Shambhala Publications).

130. *rin chen gter gyi mdzod chen po*. Compiled by Jamgön Kongtrul Lodrö Taye.

131. *'gyur med nges don dbang po*, Dudjom Rinpoché's root Lama. Dudjom Rinpoché writes in his *Nyingma School* that Gyurmé Ngédon Wangpo, the all-pervading lord, was the magical emanation of Bérotsana. Dudjom Rinpoché writes that Jamgön Kongtrul entrusted his entire teachings to several masters, including Dudjom Rinpoché's two root Lamas, Gyurmé Ngédon Wangpo and Jedrung Trinlé Campéi Jungné. CWDR, vol. *ka*, p. 693.

132. *rin chen gter gyi mdzod chen po*.

133. *sgrub thabs 'dod 'jo'i bum bzang*.

134. *smin gling gter chen gter bdag gling pa 'gyur med rdo rje*. Minling Terchen Terdak Lingpa, Gyurmé Dorjé: 1646–1714. Rikdzin Terdak Lingpa was the speech emanation of the great translator Bérotsana. For a detailed description of his life written by Dudjom Rinpoché, please see NSTB, pp. 825–33.

135. *mkhyen brtse'i dbang po*.

136. Refers to Dudjom Lingpa's treasures.

137. *mdzod bdun*. Kunkhyen Longchenpa's seminal work that consists of *The Treasury of the Basic Space of Phenomena* (*chos dbyings rin po che'i mdzod*); *The Treasury of the Way of Abiding* (*gnas lugs rin po che'i mdzod*); *The Treasury of Pith Instructions* (*man ngag rin po che'i mdzod*); *The Treasury of Philosophical Views* (*grub mtha' rin po che'i mdzod*); *The Treasury of the Supreme Vehicle* (*theg mchog rin po che'i mdzod*); *The Treasury of Words and Meanings* (*tshig don rin po che'i mdzod*); *The Wish-fulfilling Treasury* (*yid bzhin rin po che'i mdzod*).

138. One of the foremost scholars of the Nyingma tradition, Patrul Rinpoché (*dpal sprul rin po che*) (1808–87) was a great accomplished master and a great non-sectarian master of the nineteenth century who was regarded as the speech emanation of Jigmé Lingpa. His principal teacher was Jigmé Gyalwé Nyugu, one of Jigmé Lingpa's main disciples. Two of Patrul Rinpoché's most famous works have been translated into English: *The Words of*

My Perfect Teacher (*kun bzang bla ma'i zhal lung*), a commentary to the common and extraordinary preliminary practices; and his commentary on the *Three Lines of Garab Dorjé* (*tshig gsum gnad brdegs*) called *The Special Commentary of the Wise Glorious King* (*mkhas pa shri rgyal po'i khyad chos*), the epitome of the Great Perfection teachings of Cutting through Solidity. For a brief discussion of Patrul Rinpoché's life see *The Words of My Perfect Teacher*, pp. xxxi–xxxiv.

139. The creation stage (*skyes rim*) and the perfection stage (*rdzogs rim*).

140. *mnyam med lha rtse pa chen po*, 1546–1615.

141. *'gyur med phan bde'i 'od zer*, also known as Lord of the Mandala Circle Jampal Dewé Nyima (*'khor lo'i mgon po 'jam dpal bde ba'i nyi ma*), was one of the Mindroling Trichens and a teacher of Dudjom Rinpoché. He is also mentioned by Dudjom Rinpoché as one whose physical body mostly vanished into light accompanied by sound, light, earthquakes, and other miracles. CWDR, vol. *ka*, pp. 773–4

142. This is a contraction for *The Sovereign All-Creating Mind Sutra* (*kun byed rgyal po'i mdo*), *The Secret Essence Tantra* (*sgyu 'phrul gsang ba'i snying po*), and *The Eighteen Tantras of the Mind Class* (*sems mde bco brgyad*).

143. *bka' brgyad bde gshegs 'dus pa*. A treasure text revealed by Nyang-ral Nyima Öser (1124–92) in nine or thirteen volumes.

144. *rdzogs chen snying thig ya bzhi*. These are some of the most important texts and writings on the *Heart Essence* (*snying thig*). Tulku Thondup, in *The Practice of Dzogchen*, explains: "Longchen Rabjam wrote a volume of commentarial and supplemental texts on *Vima Nyingtig* known as *Vima Yangtig* (*vima yang thig*) and one volume on *Khadro Nyingthig* known as *Khadro Yangtig* (*mkha-'gro yang-tig*). He also wrote a volume on both *Nyingthigs* known as *Lama Yangtig* (*bla ma yang thig*) or *Yangtig Yidzhin Norbu* (*yang-thig yid-bzhin nor bu*). These two root scriptures and two commentorial texts are known as the *Nyingthig Yazhi* (*snying thig yab zhi*), the Four Volumes of *Nyingthig*. They are some of the most important texts and writings on *Nyingthig*." (p. 35)

145. *dpal gsang ba snying po'i rgyud*. The *Guhyagarbha-tantra* is the main Mahayoga tantra of the Nyingmapa tradition.

146. The *Seven Treasuries* (*mdzod bdun*) of the omniscient Longchenpa.

147. The *Trilogy of Natural Rest* (*ngal gso skor gsum*) by the omniscient Longchenpa are *Naturally Resting in the Nature of Mind* (*sems nyid ngal gso*); *Naturally Resting within the Magical Display* (*sgyu ma ngal gso*); and *Naturally Resting within Meditation* (*bsam gtan ngal gso*).

148. *Ascertaining the Three Vows* (*sdom gsum rnam nges*). This is a work by Ngari Panchen Péma Wangyal (*mnga' ris pan chen pad ma dbang rgyal*).

149. *yon tan rin po che'i mdzod*. *The Precious Treasury of Noble Qualities*, by Jigme Lingpa.

150. *shes bya kun khyab mdzod*. *The Treasury of All-Encompassing Knowledge*. One of the five treasuries of Jamgön Kongtrul containing an encyclopedia of Buddhism and Buddhist culture in three volumes.

151. The creation stage (*bskyes rim*) and the completion stage (*rdzogs rim*).

152. Orgyen Namdrol Gyatso (*o rgyan rnam grol rgya mtsho*) was a holder of the Mindroling lineage.

153. Guru Chökyi Wangchuk (*gu ru chos kyi dbang phyug*).

154. *thugs rje chen po yang snying 'dus pa*. This is a treasure text revealed by Guru Chökyi Wangchuk, 1212–73.

155. *The Ancient School's Collection of Tantras (rnying ma rgyud 'bum)*. This is a collection of the three inner tantras gathered and arranged by Ratna Lingpa and edited by Jigmé Lingpa. Various editions exist, but the numbering of the volumes used in this book are from the version in thirty-six volumes published by His Holiness Dilgo Khyentse Rinpoché, New Delhi, 1974. Structure of this edition: ten volumes of Atiyoga, three volumes of Anuyoga, six volumes of the tantra section of Mahayoga, thirteen volumes of the sadhana section of Mahayoga, one volume of protector tantras, and three volumes of catalogues and historical background.

156. *o rgyan chos 'byor rgya mtsho*.

157. *bka' brgyud sngags mdzod*. One of the five treasuries of Jamgön Kongtrul containing the main Kagyu empowerments.

158. *thugs sgrub bar chad kun sel*. *The Heart Practice That Dispels All Obstacles* is a cycle of teachings revealed by Chokgyur Lingpa together with Jamyang Khyentse Wangpo consisting of about ten volumes. For details, see the foreword to *The Great Gate* (Rangjung Yeshe Publications).

159. *zhal gdams snying byang yid bzhin nor bu*. The complete title of this text is *The Wish-fulfilling Jewel, Essential Manual of Heart Advice*. It is the main root text and first volume of the *Dispels All Obstacles (bar chad kun sel)* cycle revealed by Chokgyur Lingpa (*mchog 'gyur gling pa*) (1829–70).

160. A great awareness-holder and treasure-revealer, Jatson Nyingpo (*'ja' tshon snying po*) (1585–1656) bestowed many empowerments, pith instructions, guidance, and his own profound treasures upon Düdül Dorjé, a former incarnation of Dudjom Rinpoché.

161. Rikdzin Dorjé Tokmé (*rig 'dzin rdo rje thogs med*) (1746–97), Chöling Garwang Chimé Dorjé (*chos gling gar dbang 'chi med rdo rje*), and Gampopa Orgyen Drodül Lingpa (*sgam po pa o rgyan 'gro 'dul gling pa*) were renowned as the "nirmanakaya awareness-holders who opened the secret land of Péma Kö (*pad ma bkod*) as a pilgrimage place." Péma Kö is Dudjom Rinpoché's native homeland. CWDR, vol. *ka*, p. 830.

162. Gampo Orgyen Drodül Lingpa (*sgam po o rgyan 'gro 'dul gling pa*) (1757–?), also known as Tertön Déchen Dorjé (*gter ston bde chen rdo rje*), was a contemporary of Chöling Garwang Chimé Dorjé and Rikdzin Dorjé Tokmé.

163. Garwang Sangyé Dorjé (*gar dbang sangs rgyas rdo rje*) was a disciple of one of Dudjom Lingpa's sons.

164. The great treasure-revealer and awareness-holder Rikdzin Düdül Dorjé (*rig 'dzin bdud 'dul rdo rje*) (1615–72) was a later incarnation of the translator Drokben Khyé'u Chung and a previous incarnation of Dudjom Rinpoché. See NSTB, pp. 813–17.

165. *ngag dbang dge 'dun rgya mtsho*.

166. The great treasure-revealer Péma Lingpa (1450–1521) is praised as the fourth of five royal treasure-revealers (*gter ston rgyal po lnga*) and was the last pure incarnation of Princess Péma Sel (*pad ma gsal*), the daughter of King Trisong Déutsen. Péma Lingpa's previous life was as the omniscient Longchenpa. CWDR, vol. *ka*, pp. 583–88. See NTBS, pp.796–8.

167. *ngag dbang 'jigs med blo gros*.

168. The *Kangyur (bka' 'gyur)*. According to Tulku Thondup (*Buddhist Civilization in Tibet*, pp. 40–1), the *Kangyur* is the collection of Buddha's teachings. It contains 1,046 treatises in 104 volumes, including most all of the Buddha's teachings in the categories of the sutras, the Abhidharma, the Vinaya, the Prajnaparamita, and the tantras.

169. Taklung is a place in the region of Ü in central Tibet.

170. *ngag dbang dpal ldan bzang po.*

171. The two systems are that of Nagarjuna and Asanga. For a detailed discussion of the bodhi-sattva vows see *Perfect Conduct: Ascertaining the Three Vows* by Ngari Panchen, Péma Wangyi Gyalpo, with a commentary by His Holiness Dudjom Rinpoché. Translated by Khenpo Gyurme Samdrub and Sangye Khandro (Wisdom Publications).

172. Jigmé Trogyal Dorjé (*'jigs med khro rgyal rdo rje*) otherwise known as Chadral Rinpoché. Kyabjé Chadral Rinpoché, born in the province of Kham in the year 1913, is one of the greatest Lamas of our time. He is a lineage holder of many lineages, including his primary lineage of the *Longchen Nyingtik* as well as Dudjom Rinpoché's New Treasure lineage. In a treasure prophecy by the treasure-revealer Péma Dügyal it was said, "Supreme heart emanation of Guru Rinpoché, a son blessed by Vimalamitra, will be born in the Ox Year with the name of 'Dorjé,' will propagate the practice lineage, and will make it flourish." According to Lopön Jigmé, Chadral Rinpoché received the transmission of the cycle of hidden treasure texts of Dudjom Lingpa directly from Dudjom Lingpa's youngest son, Dorjé Dradül (1891–1959). Tulku Thondup writes that Chadral Rinpoché also received Sera Khandro's cycle of hidden treasure texts directly from Sera Khandro herself. For a concise life story of Chadral Rinpoché, see *Masters of Meditation and Miracles* by Tulku Thondup, pp. 296–7.

173. Tantras, transmissions, and pith instructions refer to the three inner tantras, Mahayoga, Anuyoga, and Atiyoga, respectively.

174. *phur 'grel 'bum nag.* The complete title is *A Collection of Explanations on Vajrakilaya, As Was Transmitted to the Princess/Lady of Kharchen (Yeshé Tsogyal) by the Sublime Spiritual Master (Padmasambhava) in Accord with the Realization of the Three Spiritual Masters (Padmasambhava, Vimalamitra, and Newar Shilamanju)* (*rdo rje phur pa'i bshad 'bum slob dpon rnam gsum gyi dgongs pa slob dpon chen po pad mas mkhar chen bza' la gdams pa*). It can be found in the *Nyingma Kama*, volume *tha.*

175. Déchen Déwé Dorjé (*bde chen bde ba'i rdo rje*) was otherwise known as Sera Khandro (1899–1947). Lama Ngawang Zangpo mentions in his introduction to *The Immaculate White Lotus: The Life of the Master from Oddiyana* that was revealed by Sera Khandro that, "Sera Khandro was a prolific treasure-revealer: four hefty volumes of her treasures are preserved in their modern edition. She also composed texts, including two autobiographies." See *Guru Rinpoché: His Life and Times,* p. 132.

176. The treasure-revealer Chokgyur Lingpa (*mchog gyur bde chen zhig po gling pa*) (1829–70) was the incarnation of Murup Tsépo, also called Yeshé Rolpatsel, who was the son of Trisong Déutsen. CWDR, vol. *ka,* pp. 646–58. For an English translation, see NSTB, pp. 841–8.

177. *o rgyan tshe dbang dpal 'bar.*

178. *nges don chos kyi rgya mtsho.*

179. The great treasure-revealer Ratna Lingpa Rinchen Palzangpo (*rat na gling pa rin chen dpal bzang po*) (1403–78) is considered to be an incarnation of Langdro Könchok Jungné, a minister at the court of Trisong Déutsen who later became one of Guru Rinpoché's twenty-five disciples. CWDR, vol. *ka,* pp. 580–83. For an English translation, see NSTB, pp. 793–95.

180. *'dus pa skor bzhi.*

181. *rim lnga dmar khri.*

182. *pad ma dkon mchog rab brtan.*

183. *rdzogs chen snying thig ya bzhi*. This contains the four branches of the *Heart Essence* teachings: *bi ma snying thig; bla ma yang thig; mkha' 'gro snying thig; mkha' 'gro yang thig;* and *zab mo yang thig*.

184. The omniscient Jigmé Lingpa (*'jigs med gling pa*) (1729–98) was the inseparable incarnation of the great pandita Vimalamitra, the Dharma king Trisong Déutsen, and Gyalsé Lharjé (*rgyal sras lha rje*). He discovered the vast and profound *Longchen Nyingthik* cycle of teachings as a mind treasure. CWDR, vol. *ka*, pp. 636–46. For an English translation, see NSTB, pp. 835–40.

185. This refers to Jikmé Lingpa's collected works. His most prominent works are: *The Heart Essence of Longchenpa* (*klong chen snying thig*), a collection of meditation instructions and ritual texts in two or three volumes; *The Methods of the Vajrakilaya Lineage* (*phur ba rgyud lugs*), a volume on Vajrakilaya practice; *The Precious Treasury of Noble Qualities* (*yon tan rin po che'i mdzod*), including its two-volume autocommentary; and *Wisdom Lama* (*ye shes bla ma*), a Great Perfection practice manual.

186. *byang chub sems dpa'i spyod pa la 'jug pa*, the *Bodhicaryavatara* by Shantideva.

187. *sdom gsum rnam nges*, a work by Ngari Panchen Péma Wangyal (*mnga' ris pan chen pad ma dbang rgyal*) translated into English by Khenpo Gyurme Samdrub and Sangye Khandro, under the title *Perfect Conduct: Ascertaining the Three Vows*, with a commentary by His Holiness Dudjom Rinpoché (Wisdom Publications).

188. Jigme Lingpa's *Precious Treasury of Noble Qualities* (*yon tan rin po che'i mdzod*).

189. Probably *The Mirror of Poetics* (*snyan ngag me long dbyug pa can gyi gzhung*).

190. *ka thog pa*.

191. Rongzom Chökyi Zangpo (*rong zom chos kyi bzang po*) (1012–88), born in Narlung Rung in lower Tsang in central Tibet, was renowned as the supreme mahapandita of Tibet. CWDR, vol. *ka*, pp. 452–64.

192. For an explanation of the Zur lineage, see NSTB, pp. 617–87.

193. *ka rma legs bshad phun tshogs*.

194. *bde mchog 'khor lo*.

195. *rdo rje phag mo*.

196. *ngag dbang 'jam dbyangs blo gros rgya mtsho*.

197. *tshe dbang bstan 'dzin bzang po*.

198. *brtag pa gnyis pa*, the condensed version of the *Hévajra Tantra*.

199. *rgya chen bka' mdzod*. One of the five treasuries of Jamgön Kongtrul Lodrö Tayé, which contains his collection of various writings.

200. *rig 'dzin pad ma dbang drag*.

201. The oral transmission is the third of three aspects of transmission of the tantric teachings. According the Nyimgma teachings, there are three aspects to the long transmission of the tantric teachings. The first is the wisdom mind transmission (*dgongs brgyud*), in which Kuntu Zangpo transmits his realization directly to the sambhogakaya buddhas who are inseparable from himself, without symbols or words. The second is the symbolic transmission (*brda brgyud*) of the sambhogakaya buddhas to the nirmanakaya buddhas, such as from Vajrasattva to Garab Dorjé, which occurs through symbols or gestures. The third is the oral transmission (*snyan brgyud*) in which sublime noble beings transmit the teachings to their sublime disciples, such as Padmasambhava, Vimalamitra, and so forth.

202. *o rgyan gsang sngags bstan 'dzin*.

203. *khrag 'thung rnam mkha 'jigs med.*

204. *'gyur med dge 'dun rab rgyas.*

205. *'jigs med kun bzang rdo rje.*

206. *pad ma rin chen nor bu.*

207. *sdom gsum rnam nges.* Written by Ngari Panchen Wangyal (*mnga' ris pan chen pad ma dbang rgyal*).

208. *lam rim ye shes snying po.* See *Light of Wisdom,* vol. 1 (Shambhala Publications).

209. Jigdral Yeshé Dorjé (*'jigs bral ye shes rdo rje*). The definitive detailed commentary on this text was written by Dudjom Rinpoché's son, Kyabjé Dungsé Thinley Norbu Rinpoché. The Tibetan version may be completed within the year. We make prayers that an English translation will be available in the coming years.

210. *nus ldan rdo rje 'chang.* The Buddha who bestowed empowerments upon the thousand buddhas of this current fortunate eon.

211. That is, the *kaliyuga.*

212. *'phags pa sha' ri'i bu.* One of Buddha's main disciples. The *Heart Sutra* (*Bhagavati-prajnaparamita-hridaya*) was delivered through the dialogue of Shariputra and Avalokiteshvara by the power of Buddha's samadhi.

213. *bram ze sa ra ha.* Saraha, "he who shot the arrow," took birth in the fourth century B.C.E. (before the Christian era) in southern India. He was one of the greatest accomplished masters (*mahasiddha*), of India, and His Holiness Dudjom Rinpoché was his incarnation. He is well known for his *Three Cycles of Songs of Tantric Realization* (*do ha skor gsum*): the *King Song of Tantric Realization* (forty verses); the *Queen Song of Tantric Realization* (eighty verses); and the *People Song of Tantric Realization* (one hundred sixty verses). For a translation of these songs of tantric realization, see *Ecstatic Spontaneity: Saraha's Three Cycles of Dohas,* translated by Herbert Guenther.

214. *chos blon kri shna 'dzin.* Krishnadhara was the religious minister of the king of Oddiyana, Indrabhuti, who had no son. The king sent Krishnadhara to a special island to bring back the wish-fulfilling gem. On his return he noticed a young boy. The king then brought this child back to his palace to become his adopted son. At this time the boy received the name Péma Jungné, the Lotus-Born; and Tsokyé Dorjé, Lake Born Vajra. CWDR, vol. *ka,* p. 93.

215. *slob dpon hung ka ra.* The master Hungkara was the holder of the Buddha's Word of Yangdak. Hungkara was born to a Brahmin family in Nepal and studied the Vedas and various other non-Buddhist systems. Eventually, he studied and practiced at the great Nalanda University in central India. He studied everything from the Perfection of Wisdom sutras through the outer and inner Secret Mantra. In particular, when he was empowered into the mandala of Yangdak Héruka, his flower fell on the wrathful deity Hungkara, on which he did a six-month retreat culminating in the full attainment of the supreme accomplishment of Mahamudra. CWDR, vol. *ka,* pp. 103–6.

216. *'brog ban khye'u chung lo tsa.* One of Guru Rinpoché's twenty-five disciples who was a great translator and was famous for the ability to summon birds from the sky merely by his gaze.

217. That is, Manjushri.

218. Lord Smriti Jñana (*jo bo smri ti dza nya na*) was a great wisdom scholar who came to Tibet toward the end of the early spread of the Buddha's teachings in Tibet.

219. *s'a la'i ljongs* is an abbreviation for *bsil ldan s'a la'i sman ljongs.* This refers to Tibet.

220. Rongzom Chökyi Zangpo (*rong zom chos kyi bzang po*), born in Narlung Rung in lower Tsang in central Tibet, was renowned as the supreme, great scholar of Tibet. CWDR, vol. *ka*, pp. 452–64.

221. Dampa Deshek (*dam pa bde gshegs*) was the person who made the Nyingma teachings well known in the Kham region of eastern Tibet and founded the distinguished Kathok Monastery in 1159. For a brief biography, see NSTB, pp. 688–91.

222. Palden Lingjé Répa (*dpal ldan gling rje ras pa*) (1128–88).

223. *'gro mgon chos rgyal 'phags pa* (1235–80).

224. *grum gyi mkhar nag pa.*

225. *he pa chos 'byung.*

226. *khrag 'thung bdud 'dul rdo rje* (1615–72). Düdül Dorje was a great treasure-revealer and awareness-holder (*rig 'dzin*). CWDR, vol. *ka*, pp. 604–10.

227. That is, Dorjé Drolö.

228. Gyalsé Sönam Déutsen (*rgyal sras bsod nams lde'u btsan*) received the transmission of the Buddha's Word of the Nyingma tradition from Terdak Lingpa of Mindroling and restored them at the vajra seat of Khatok, where these teachings were becoming progressively rarer over time. CWDR, vol. *ka*, pp. 503.

229. *bdud 'dul rol pa rtsal.*

230. *gar dbang bdud 'joms dpa' bo.*

231. An extraordinary abode of cannibals, Tail-Fan (*Camaradvipa; rnga yab*) is blessed by all the buddhas of the three times and is the location of the Glorious Copper-Colored Mountain Pure Land where Padmasambhava actually resides in the Palace of Lotus Light, in the form of Guru Lotus Skull-garlanded Adept. (From *An Encyclopaedic Tibetan-English Dictionary.*)

232. *'jigs bral ye shes rdo rje*, 1904–87.

233. *rdo rje rnon po.*

234. *bde gshegs mos pa 'od mtha' yas pa.*

235. The four immeasurable methods are: love (*byams pa*), compassion (*snying rje*), joy (*dga' ba*), and impartiality (*btang snyoms*).

236. Drokben (*'brog ban*), also known as Khyé'u Chung, was a tantric lay practitioner (*ngags pa*) and one of Padmasambhava's twenty-five disciples. He later reincarnated at Khatok as the treasure-revealer Düdül Dorjé Lingpa, and eventually as Dudjom Rinpoché himself.

237. The six classes of beings are: hell beings, starving spirits, and animals—populating the three lower realms; and humans, demi-gods, and gods—populating the three higher realms.

238. The mind of awakening of aspiration is the wish to attain enlightenment for the benefit of all sentient beings. The mind of awakening of application is actually to engage in practice to actualize the mind of awakening of aspiration. The metaphor usually given is the wish to go somewhere, and the actual preparations and travel that get you there. For an in-depth explanation, see *The Words of My Perfect Teacher*, pp. 222–61.

239. The four empowerments are the vase empowerment, secret empowerment, wisdom empowerment, and word empowerment, which is also referred to as the fourth empowerment. For a detailed explanation, see *Perfect Conduct*, pp. 107–8.

240. The four obscurations (*sgrib pa bzhi*) are karmic obscurations (*las kyi sgrib pa*); the obscuration of passions (*nyon mongs kyi sgrib pa*); conceptual obscuration or the obscuration of not knowing (*shes bya'i sgrib pa*); and the obscuration of habitual tendencies (*bag chags kyi sgrib pa*). When referred to as two obscurations, they are the obscurations of the passions and conceptual obscurations. Karmic obscurations come from performing non-virtuous actions, such as the ten non-virtuous actions (*mi dge ba bcu*). The obscuration of the passions refers to the obscurations caused by the three passions—anger, desire, and ignorance. The three passions are often categorized as five—anger, desire, ignorance, jealousy, and pride. The obscuration of not knowing is to take the threefold sphere (*'khor gsum*) of subject, object, and action as solid, material, truly existent. From the perspective of the vehicle of discourses (Sutrayana), the obscuration of habitual tendencies is a very subtle form of the obscuration of not knowing. From the Vajrayana perspective it is the basis for sentient beings' habits of ordinary body, speech, and mind.

241. The four wisdom bodies, or *kaya*s, are dharmakaya, sambhogakaya, nirmanakaya, and svabhavikakaya. For an excellent and concise understanding of the wisdom bodies I highly recommend Dungsé Thinley Norbu Rinpoché's *Small Golden Key*, pp. 68–93.

242. The three kindnesses are: to confer empowerments (*dbang bskur*); to give transmissions (*lung*); and to give pith instructions (*man ngag*).

243. *chos nyid mngon sum*. The first of the four visions in *tögal* practice.

244. *nyams snang gong 'phel*. The second of the four visions in *tögal* practice.

245. *rig pa tshad phebs*. The third of the four visions in *tögal* practice.

246. *chos nyid zad sar 'khyol ba*. The fourth of the four visions in *tögal* practice.

247. *slob dpon sngags 'chang*.

248. The Tibetan word *rig byed* in this case means "tantric activity" and not the Hindu "Vedas."

249. *nyi ma rgyal mtshan*.

250. This refers to Dudjom Rinpoché's biological father.

251. *'jam dpal nor bu*.

252. *ye shes rdo rje*.

253. *nam mkha'i rnal 'byor*. This is probably another name for the fifteenth Karmapa, Kakyab Dorjé, who gave His Holiness the "Jigdral" part of his name (Jigdral Yeshé Dorjé).

254. *'jigs bral bde chen rdo rje drag po*.

255. This name for Dudjom Rinpoché can be translated as "Unprecedented, Extraordinary Moon," which means a moon that is so bright as never to have been seen before.

256. *'gyur med dge legs phyogs kun las*.

257. *ngag dbang dpal ldan*.

258. *rgyal sras blo gros dri med phan bde'i zla 'od gsal dpal 'bar*.

259. *rdo rje 'dus rtsal*.

260. This does not refer to the present-day Trulzhik Rinpoché but to the Trulzhik Rinpoché from Sikkim who built the stupa in Gangtok.

261. *yan pa blo bde*.

262. *pad ma thod phreng rtsal*.

263. Drodül Lingpa (*'gro 'dul gling pa*), also known as Ratna Lingpa, discovered the treasures of three lifetimes in one single life and is therefore known under three names: Zhikpo Lingpa, Drodül Lingpa, and Ratna Lingpa. See NSTB, pp. 791–95

264. Nangsi Zilnön Péma Tötreng Tsal (*snang srid zil gnon pad ma thod phreng rtsal*). Péma Tötreng Tsal is a name of Guru Rinpoché. As explained in the biography of Guru Rinpoché by Jamgön Kongtrul: "To guide the kingdom of Oddiyana on the path to enlightenment, he traveled there as a beggar. The people of the kingdom recognized him, and the malevolent government minister [whose son he killed] and others tried to burn him on a pyre of sandalwood. He again demonstrated a miracle by appearing with his consort on a lotus in the center of a lake. As a symbol of liberating beings from the wheel of life he wore a garland of skulls. Thus, he became known as Lotus Skull-garlanded Adept (Péma Tö-treng Tsal)." From *Guru Rinpoché: His Life and Times*, translated by Ngawang Zangpo, p. 121.

265. Drokben Khyé'u Chung Lotsawa (*'brog ban khye'u chung lo tsa ba*), one of Guru Rinpoché's twenty-five disciples and a past incarnation of Dudjom Rinpoché.

266. Yingchuk Déchen Tsogyal (*dbyings phyug bde chen mtsho rgyal*). Yeshé Tsogyal was the Tibetan consort of Guru Rinpoché who attained the same level of realization as Guru Rinpoché, that of a fully enlightened buddha. As Lama Ngawang Zangpo writes: "Yeshé Tsogyal was Guru Rinpoché's most gifted Tibetan disciple, the main recorder of his instructions, and one of the greatest meditation masters Tibet ever produced. She was his principal intimate companion during his stay in Tibet and one of his main representatives after his departure." *Guru Rinpoché: His Life and Times*, p. 304. For a concise biography of Yeshé Tsogyal written by Jamgön Kongtrul, see the same book, pp. 302–3. For Yeshé Tsogyal's extensive life story, see *Lady of the Lotus-Born: The Life and Enlightenment of Yeshé Tsogyal*, translated by the Padmakara Translation Group. This is a translation of a treasure text that was revealed by the treasure-revealer Samten Lingpa and committed to writing by Gyalwa Changchub and Namkhai Nyingpo.

267. The three places are on, under, and above the ground.

268. The Tibetan word *rikden* (*rigs ldan*), meaning "ruler," refers to Shambhala's kings; here it is used as an honorific for a ruler. Dudjom Rinpoché is lauding a local ruler as a lineage-bearing ruler of Shambhala.

269. The three roots are the Lama, Wisdom Deity (*yi dam*), and Dakini (*mkha' 'gro*).

270. The three blazes (*'bar ba gsum*) are: the blazing of blissful warmth in the body (*lus la bde drod 'bar ba*); the blazing of potency in speech (*ngag la nus pa 'bar ba*); and the blazing of realization in the mind (*sems la rtogs pa 'bar ba*).

271. The three gatherings (*'du ba gsum*) are: the gathering of people during the day (*nyin mor mi 'du ba*); the gathering of dakinis by night (*mtshan mor mkha' 'gro 'du ba*); and the gathering of material resources at all times (*rtag tu zas nor 'du ba*).

272. The three bodhisattvas' names are woven in the praise in this first verse. Sun of Speech (*smra ba'i nyi ma*) is an epithet of Manjushri; Treasure of Compassion (*snying rje'i gter*) refers to Chenrezi; and Lord of Secrets (*gsang bdag*) is Vajrapani.

273. In the text, *brag mgo* is a spelling mistake for *brag 'go*, which the locals in eastern Tibet pronounce Drango. It's a town at a junction in eastern Tibet; from there one road goes toward Ganzé, the other toward Sertak, Dudjom Lingpa's home town.

274. Zhogpa is a place in the region of upper Ü east of Lhasa.

275. In the Tibetan, marks are used to designate the syllables that comprise Dudjom Rinpoché's name, Ye-shé [primordial wisdom] Dor-jé [vajra]. In the body of this prayer italics have been used to replicate the Tibetan.

276. Blessed by all the buddhas of the three times, Glorious Copper-Colored Mountain (*rnga g.yab zangs mdog dpal gyi ri bo*) on Tail-Fan Island is an extraordinary abode of cannibals and is the location of the Glorious Copper-Colored Mountain Pure Land where Padmasambhava actually resides in the Palace of Lotus Light, in the form of Guru Lotus Skull-garlanded Adept. (From *An Encyclopaedic Tibetan-English Dictionary*).

277. Twofold supreme knowledge (*mkhyen pa gnyis*) refers to the primordial wisdom that knows the abiding nature as it is (*gnas lugs ji lta ba mkhyen pa'i ye shes*) and the primordial wisdom that perceives all that exists (*shes bya ji rnyed pa gzigs pa'i ye shes*). Translation note: I am using the superlative "supreme" to distinguish between "intellectual" knowledge and the knowledge of a realized being, translated here as "supreme knowledge" (*mkhyen*). A precedent for this can be found in Sanskrit and Tibetan Buddhist language. For instance, to distinguish the ultimate, non-dualistic state of emptiness—*mahashunyata* in Sanskrit—from the various levels of emptiness— *shunyata*— the modifier *maha* ("great") is used. In Tibetan, the adjective *chen po* ("great") is added to *tong-nyi* ("emptiness").

278. This and the two lines above contain the name of Dudjom Rinpoché, Jigdral Yeshé Dorjé.

279. Orgyen Dorjé Chang is the dharmakaya aspect of Guru Rinpoché.

280. There is a spelling mistake in the last line in Tibetan: *dben sbyor* should be *dbyen sbyor*, meaning "to disrupt" or "to agitate."

281. Literally, "forces my heart's circulating energy into my upper body."

282. As recounted in *A Biography of Guru Rinpoché by Jamgön Kongtrul*: "In thirteen places named 'Tiger's Den,' such as Néring Sengé Dzong in Mönka [Bhutan], he took the form of an uncontrollably wrathful deity, bound all the major and minor arrogant gods and cannibal demons of Tibet under oath, and entrusted them with guardianship of the treasure texts. At that time he [Guru Rinpoché] was known as Vajra Sagging Belly [Dorjé Drolö]." *Guru Rinpoché: His Life and Times*, translated by Ngawang Zangpo, p. 126. According to another tradition for understanding the meaning of the name Drolö (*gro lod*), Dro (*gro*) refers to liberation, and *lö* (*lod*) refers to the world. Dorjé Drolö could then be translated as Vajra Liberator of the World.

283. My Lama explains *yidam* as follows. *Yid* means "mind," and *dam* refers to an inseparable bond based upon pure samaya. Each practitioner has a special deity with whom they have a connection.

284. Orgyen, the second Buddha, is Guru Rinpoché. This prayer is to the master, Guru Rinpoché; the scholar, Shantarakshita; and the king who protects the Buddha's teachings, Trisong Déutsen. Together they are sometimes referred to in prayers and texts as "the master, the scholar, and the king who protect the Buddha's teachings."

285. "The Teacher" refers to Buddha.

286. Shantarakshita (*mkhan chen zhi ba 'tsho*), also known as Khenpo Bodhisattva, who introduced the monastic lineage to Tibet. See NSTB, pp. 512–21; and in Tibetan, see CWDR, vol. *kha*, pp. 154–66.

287. King Trisong Déutsen, the king of Tibet who invited Guru Rinpoché and Shantarakshita to Tibet in order to spread the Buddhist teachings. See NSTB, pp. 512–21; and in Tibetan, CWDR, vol. *kha*, pp. 154–66.

288. In this last verse, Dudjom Rinpoché has used the numbers one, two, three, and four, one per line. In order to indicate this, the English numbers have been italicized.

289. Nüden Dorjé Tsal (*nus ldan rdo rje tshal*) was the teacher of the 1,002 buddhas who will appear in this fortunate eon. Dudjom Rinpoché is his incarnation.

290. The Joyful Buddha Möpa Tayé (*mos pa mtha' yas*) was the spiritual master of the 1,000 buddhas of our current fortunate eon.

291. The five degenerations are: the degeneration of longevity (*tshe'i kyi snyigs ma*), that is, beings live for a shorter time; the degeneration of view (*lta ba'i snyigs ma*); the degeneration of the passions (*nyon mongs kyi snyigs ma*); the degeneration of sentient beings (*sems can gyi snyigs ma*); the degeneration of our present age (*dus kyi snyigs ma*).

292. Wind (*rlung*), bile (*mkhris*), and phlegm (*bad kan*).

293. From "The Sublime Quintessence," p. 269.

294. The Glorious Copper-Colored Mountain is the pure land where Guru Rinpoché abides.

295. The ten leisures: the five leisures based upon oneself are to be born: with a precious human birth; in a country where the Buddhist teachings are available; with all sense faculties intact; without involvement in negative acts; and with faith in the Buddhist teachings. The five leisures based upon circumstances are being born in a time: in which a buddha has appeared; in which a buddha has taught; in which his teachings still exist; and in which his followers act on behalf of others; and in which there is the kindness of a Lama who has compassion for others. The eight opportunities are the freedoms from: birth in the hell realms; birth in a starving spirit realm; birth in an animal realm; birth among barbarians; birth among those who hold extreme views; birth in the realm of long-lived gods; birth in a place where the Buddhist teachings do not exist; or being born deaf and dumb. For a detailed discussion of this topic, see *The Words of My Perfect Teacher*, pp. 22–33.

296. Grass (*ka rtswa*) represents something you carry around that is useless, so you should just throw it away. Why carry it around?

297. Literally, "wrap your nose-rope on your own head" (*sna thag rang mi mgo*). This means not to allow yourself to be led around by others.

298. When a deer is attacked by a wild animal, it would seem that it needs its antlers for protection, but in fact they are useless.

299. This is a common simile. Family or close ties that seem so solid are likened to a crowd at the mall: Everyone has come from different places and then they all depart at random, each in separate directions.

300. That is, something that is momentary and inconsequential.

301. That is, temporary springs. In Tibet, there are springs that only temporarily last due to the summer rains. In California, these temporary springs caused by seasonal rain occur in the winter.

302. In Tibet, sometimes it would look as though it was going to rain in the valley on the crops where it was needed, but the rain would only fall high in the mountains.

303. This means that your pure vision is unstable, so do not be deluded by your practice-related experiences.

304. In Tibet, butter was stored in sacks made of gut.

305. A type of craving spirit who consumes the potent essences of food and wealth. This type of spirit personifies ultimate envy and miserliness and is usually exorcized during rituals to promote wealth and prosperity.

306. *dbu ma chenpo*, Maha-Madhyamaka.

307. A good reference book for teachings on the intermediate state is *The Mirror of Mindfulness*, by Tsele Natsok Rangdrol and translated by Erik Pema Kunsang.

308. See *The Mirror of Mindfulness*, p. 29.

309. According to the sutra tradition, the three kindnesses of the guru are: (1) giving precepts (*sdom pa*), (2) reading authorizations (*lung*), and (3) giving teachings (*khrid*). Alternately, according to the tantric tradition: (1) conferring empowerments (*dbang bskur*), (2) explaining the tantras (*rgyud bshad*), and (3) giving pith instructions (*man ngag gnang ba*).

310. *gsang sngags snga 'gyur rnying ma ba'i bstan pa'i rnam gzhag mdo tsam brjod pa legs bshad snang ba'i dga 'ston*, from CWDR, vol. *kha*, pp. 277–423.

311. Ibid., pp. 438–56.

312. The six perfections are: the perfection of generosity (*sbyin pa*), discipline (*tshul khrims*), patience (*bzod pa*), diligence (*brston 'grus*), meditation (*bsam gtan*), and incisive knowledge (*shes rab*). When speaking of ten perfections the following are added to this list: skillful means (*thabs*), aspiration prayer (*smon lam*), power (*stobs*), and primordial wisdom (*ye shes*).

313. The four paths of learning (*slob pa'i lam bzhi*) are the path of accumulation (*tshogs lam*); path of application (*sbyor lam*); path of seeing (*mthong lam*); and path of meditation (*sgom lam*).

314. The four essential recollections (*dran pa nyer gzhag*) are: the recollection of the body (*lus dran pa nyer gzhag*); the recollection of feeling (*tshor ba dran pa nyer gzhag*); the recollection of mind (*sems dran pa nyer gzhag*); and the recollection of phenomena (*chos dran pa nyer gzhag*).

315. The four aspects of correct renunciation (*yang dag spong bzhi*) are: renouncing giving rise to non-virtuous actions; renouncing non-virtuous actions that have arisen; generating virtues that have not yet arisen; and expanding virtues that have already arisen.

316. The four aspects of miraculous power (*rdzu 'phrul rkang bzhi*) are: the aspects of miraculous power that combine training in aspirational samadhi; mind samadhi; dilgence samadhi; and analysis samadhi.

317. The five faculties (*dbang po lnga*) are: faith (*dad pa*); diligence (*brtson 'grus*); mindfulness (*dran pa*); samadhi (*ting nge 'dzin*); and incisive knowledge (*shes rab*).

318. The five powers (*stob lnga*) are: the power of faith (*dad pa'i stob*); the power of recollection (*dran pa'i stob*); the power of diligence (*brtson 'grus kyi stob*); the power of samadhi (*ting 'dzin gyi stob*); and the power of incisive knowledge (*shes rab kyi stob*).

319. The seven branches of enlightenment (*byang chub yan lag bdun*) are: the branch of perfect enlightenment of mindfulness; the branch of enlightenment of extremely precise analysis of phenomena; the branch of enlightenment of diligence; the branch of enlightenment of joy; the branch of enlightenment of mental flexibility (*shin tu sbyang ba*); the branch of enlightenment of samadhi; and the branch of enlightenment of equanimity.

320. The eightfold path (*'phags lam yan lag brgyad*) is right view; right thought; right speech; right action; right livelihood; right effort; right recollection; and right samadhi.

321. The two kayas refer to the two wisdom bodies of a Buddha: the rupakaya, or form wisdom body that includes both the nirmanakaya, or manifestation body, and the sambhogakaya, or body of perfect rapture; and the dharmakaya.

322. The three whites are milk, butter, and yogurt. The three sweets are sugar, honey, and molasses.

323. Often five families are referred to: Tathagatha (*de bzhin gshegs pa'i rigs*), Vajra (*rdo rje'i rigs*), Jewel (*rin chen rigs*), Lotus (*padma rigs*), and Action (*las kyi rigs*). According to Kriyatantra there are three families: Tathagatha, Lotus, and Vajra. Upatantra refers to

four families: Tathagatha, Lotus, Vajra, and a fourth family that combines the Action with the Jewel family.

324. *Buddhist Civilization in Tibet*, p. 44.

325. *The Festival of Delight in Which the Expression of Eloquent Teachings Manifests: A Concise Detailed Classification of the Nyingmapa Teachings, the Ancient Translation School of Secret Mantra (gsang sngags snga 'gyur rnying ma ba'i bstan pa'i rnam gzhag mdo tsam brjod pa legs bshad snang ba'i dga 'ston)*, from CWDR, vol. *kha*, pp. 277–423.

326. Mantrayana is synonymous with the terms Vajrayana and Tantric Vehicle (Tantrayana).

327. The four extremes are: existence, non-existence, both existence and non-existence; and neither existence nor non-existence.

328. *Magical Net* is an important Mahayoga tantra.

329. Vimalamitra's *phyag rgya bsam gtan gyi 'grel pa*.

330. The four pillars are: Kyotön Shakyé of Gungbu, the pillar of the Mind Class; Yangkeng Lama of Kyong-lung, the pillar of the *Sutra That Gathers All Intentions*; Len Shakya Zangpo of Chuwar, the pillar of the *Magical Net*; and Datik Chö Shakya of Nakmo-ré, the pillar of activity and means for attainment. See *gangs ljongs rgyal bstan yongs rdzogs kyi phyi mo snga 'gyur rdo rje theg pa'i bstan pa rin po che ji ltar byung ba'i tshul dag cing gsal bar brjod pa lha dbaang g.yul las rgyal ba' rnga bo che'i sgra dbyangs*, pp. 353–4.

331. Those who hold to the three or five buddha families refer to adherents of the lower tantras. The common vehicles refer to those of the Mahayana.

332. Datik Chö Shakya (*mda' tig chos sha ka*), one of four disciples of Zurchungpa, was known as one of the four pillars. He was the pillar of ritual and means for attainment (*sadhana*).

333. Lharjé Rok studied and held the lineage of many traditions. For instance, he extensively spread the commentaries to the *Sutra That Gathers All Intentions* and the *Magical Net*. He studied these texts under the So, Kyo, and Zur traditions.

334. The ten factors of tantra (*rgyud kyi dngos po bcu*) are: the view of ultimate reality as it is (*de kho na nyid lta ba*); determinate conduct (*la dor ba spyod pa*); mandala arrangement (*bkod pa dkyil 'khor*); sequential degrees of empowerments (*rim par bgrod pa dbang*); tantric commitments not to be transgressed (*mi 'da' ba dam tshig*); enlightened activity displayed (*rol pa phrin las*); fulfillment of aims (*don du gnyer ba sgrub pa*); offerings that bring the goal to fruition (*gnas su stob pa mchod pa*); unmoving samadhi (*mi g.yo ba ting nge 'dzin*); mantra recitation together with the binding seal (*zlos pa sngags 'ching ba phyag rgya*).

335. Menyak Jung-drak (*me nyag 'byung grags*) is Lharjé Zurpoché's disciple, who arrived at the summit of the explanation of the *Tantra of the Magical Net (sgyu 'phrul)*. CWDR, vol. *ka*, p. 313.

336. The three mandalas (*dkyil 'khor gsum*) are those mentioned above: the primordial mandala just as it is of the female consort Kuntu Zangmo; the mandala of self-manifest light of the male consort; and the mandala that is the inseparable illumination of these two mandalas, which is the great exa

336. The three mandalas (*dkyil 'khor gsum*) are those mentioned above: the primordial mandala just as it is of the female consort Kuntu Zangmo; the mandala of self-manifest light of the male consort; and the mandala that is the inseparable illumination of these two mandalas, which is the great exaltation child of the non-duality of stainless space and primordial wisdom.

337. *The Festival of Delight in Which the Expression of Eloquent Teachings Manifests: A Concise Detailed Classification of the Nyingmapa Teachings, the Ancient Translation School of Secret Mantra (gsang sngags snga 'gyur rnying ma ba'i bstan pa'i rnam gzhag mdo tsam brjod pa legs bshad snang ba'i dga 'ston)*, in CWDR, vol. *kha*, pp. 62–107.

338. The three kinds of valid cognition are: direct perception (*mgon sum tshad ma*); inference (*dngos stobs rjes dpag gi tshad ma*); and scriptural authority (*lung*).

339. Skt. *Prajnaparamita-samcayagatha.*

340. Skt. *Manjushri-namasamgiti.*

341. Skt. *Ashtasahasrika-prajnaparamita-vyakhyabhisamayalamkaraloka.*

342. Skt. *Prasannapada.*

343. Skt. *Caturdevi-pariprccha.*

344. Skt. *Guhyagarbha-tantra.*

345. The three higher trainings are discipline (*tshul khrims*), samadhi (*ting nge 'dzin*), and incisive knowledge (*shes rab*).

346. Skt. *Prajnashatakanamaprakarana.*

347. Skt. *Pradipodyotana*